THE RIVER VER
A Meander Through Time

Jacqui Banfield-Taylor

Based on the original notes of Ted Banfield

HALSGROVE

First published in Great Britain in 2012

British Library Cataloguing-in-Publication Data
A CIP record for this title is available from the British Library

ISBN 978 0 85704 160 9

HALSGROVE
Halsgrove House,
Ryelands Business Park,
Bagley Road, Wellington, Somerset TA21 9PZ
Tel: 01823 653777   Fax: 01823 216796
email: sales@halsgrove.com

Part of the Halsgrove group of companies
Information on all Halsgrove titles is available at: www.halsgrove.com

Printed in China by Everbest Printing Co Ltd

Contents

Acknowledgements

Many people have kindly offered help, advice and contributions in so many ways since I began to complete this book and to dad before me, but I know by the unusual way it has been started and completed by two different authors that there will undoubtedly be missing names and acknowledgments. For this I can only apologise and offer my thanks to those I either missed, do not yet know (but please come forward) or for various reasons may never get to meet. The list below is in alphabetical order and contains some lovely people sadly no longer with us but my and of course dad's heartfelt thanks and gratitude is offered to everyone for helping to make this long, sometimes frustrating but amazingly interesting and pleasurable journey just that little bit easier!

Alan Malin (memories/images)
Allen Beechey (Chilterns Conservation Board – image)
Amy Warner (St Albans Museums – information/ images)
Andy Lawrence (images)
Ann Smith (memories/images)
Annette Smith (Environment Agency – information)
Arthur Melbourne-Cooper(Alpha St Albans – images)
Bernard Smith (memories)
Betty Sawers (images)
Brenda Toussaint (Equity – information)
Bruce Banfield-Taylor (for more than I have space to mention)
Charles Chapman (memories/information)
Charles Cockell (memories)
Claire Thornton (St Albans Museum Service – Information)
Clare Bourke (*Hertfordshire Life* magazine)
Claude Pinnock (memories)
Cyril Martin (information from books/images and talking to dad)
Daphne Bunker (Images)
David Thorold (Archaeologist St Albans Museums – information)
Dick Hogg (Markyate History Society – information and images)
Dilys Hudson (images)
Dr Isobel Thompson (Archaeologist, Historic Environment Record, Herts County Council – information)
Eleanor Cowland (St Albans Museums – information and images)
Elizabeth Adey (Luton Museum – information)
Ellie Powers and Rob Sage (Veolia Central Water – information and images)
English Heritage Archives/Alice Stacey (images)
Eric Edwards (information and images)
Geoff Webb (information and images)
Giuseppe Petruccelli (Granada /*Inpector Morse* – images)
GL Draper (memories)
Helen Olive (www.redkites.net – information and images)
Hertfordshire Archives and Local Studies (HALS) (information and images)
Jane Hammond (Production Manager *Time Team* – information)
Joan Forder (memories)
Joanne Turner (information and images)
John Buckingham (memories and images)
John Dunkley (Redbournbury Fishery – information)
John Sainsbury (information)
Kate Warren (St Albans Museums – information)
Kathy Sinfield (memories and images)
Laurie Hart (Bricket Wood History Society – information and images)
Lil Day (memories)
Lord and Lady Verulam (Use of Gorhambury material)
Lorraine Mepham (Wessex Archaeology/*Time Team* – information)
Mandy James (Redbournbury Mill – information and images)
Margaret and Jim Wickens (memories and images)
Markyate History Society (information)
Maxine McCourt (Veolia Environmental Services (UK) Plc – information)
Mike Richardson (memories and images)
Mike Sammons (Veolia ES (UK) Limited – information)
Mr Dunkley (memories)
Mrs Terry (memories)
Noel Godman (memories and images)
Norah King (memories)
Paul Rolfe, Susan Heale, Dr Avice M Hall, University of Hertfordshire (information)
Pauline Day (memories)
Peggy Pollock (Information given to dad including from VVS archives and through many hours talking)
Peter O'Connell (Bluesky International Ltd – image)
Rachel King (memories)
Ralph Hawkins (memories)
Richard Hale (image)
RS Dew (memories)
Sandra Muggleton-Mole (memories and images)

Sandy Norman (Sopwell Residents Association – information and images)

Sarah Hinchliffe (Head St Michael's School for use of image)

Simon West (District Archaeologist, St Albans District Council – information)

St Albans City and District Council/Laura Levitt (images)

Stephen Coleman (Historic Environment Information Officer Central Bedfordshire Council – information)

Steve Simpson (Watercress Wildlife Association – information and images)

Stuart Antrobus (For use of information and image from his book – *We wouldn't have missed it for the world: the Women's Land Army in Bedfordshire, 1939-1950*)

Ted Turner (information)

Tony Stevens (Park Street and Frogmore History Society – information, images and many lovely hours chatting!)

Tony Willett (image)

Thames Valley Water (information)

Ver Valley Society (information)

Verulam Angling Club (images)

Dedication

This book is based on an idea started by my dad, Ted Banfield. When he became unwell he made me promise that if anything should happen to him I would finish it for him. Dad died on 19 February 2004 after a long bravely fought battle, my mum Audrey joined him ten months later.

It is dedicated to the three most important men that I have had the privilege to love – My darling Daddy, Pa my beloved granddad and my wonderful husband, best friend and soul-mate Bruce – who dad loved as a son.

And of course this book is also dedicated to the River Ver, a small chalk stream whose presence has supported life and influenced so many.

Foreword

The red spotted, black speckled gently twisting body of a trout in a clear stream veiled by fronds of jade weed, dancing with its own shadow is a delightful vision. A demoiselle flitting on fragile slivers of electric blue, the plop of a diving water vole, the bouncing wagtail on the bank and the sound of winter reeds singing in a dry breeze are still more gems which materialise on and around one of Britain's most valuable habitats – the chalk stream. These cool, clean, rich ribbons of water are globally important and urgently in need of conservation and restoration. This deeply personal treatise on the beautiful River Ver illustrates how this particular chalk stream is an environment which has had a chequered human history. Once a strategic route to rout Romans, an important source of 'millpower' to pump and grind and then a bed to sprout watercress and a water meadow system to maximise fertility for grazing. Coincidentally the fortunes of its natural history have waxed and waned, indeed they have been keenly monitored by the author and her late father whose lifelong passion for the Ver has been the inspiration for the book. Ted Banfield was made of the Ver; it coursed through his body and fuelled a lifetime of varied interests. But perhaps most importantly he infused his love of this 24km stretch of river firmly into the soul and psyche of his daughter Jacqui.

I hope that this book will further spread an appreciation of this valuable resource so that many future generations can swim, fish, canoe and paddle in the crystal waters of the Ver.

Chris Packham

Introduction

Concerning rivers: there be so many wonders reported and written of them, and of the several creatures that be bred and live in them; and those by authors of so good credit, that we need not deny them an historical faith.

Walton, 1653.

Writing a book is not always an easy task. Some are lucky enough to be born with the gift of being able to transfer thoughts onto paper in a creative and imaginative way. Others are drawn into writing by an event or happening in their life or by their work. My reason is a little more unusual; I have completed a book started by another author – my darling dad, Ted Banfield, who died before he could complete the story of the Ver – a river that was part of his life and soul.

Like dad, I was bought up to appreciate and respect the countryside and the flora and fauna that are an integral part of this small island of ours. I have many happy memories of dad, a good amateur naturalist and fisherman, pointing out and naming the plants and creatures to me of land and river. Occasionally we would take home specimens, including water from the river so we could explore the minute, teeming organisms under his ancient microscope. As with most children living near water I was taught to fish for 'tiddlers' which led to becoming a match angler and pleasure fisherwoman from my early teens onwards. We would paddle on warm balmy days or briskly stroll along our river in the depth of winter stopping occasionally to feed fish and ducks. From my earliest memories, the River Ver has always been a constant part of my life and many photos and family films show us in or around this small yet beautiful river. Our various dogs as I grew up, were particularly fond of splashing around with us and even fonder of shaking their very wet coats all over us!

Rivers large and small are the life-blood of our planet, the arteries feeding that precious, often abused and taken for granted commodity – water to the animals and plants that could not exist without it. Indeed life itself began in water. There are some estimated 40,000 miles of waterways in this land of

Ted Banfield and Jacqui (with Lassie) enjoying the river (JBT)

ours, from the mightiest river to the smallest rivulet and all have a story to tell, a history waiting to be discovered and developing around us as we go about our day-to-day life.

From its source 180m above sea level, at Kensworth Lynch in the foothills of the Chilterns, the River Ver, when in full flow, meanders roughly south for approximately 24km through its valley to Bricket Wood where it joins the River Colne, approximately 60m above sea level. The groundwater catchment area covers around 100 sq km.

Aquifers are water-bearing layers of rock, such as chalk, that are porous enough to store water but permeable enough to allow significant amounts of it to pass through the rock. Formed by rainwater soaking through the fissures in the chalk aquifer, this process creates alkaline nutrient-rich water at a constant temperature, which emerges as springs feeding the chalk streams – globally scarce and fragile ecosystems containing rich and varied flora and fauna. There are only 163 chalk streams in the world, two in France and the rest here in the UK.

Throughout the world, aquifers contain more fresh water than all the lakes and rivers put together. In *Introducing Ground Water* by Michael Price it states *'It is estimated that the total amount of water on the Earth is a little over 1400 million cubic kilometres..... about 95% is sea water.... about 2% of the total – occurs in solid form in glaciers and polar ice caps. Virtually all the remaining water....is groundwater. The water in rivers and lakes, in the atmosphere and in the unsaturated zone, together amounts to only about 1/50th of 1% of the world's total water supply'.*

Being winterbourne, the river's flow is at its best during periods of heavy rain and snow. During the warmer months the water table fluctuates due to less rain, evaporation, plant absorption and of course the constant threat of abstraction, taking yet more potential river water for domestic use, which has often contributed in making the upper reaches of the river dry. In fact between the 1950s and 1990s the course of the Ver above St Albans was shortened by 10km and it has been known to be dry as far as Park Street, largely due to abstraction and reduced rainfall, which results in devastating effects on the flora and fauna. In 2011 the Environment Agency warned that the vast majority of rivers in England and Wales have reached the limit of what can be sustainably taken from them, the same year as the driest spring since records began 100 years ago was recorded.

The water meadows at the north end of the valley are still abundant in wildlife and improving, though not quite as it was in the past before abstraction caused a great decline in flora and fauna. A letter from wildlife artist and life-long friend of dad, Gordon Benningfield, written in the 1980s quotes, *"At the time of the enquiry into the planning application for the toxic waste plant near Redbourn, the bird life that I observed included moorhen, coote, dabchick, water rail, reed warbler, reed bunting, chiffchaff, snipe, woodcock, marshtit, woodpecker-great and spotted, tree creeper, heron, kingfisher, partridge and mammals: water vole, water shrew, bank and field vole and harvest mice. There is quite a good collection of butterflies that you would expect to see in this type of habitat and there were other species of wildlife seen occasionally".*

In the past water was pumped from the chalk aquifer faster than nature could replenish it, causing some springs to run dry or become intermittent, giving a reduced yield. The lowering of the water table has altered the flow of upper parts of many streams including the Ver, which originally rose several miles above its present source. In medieval times it powered many mills and is even thought to have once been navigable for large boats.

Due to abstraction at Friars Wash, Bow Bridge and Kensworth, these meadows diminished, but things began to look brighter. In the mid 1980s almost 70% of available water from normal rainfall conditions was being abstracted, therefore the Thames Water Authority commissioned a survey to investigate a way to limit the water abstraction from the river and surrounding water table.

Historically, the Ver catchment has had significant quantities of groundwater abstracted and there was a considerable increase in the 1940s and 1950s. Out of the 22 boreholes between Redbourn and Park Street, 16 were created during this time. These bore holes fall into two categories, those for water abstractions e.g. Bow Bridge, and those for water supply e.g. watercress beds and farms.

There was already concern about the level of the water table at an earlier date when in 1923 St Albans waterworks sank bore holes at Holywell. The well at Pré sawmills was pumped dry in three hours.

Although, as pointed out by W. Branch Johnson in *Industrial Archaeology of Hertfordshire*, this decline was partly due to the development of large urban areas, it was noticeable in Hertfordshire by the steady fall of the water table, which put one water powered mill after another out of action. Cassey's Directory listed 65 working mills in 1902, but by 1937 only 19 were working, a decline of 46 working mills in thirty-five years. These mills were all over Hertfordshire and we know that some on the Ver did stop working during this time, one of which was Park Mill in Park Street.

So we find that way back in the 1920s and '30s there was a drop in the water table and a decline in the River Ver. It was not just during the drying up of the river in the drought of 1976 that the drop in the water table was noticed.

It seems that a number of people knew that the water table in the Ver valley was falling, but the water was needed elsewhere and taken. This was especially so in the 1950s, when pumping from Bow Bridge, Friars Wash and Kensworth were started. Although not surprising, in the context of the 1950s, when Britain was beginning to recover from the Second World War and putting its energy into building a new technologically-orientated society, it was only relatively recently that some of the snags of this technology have been realised, from the disadvantages of high-rise flats to pollution.

Today abstraction from Friars Wash has been

limited and is now only used in emergencies, thanks in part to the campaigning of the Ver Valley Society.

Because of the abundance and purity of its water supply, Hertfordshire was one of the first counties to develop watercress growing. This has been a traditional occupation in the Ver Valley since it was introduced into England in the early part of the nineteenth century. But today the watercress beds have gone. Even in 1943, Mr Bozier found it necessary to have three bore holes sunk at New Jerome's Farm on the Redbourn Road, in order to supply sufficient water for his cress beds.

There is evidence of settlements around the River Ver as far back as 3000BC. The name of our river the Ver is said to date from around the first century AD. When Caesar invaded Britain in 55BC the Belgic settlers under their leader, Cassivellaunus, were driven out of their encampment at Devils Dyke near Wheathampstead, which had its own river route down the Lee to Londinium and into the sea. They then settled on the northern bank of the River Ver and constructed an earthwork at Beech Bottom. They preferred to travel by boat and ventured south along the river. Their camp was then changed from Beech Bottom to a higher point nearer the Ver for strategic purposes and a more direct route along the river. The new site at the time of Tasciovanus, their leader AD 1-10, was called Verlamion, a Celtic metropolis; hence the river was known as the Ver.

The river has had an astonishing number of names throughout history – the ones below are only those I have come across in my research but I am sure there are more out there. I have added dates where known, some crop up, miss a century or two and reappear, some are only used once and never seen again! Different parts of the river have sometimes been given their own title ie the different variations given to the river at the bottom of Holywell Hill. And there are variations of the same spelling, not unusual on old documents.

Many theories are attached to the names. The modern day name of our river is an obvious shortening of those starting with 'Ver', however in the 1903 book *Hertfordshire, A Reading Book of the County* HR Wilton Hall says that 'The Ver gets its name from a British word which means "the water". This stems from the word 'yar' or 'war' which signifies water.

Cole	sixteenth century
Colne	nineteenth, twentieth century
Colne Fluvius	eighteenth century map of Roman Verulamium *fluvius = stream
Haliwell/Halywelle/ Holywell Water	thirteenth, twelfth, twelfth century
Halywell	fifteenth century
Holystreme	thirteenth century
Holywell River	seventeenth-nineteenth century
Holywell Stream	
Meure	nineteenth century
Mure	sixteenth/eighteenth/ nineteenth century
Murus	
Muse	seventeenth/eighteenth century. May come from the name used for the Ver in the seventeenth century Poly-Olbion by Michael Drayton.
St Michael's River	seventeenth century
Tar	nineteenth/twentieth century
Ver	seventeenth-twenty-first century
Vere	sixteenth century
Verlam	nineteenth century
Verlume	sixteenth century
Verlumus	
Verulam	eighteenth century
Wemere	fifteenth century
Wenmer	seventeenth century
Werlam	thirteenth century
Woborne Mere	eighteenth century
Womer	seventeenth century
Womere	fifteenth, sixteenth century

The complexities of taking over from another author, especially when they are no longer around to ask the myriad of questions that have cropped up in the past years whilst writing this book are vast. I have, wherever possible checked dad's work and where necessary tried to trace the owners and contributors of information and illustrations: inevitably there will be the odd error or missed or wrongly placed acknowledgement for which I apologise.

A book such as this is never really complete, its subject is ongoing and I am certain other interesting facts will come to light once published. Despite the feeling I could probably go on for many more months adding more details and illustrations, my publisher would disown me if I didn't stop and publish at some point and so hope that any reader who has further information, especially photos and memories will contact me. My lifelong passion for our river is insatiable and maybe one day this book will be joined by a partner!

Whenever I have mentioned the Ver to various people throughout the writing of this book, the reactions have been varied from great encouragement and wishes of good luck to 'what river?' and 'that part-time puddle' and even 'how can something so small and insignificant have any history at all!' Well this book shows the believers and the doubters that our river does indeed have a wonderful story to tell and that rivers shape not only our landscapes but also our lives.

For nearly seventy years dad fished, swam, canoed, walked and frequently fell into the River Ver. With my parents, family, friends and pets I spent many pleasant hours simply enjoying our river and as I grew into adulthood I became fascinated by the connections between the history of the river, its nature and man's relationship and involvement with it.

This book is written how dad and I see and have learnt about the River Ver from experience, research and, more importantly, people's memories – every person is a unique, individual and fascinating library of experiences, information and recollections which if not gathered and recorded are lost forever.

I find that there is always more pleasure and appreciation of a place be it a town, building or waterway by knowing even a little of its history and it is hoped that this book helps to show just how lucky we all are to have our local river, encourages people to take an interest in using and caring for it and its surroundings and that it helps to give the Ver its rightful importance now and for future generations.

"If the crown jewels of the landscape are stolen,
Then when the final history books are written,
It will be not just the thief, who will be remembered
  and blamed,
But also the slumbering guard".
    (From *Taming the Flood* by Jeremy Purseglove)

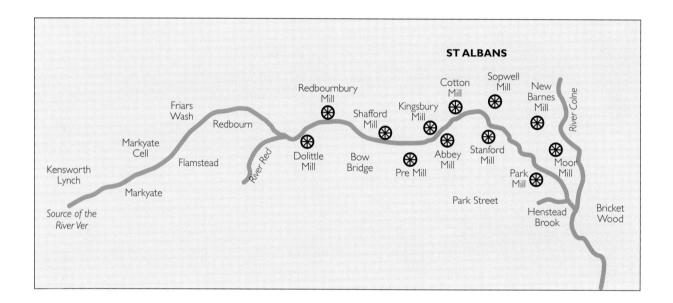

Rainfall, Aquifer and Abstraction Tables

Rainfall

Month 2010	Actual rainfall (2010) Millimetres	Average Rainfall in Millimetres	+/- mm Average	Percent Average
January	47.3	69.7	-22.4	67.9%
February	77.2	48.8	28.4	158.2%
March	45.2	53.9	-8.7	83.8%
April	18.7	53.4	-34.7	35.0%
May	38.4	49.7	-11.3	77.3%
June	23.5	60.2	-36.7	39.0%
July	31.6	42.1	-10.5	75.1%
August	127.6	53.5	74.1	238.3%
September				
October				
November				
December				
TOTALS	409.5	431.3	-21.8	94.9

Month 2009	Actual rainfall (2009) Millimetres	Average Rainfall in Millimetres	+/- mm Average	Percent Average
January	70.4	69.7	0.7	101.0%
February	73.9	48.8	25.1	151.4%
March	37.3	53.9	-16.6	69.2%
April	46.7	53.5	-6.8	87.3%
May	24.8	49.7	-24.9	49.9%
June	68.1	60.2	7.9	113.1%
July	73.3	42.1	31.2	174.1%
August	63.4	53.7	9.7	118.1%
September	15.9	61.0	-45.1	26.1%
October	39.1	74.7	-35.6	52.4%
November	146.1	66.2	79.9	220.6%
December	105.2	70.1	35.1	150.0%
TOTALS	764.2	703.6	60.6	108.6%

Month 2008	Actual rainfall (2008) Millimetres	Average Rainfall in Millimetres	+/- mm Average	Percent Average
January	103.20	69.70	33.50	148.1%
February	21.90	48.80	-26.90	44.9%
March	108.50	53.90	54.60	201.3%
April	53.50	53.50	0.00	100.0%
May	87.00	49.70	37.30	175.1%
June	35.30	60.20	-24.90	58.6%
July	90.3	42.00	48.30	215.0%
August	107.8	53.70	54.10	200.7%
September	66.2	61.00	5.20	108.5%
October	74.3	74.7	-0.40	99.5%
November	91.1	66.2	24.90	137.6%
December	42.0	70.1	-28.10	59.9%
TOTALS	881.10	703.50	177.60	125.2%

Month 2007	Actual rainfall (2007) Millimetres	Average Rainfall in Millimetres	+/- mm Average	Percent Average
January	91.60	69.70	21.90	131.4%
February	97.44	48.60	48.84	200.5%
March	57.60	53.90	3.70	106.9%
April	2.80	53.50	-50.70	5.2%
May	135.80	49.70	86.10	273.2%
June	72.40	60.20	12.20	120.3%
July	86.8	44.60	42.20	194.6%
August	64.6	53.90	10.70	119.9%
September	29.2	61.00	-31.80	47.9%
October	57.1	74.7	-17.60	76.4%
November	80.0	66.2	13.80	120.8%
December	67.1	70.1	-3.00	95.7%
TOTALS	842.44	706.10	136.34	119.3%

Month 2006	Actual rainfall (2006) Millimetres	Average Rainfall in Millimetres	+/- mm Average	Percent Average
January	29.20	69.70	-40.50	41.9%
February	41.40	48.80	-7.40	84.8%
March	49.50	53.90	-4.40	91.8%
April	51.00	53.50	-2.50	95.3%
May	89.00	49.70	39.30	179.1%
June	15.00	60.20	-45.20	24.9%
July	35.60	42.10	-6.50	84.6%
August	110.00	53.70	56.30	204.8%
September	54.20	61.00	-6.80	88.9%
October	105.00	74.70	30.30	140.6%
November	104.40	66.20	38.20	157.7%
December	95.00	74.10	20.90	128.2%
TOTALS	779.30	707.60	71.70	110.1%

Month 2005	Actual rainfall (2005) Millimetres	Average Rainfall in Millimetres	+/- mm Average	Percent Average
January	33.8	69.7	-35.9	48.5%
February	36.2	48.8	-12.6	74.2%
March	43.2	53.4	-10.2	80.9%
April	65.6	53.5	12.1	122.6%
May	44.4	49.7	-5.3	89.3%
June	44.0	60.2	-16.2	73.1%
July	39.0	42.1	-3.1	92.6%
August	58.6	53.7	4.9	109.1%
September	65.0	61.0	4.0	106.6%
October	88.4	74.7	13.7	118.3%
November	53.8	66.8	-13.0	80.5%
December	53.0	74.5	-21.5	71.1%
TOTALS	625.0	708.1	-83.1	88.3%

Aquifer

Month 2010	Actual Aquifer (metres)	Average Aquifer (metres)	Difference (metres)
January	128.49	130.92	-2.43
February	129.04	131.60	-2.56
March	131.94	132.38	-0.44
April	135.52	133.60	1.92
May	135.70	134.10	1.60
June	134.97	133.32	1.65
July	131.99	133.25	-1.26
August	132.51	132.56	-0.05
September			0.00
October			0.00
November			0.00
December			0.00

Month 2009	Actual Aquifer (metres)	Average Aquifer (metres)	Difference (metres)
January	133.10	131.36	1.74
February	134.62	132.38	2.24
March	136.57	132.79	3.78
April	136.64	133.60	3.04
May	135.85	134.10	1.75
June	134.61	133.30	1.31
July	131.57	133.22	-1.65
August	132.30	132.56	-0.26
September	131.24	130.87	0.37
October	130.09	130.93	-0.84
November	128.80	130.91	-2.11
December	128.24	130.50	-2.26

Month 2008	Actual Aquifer (metres)	Average Aquifer (metres)	Difference (metres)
January	131.26	131.36	-0.10
February	134.22	132.38	1.84
March	134.90	132.79	2.11
April	135.53	133.60	1.93
May	134.84	134.10	0.74
June	134.52	133.32	1.20
July	133.88	133.23	0.65
August	133.07	132.56	0.51
September	132.29	130.87	1.42
October	131.60	130.91	0.69
November	131.40	130.90	0.50
December	131.62	130.56	1.06

Month 2007	Actual Aquifer (metres)	Average Aquifer (metres)	Difference (metres)
January	128.94	131.36	-2.42
February	132.60	132.38	0.22
March	135.67	132.79	2.88
April	136.26	133.60	2.66
May	135.60	134.10	1.50
June	134.79	133.32	1.47
July	133.78	133.23	0.55
August	132.83	132.56	0.27
September	131.82	130.83	0.99
October	131.40	130.87	0.53
November	130.90	130.91	-0.01
December	130.66	130.56	0.10

Month 2006	Actual Aquifer (metres)	Average Aquifer (metres)	Difference (metres)
January	126.09	131.36	-5.27
February	126.03	132.38	-6.35
March	126.63	132.79	-6.16
April	126.63	133.60	-6.97
May	126.70	134.10	-7.40
June	126.71	133.32	-6.61
July	126.77	133.23	-6.46
August	126.45	132.56	-6.11
September	125.81	130.87	-5.06
October	125.49	130.93	-5.44
November	125.34	130.91	-5.57
December	126.47	130.56	-4.09

Month 2005	Actual Aquifer (metres)	Average Aquifer (metres)	Difference (metres)
December	126.15	130.56	-4.41
November	126.15	130.91	-4.76
October	126.17	130.93	-4.76
September	126.17	130.87	-4.70
August	126.68	132.56	-5.88
July	127.24	133.23	-5.99
June	127.93	133.32	-5.39
May	127.76	134.10	-6.34
April	127.27	133.60	-6.33
March	127.77	132.79	-5.02
February	127.25	132.38	-5.13
January	128.15	131.36	-3.21

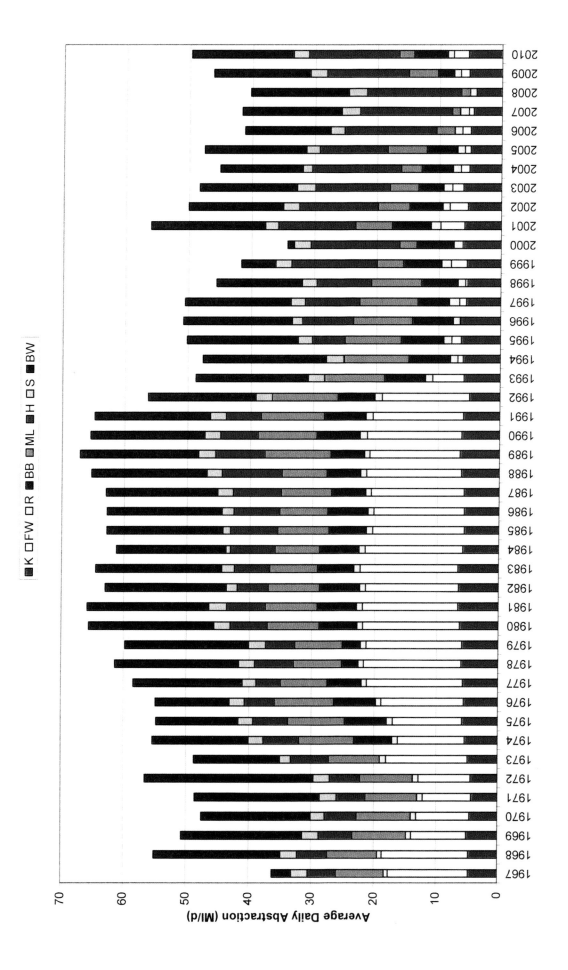

Abstraction details 1967–2010 of pumping stations between the source and confluence. (Veolia Water Central)

Flora and Fauna seen in and around the Ver and its Valley since 2000

Fish (JBT)
Brown Trout
Chub
Dace
Millers Thumbs
Minnows
Perch
Pike
Rainbow trout
Roach
Roach/rudd hybrid
Rudd
Sticklebacks

Dragonflies (VVS and JBT)
Banded Demoiselle
Blue-tailed Damselflies
Brown Hawker
Common Darter
EmperorRuddy Darter
Soutern Hawker

Butterflies (VVS and JBT)
Brimstone
Comma
Gatekeeper
Green-veined White
Large and Small Whites
Meadow Brown
Orange Tip
Peacock
Red Admiral
Small Tortoiseshell
Speckled Wood

Some of the many Ver Valley water and wet meadow flowers and trees (VVS and JBT)
Bee Orchid
Bluebells
Brambles Bugle
Brooklime
Bullrush
Bur-reed
Butterbur
Buttercups – meadow and creeping

Celandine
Celery-leafed Buttercup
Coltsfoot
Comfrey
Common Reed
Cowslips
Cranesbills
Dog Rose
Gorse
Herb Robert
Himalayan Balsam * Invasive alien
Hogweed
Japanese Knotweed * Invasive alien
Lady's Smock or Cuckoo Flower
Marestails
Marsh Marigold
Oxeye Daisy
Ragged Robin
Red Campion
Speedwell
Various Fungi
Vetches, various
Violets
Water Cress
Water Crowfoot
Water Figwort
Water Forget-Me-Not
Water Mint
Willowherb
Yellow Flag Iris

Alder
Ash
Elder
Guelder Rose
Hawthorn
Horse Chestnut
Oak
Spindle
Sycamore
Wayfaring Tree
Wild Cherry
Willows – Crack, Pussy and Weeping

Bird Species

Species	Status	Season	Breeding	Comments
Little Grebe	Common	All Year	Yes	
Great Crested Grebe	Common	All Year	Yes	
Cormorant	Common	All Year	Yes	
Little Egret	Common	All Year	No	Bred in Herts 2011
Grey Heron	Common	All Year	Yes	Breeding Colony at Lake
Mute Swan	Common	All Year	Yes	
Greylag Goose	Common	All Year	Yes	
Canada Goose	Common	All Year	Yes	
Ruddy Shelduck	Rare	Vagrant		1 seen 2009
Mandarin	Rare	Vagrant		
Wigeon	Rare	Winter Visitor		
Gadwall	Common	All Year	Yes	
Teal	Common	Winter Visitor		
Mallard	Common	All Year	Yes	
Pintail	Very Rare	Vagrant		
Shoveler	Common	Winter Visitor		
Pochard	Common	Winter Visitor		
Ruddy Duck	Common	Winter Visitor		
Osprey	Very Rare	Vagrant		1 seen Sept 2009 - Park Street
Red Kite	Common	All Year	Yes	Seen regularly since 2006
Marsh Harrier	Very Rare	Vagrant		1 seen 2001
Goshawk	Very Rare	All Year	Possible	
Sparrowhawk	Common	All Year	Yes	
Buzzard	Common	All Year	Yes	
Kestrel	Common	All Year	Yes	
Merlin	Very Rare	Vagrant		Female present for few days in Nov 2008
Hobby	Common	Summer Visitor	Some Years	Seen mainly on passage
Peregrine	Very Rare	Vagrant		Passage only
Red-legged Partridge	Common	All Year	Yes	Introduced species bred for shooting
Grey Partridge	Common	All Year	Yes	Declining breeding species
Pheasant	Common	All Year	Yes	Introduced species bred for shooting
Water Rail	Rare	Winter Visitor		
Moorhen	Common	All Year	Yes	
Coot	Common	All Year	Yes	
Crane	Very Rare	Vagrant		5 birds flew over in 2005
Little Ringed Plover	Very Rare	Vagrant	Yes	Bred in 2001 and 2009
Ringed Plover	Very Rare	Vagrant		
Golden Plover	Common	Winter Visitor		Passage only
Lapwing	Common	All Year	Yes	Passage and breeding bird
Dunlin	Very Rare	Vagrant		6 seen 2001
Jack Snipe	Very Rare	Vagrant		Passage only
Snipe	Common	Winter Visitor		Previously breeding species
Woodcock	Very Rare	Vagrant		Passage only
Redshank	Rare	Vagrant		Passage only

Greenshank	Rare	Winter Visitor		Passage only
Green Sandpiper	Rare	Winter Visitor		Passage only
Common Sandpiper	Very Rare	Vagrant		Passage only
Black-headed Gull	Common	All Year		
Common Gull	Common	All Year		
Lesser Black-backed Gull		Common	All Year	
Herring Gull	Common	All Year		
Great Black-backed Gull	Rare	Vagrant		Passage only
Common Tern	Rare	Vagrant		Passage only
Feral/ Rock Pigeon	Common	All Year	Yes	
Stock Dove	Common	All Year	Yes	
Woodpigeon	Common	All Year	Yes	
Collared Dove	Common	All Year	Yes	
Turtle Dove	Very Rare	Vagrant		Passage only - did breed previously
Ring-necked Parakeet	Rare	Vagrant		Introduced species spreading through home counties
Cuckoo	Common	Summer Visitor	Yes	Declining breeding species
Barn Owl	Common	All Year	Yes	
Little Owl	Common	All Year	Yes	
Tawny Owl	Common	All Year	Yes	
Short-eared Owl	Very Rare	Winter Visitor		Passage only
Swift	Common	Summer Visitor	Yes	
Kingfisher	Common	All Year	Yes	
Green Woodpecker	Common	All Year	Yes	
Great Spotted Woodpecker	Common	All Year	Yes	
Lesser Spotted Woodpecker	Very Rare	All Year	Possible	Declining breeding species
Skylark	Common	All Year	Yes	
Sand Martin	Rare	Summer Visitor		Passage only
Swallow	Common	Summer Visitor	Yes	
House Martin	Common	Summer Visitor	Yes	
Meadow Pipit	Common	All Year		Mainly passage only
Yellow Wagtail	Rare	Summer Visitor		Breeding some years
Grey Wagtail	Common	All Year	Yes	
Pied Wagtail	Common	All Year	Yes	
Bohemian Waxwing	Rare	Vagrant		Last influx was 2005
Wren	Common	All Year	Yes	
Dunnock	Common	All Year	Yes	
Robin	Common	All Year	Yes	
Black Redstart	Very Rare	Vagrant		Passage only
Redstart	Very Rare	Vagrant		Passage only
Whinchat	Rare	Vagrant		Passage only
Stonechat	Rare	Winter Visitor		Over winters most years
Wheatear	Rare	Vagrant		Passage only
Song Thrush	Common	All Year	Yes	
Redwing	Common	Winter Visitor		

Mistle Thrush	Common	All Year	Yes	
Fieldfare	Common	Winter Visitor		
Blackbird	Common	All Year	Yes	
Ring Ouzel	Very Rare	Passage		Male on Passage in April 2007
Grasshopper Warbler	Very Rare	Passage		Passage only - did breed previously
Sedge Warbler	Common	Summer Visitor	Yes	
Reed Warbler	Common	Summer Visitor	Yes	
Lesser Whitethroat	Common	Summer Visitor	Yes	
Whitethroat	Common	Summer Visitor	Yes	
Garden Warbler	Common	Summer Visitor	Yes	
Blackcap	Common	Summer Visitor	Yes	
Wood Warbler	Very Rare	Vagrant		Passage only - seen 2006
Chiffchaff	Common	Summer Visitor	Yes	
Willow Warbler	Common	Summer Visitor	Yes	
Goldcrest	Common	All Year	Yes	
Firecrest	Very Rare	Vagrant		
Spotted Flycatcher	Rare	Summer Visitor	Yes	Breeds most years
Long-tailed Tit	Common	All Year	Yes	
Marsh Tit	Rare	All Year		
Coal Tit	Common	All Year	Yes	
Blue Tit	Common	All Year	Yes	
Great Tit	Common	All Year	Yes	
Nuthatch	Common	All Year	Yes	
Treecreeper	Common	All Year	Yes	
Jay	Common	All Year	Yes	
Magpie	Common	All Year	Yes	
Jackdaw	Common	All Year	Yes	
Rook	Common	All Year	Yes	
Carrion Crow	Common	All Year	Yes	
Raven	Very Rare	All Year		2 sightings 2009
Starling	Common	All Year	Yes	
House Sparrow	Common	All Year	Yes	
Tree Sparrow	Rare	Vagrant		Breeding colony nearby
Chaffinch	Common	All Year	Yes	
Brambling	Rare	Winter Visitor		Good numbers some winters
Greenfinch	Common	All Year	Yes	
Goldfinch	Common	All Year	Yes	
Siskin	Rare	Winter Visitor		Good numbers some winters
Linnet	Common	All Year	Yes	
Common Redpoll	Rare	Winter Visitor		Good numbers some winters
Crossbill	Very Rare	Winter Visitor		
Bullfinch	Common	All Year	Yes	
Yellowhammer	Common	All Year	Yes	
Reed Bunting	Common	All Year	Yes	
Corn Bunting	Very Rare	All Year		

Mammal Species

Species	Status	Season	Breeding	Comments
Fox	Common	All Year	Yes	Becoming more common
Badger	Common	All Year	Yes	Nocturnal lifestyle means they are seldom seen
Stoat	Common	All Year	Yes	Few sightings
Weasel	Common	All Year	Yes	Few sightings
Water Vole	Possible	All Year		Bred prolifically until 1980s - could be reintroduced
Mink	Common	All Year	Yes	Introduced species now being trapped
Otter	Possible	All Year		Following the hunting ban they are re-establishing
Muntjac	Common	All Year	Yes	Introduced species
Hare	Common	All Year	Yes	Have declined but still seen most of the year
Rabbit	Common	All Year	Yes	Introduced species
Grey Squirrel	Common	All Year	Yes	Introduced species
Shrew	Common	All Year	Yes	Seldom seen
Water Shrew	Common	All Year	Yes	Seldom seen
Vole	Common	All Year	Yes	Seldom seen

Some Old Words Associated with Rivers and Water

Aedre (OE)	Stream	**Frogga** (OE)	Frog
Aelfisc (OE)	Eel	**Gafolfisc** (OE)	Fish paid as rent
Aewelm (OE)	Place at the river source	**Gemythe** (OE)	River junction
Ait/eyot (OE)	A small island in a river	**Gewaed** (OE)	Ford
Baece (OE)	Brook	**Grin-stun** (OH)	Grindstone
Bams (OH)	Sticklebacks/tiddlers	**Head** (OE)	Spring, source
Bammin (OH)	Fishing for tiddlers	**Her** (OE)	Heron
Bangy (OH)	Muddy	**Hippin-stones** (OE)	Stepping stones
Bekkr (ON)	Stream or brook	**Hladan** (OE)	Draw water, take in water
Bestyman (OH)	Wet, flood	**Hoddydod** (OE)	Snail
Bomby/Bumpy (OH)	Low marshy place	**Hoss-stinger** (OE)	Dragon fly
Bottom (OE)	Low, often marshy ground	**Hurlocky** (OH)	Stony chalk
Bourn (OE)	A stream, a boundary, often a deep wide ditch	**Isearn** (OE)	Kingfisher
		Jink (OH)	A small water worn pebble
Broc (OE)	Brook, Stream	**Keech** (OE)	To dip for water
Burna (OE)	Stream	**Kiddles/Kidels** (OE)	Fish weirs
Caerswill (OE)	Spring where watercress grows	**Lagu** (OE)	Flood
		Lea (OE)	Meadow
Callerboshes (OH)	Unfledged nestlings	**Leaccaerse** (OE)	Watercress
Cealcpyt (OE)	Chalk pit	**Leap** (OE)	Basket for catching or keeping fish
Cealcsead (OE)	Chalk stone		
Celde (OE)	Spring	**Legstream** (OE)	River
Cherm/Charm (OE)	Chorus of birds	**Loekr** (ON)	Brook
Claggy (OE)	Muddy	**Loop** (OE)	The winding of the river
Core (OH)	A small island in a stream	**Lugustream** (OE)	Water, stream
Cucking stool (OE)	A chair in which suspected witches or disorderly women were ducked	**Mammerin** (OE)	The small noise made by bats
		Mead (OE)	Field
Cweorn (OE)	Mill	**Mere** (OE)	Lake or pond
Dabble (OE)	To paddle in shallow water	**Meregrund** (OE)	Lake bottom
		Naca (OE)	Boat or vessel
Dale (OE)	Valley	**Neckid Snail** (OH)	Slug
Dodman (OE)	Snail	**Oshey (ozhey)** (OE)	Soft ground fit for growing osier
Ea (OE)	Water/River		
Effs/ewts/efts (OH)	Newts	**Paigle, Peggle, cow-peggle** (OE)	Cowslip
Eye/Core (OE)	Land partially/entirely surrounded by water	**Peggle peeps** (OE)	Petals of cowslips used to make cowslip wine. Issac Walton was fond of trout served with fried cowslip peeps.
Feesh (OH)	Fish		
Fisc (OE)	Fish and animals living exclusively in water		
Fiscap (OE)	Fishing	**Piscary** (OE)	The right to fish in waters owned by another/A fishery
Fiscwielle (OE)	Rich in fish		
Fleote (OE)	Small stream, especially a place where it enters or leaves a larger body of water or marshland	**Pitchins** (OH)	Rounded flint pebbles, used in Hertfordshire for paving. Often found in river-gravels and came originally from the chalk.
Flod (OE)	Flood		
Flode (OE)	Channel of water		

Plash, also **wash** (OE)	A small pool or to make a splashing sound.	**Stilttlebat/tittlebat/ tiddler /bam soldier** (OH)	Stickleback. In spring the males are tinted red and were called **fiery kings**.
Plosh (OE)	Splash		
Poliwogs/ polwygle (pol, head and wiglen, to wiggle) (OE),	Frog tadpoles. Tadpole was traditionally a young toad, not frog.	**Sun-stone/God stone** (OE)	A water-worn, transparent pebble, carried for luck.
Puddock (OE)	A frog	**Swaller** (OH)	A hole in the ground for water to run away
Pynding (OE)	Dam		
Rith (OE)	Small stream	**Thetch** (OH)	Vetch
Sallow /sollar/sally (OE)	Willow	**Thwart** (OH)	To bridge (a stream or river)
Scrumpt (OH)	Dried up	**Waeter** (OE)	Water
Seep (OE)	An oozing up or away of water	**Walley** (OH)	Valley
		Wash (OE)	A ford or occasional flood
Slabby (OE)	Muddy place or puddle	**Wæter-scipe** (OE)	A body or piece of water
Slocker (OH)	A quiet walk	**Wash** (OE)	A ford, or occasional flood.
Slud (OH)	Thick mud, slush	**Whelm** (OE)	Well up or flow
Smirry (OH)	Damp drizzly weather	**Whellum** (OH)	A roughly made bridge across a width of water for carts. They were often made of tree trunks, sawn in half lengthways. Trees were also hollowed out to use for a drain to go across or under a road leading from one field to another.
Soldier (OH)	Stickleback		
Soppy (OE)	Very (soppin) wet		
Spewy/spewyness (OH)	Damp, ooziness of the soil		
Spit (OE)	An accumulation of gravel or sand in a stream		
Splodge (OE)	To splash		
Squad (OH)	Thick mud		
Squashy (OH)	A wet patch in a meadow		
Stagnum (OE)	A pond or swamp with no outlet	**Wicker/Withy** (OE)	Willow
		Wiell (OE)	Spring or fountain
Stank (OE)	A dam/to lay boards, supported by piles or struts at sides of watercourses to strengthen the banks.	**Ylfett** (OE)	Swan

OE - Old English
ON - Old Norse
OH - Old Hertfordshire

Chapter One
Geology

....Hammers an' chisels an' a',
Chisels an' fossils an' a';
The deeper we go, the more we shall know
Of the past an' the recent an' a'.

From *Song of a Geologist* by Robert Dick a nineteenth century Scottish geologist

Geology is the building blocks of the planet we live on, shaping our Earth's past, present and future. There is an intrinsic link between geology and archaeology and the geological history of the land is paramount in the shaping of our hills, valleys and levels together with soil types which in turn influence the placing of early settlements, villages and towns along with their industries especially agriculture, throughout history. Rivers play an important part in giving shape and character to the landscape and in their natural state can be straight, meandering and multi-channelled (braided); the Ver can be found in all these variations throughout its course.

Rocks are of three main types, those created by fire called *igneous* rocks (igneous comes from the latin for fire), which were once molten.

Metamorphic rocks are the result of change in sedimentary and igneous rocks by underground conditions normally heat, pressure, fluids and strain, sometimes an interaction of some or all of these. Most of the Earth's rare minerals occur in metamorphic rocks.

Lastly *Sedimentary* rocks, in which most of the world's aquifers have their beginnings, originate in cool conditions at the Earth's surface, usually eroded and weathered from rocks then laid down under water creating beds, generally made of sand, often containing other materials such as pebbles, clay and mud or a mixture of several of these. It is the gaps that these assorted materials produce when they are laid down that give the aquifers their porosity.

The above geological deposits can be split into two: those less than two million years old are superficial sediments, softer and thinner; they usually cover the older, solid formations of harder rocks.

By geological terms Hertfordshire is comparatively young. The oldest deposits on the land surface are at the foot of the Chiltern Hills on the northern boundary of the county and are around 100 million years old. These consist of the Gault clay and upper green sand of the Upper Cretaceous period.

Gault clay, a blue/grey material which turns to a dull brown on exposure to the elements, contains many marine fossils, and is the remnant of muddy sediment once carried by rivers and deposited at the bottom of a shallow sea. It forms an area of low lying ground along the foot of the Chilterns, and has been found in bore holes to occur at depth beneath south east Hertfordshire. From medieval times it was used for brick making. Greensand was formed from sediments nearer to the sea shore and also contains abundant fossils. Moving south-east, the rocks gradually get younger.

The main Palaeocene deposit (65 million years ago) in Hertfordshire is the Reading Beds. These are made up of 30-50 foot of multicoloured clays with occasional patches of yellow sand and small black pebbles that lay over the chalk. At the base it is a shallow sea deposit but the upper parts were deposited by rivers flowing across the area.

65 million years ago large movements in the Earth's crust caused seas to retreat leaving the south of Britain with a sub tropical climate and largely covered in chalk. Later movements caused Britain to tilt 'downwards' giving rise to newly formed river estuaries in the south depositing large amounts of sand, clay and rocks up to 15 metres thick which now form the Reading Beds. Although once covering the whole of the Chilterns, it now occurs mainly in the south-eastern parts of the county, but a few outliers of this earlier cover were left in northwestern areas when most of it was eroded by rivers. There are examples of Reading Beds outliers in northern parts of St Albans. Hertfordshire puddingstones are occasionally found in these beds.

The London Clay, containing fewer animal fossils, was laid down in deeper seas, and overlies the Reading Beds in southeast Hertfordshire. Uplift, subsidence and erosion of land exposed the Reading Beds and London Clay, which is why they now cover only a small part of the county.

The superficial deposits in Hertfordshire are more variable in nature and originated in various ways.

Cretaceous (83-89 million years ago) chalk is a soft limestone composed of calcium carbonate that lies diagonally beneath most of southern England between the southeast and East Anglia, and was formed mainly by a multitude of sea life including algae and the shells and skeletons of billions of sea creatures when much of southern Britain was beneath a shallow warm sea, which over a period of

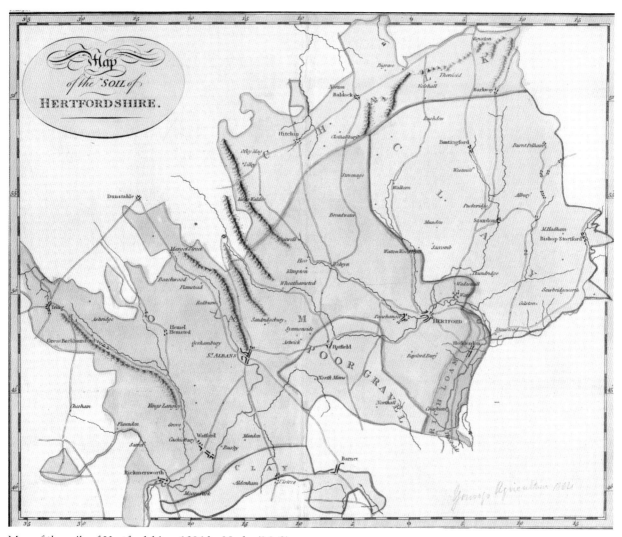

Map of the soils of Hertfordshire c1804 by Neele. (MoS)

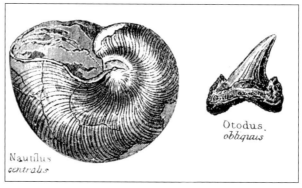

Fossils of the London Clay and Reading Beds.

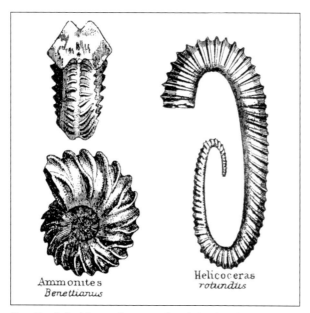

Fossils of the Upper Greensand and Gault Clay.

Examples of fossils found in the Ver Valley – sea urchin (Micraster cortestudinarium) and brachiopod (Gibbithyris semiglobosa). (DH)

 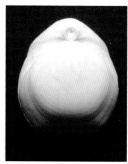

approximately 30 million years formed a chalk layer around 600 metres thick.

Fossils are the Earth's museum of life and this chalk is renowned for them – including shells, ammonites, gastropods, sea urchins and sharks' teeth. An example of a chalk 'cliff' can be seen at the former chalk works just off the Redbourn Road near the Ver.

Amongst the upper chalk can be found an abundance of flint made of a very hard type of silica.

Before the Anglian Ice Age began around 440,000 years ago, the River Thames flowed northeastwards through what is today the vale of St Albans into the sea at Suffolk. This 'proto-Thames' was much bigger than today. The Chiltern scarp was an obstacle for the ice sheets travelling from the northeast and caused them to divide down the valley of the Vale of Aylesbury and south across the lower plateau to the east of the county reaching the edge of Bricket Wood. Ice blocking the valley created a large lake to the southwest of St Albans causing the proto-Thames to re-route further south to where it flows today through London.

Once the Ice Age glaciers melted, the Thames' original valley formed the Lea and Colne rivers and their tributaries including the Ver which now flow in a southeast direction caused by the underlying rocks' gradual slope. Once the Ver reaches the east of St Albans, it makes a sharp turn to the south caused by ice blocking its escape route half a million years ago forcing the river to flow along the edge of the glacier.

The diversion of the Thames left rich deposits of gravel and these lighter soil areas were chosen for early habitation over the areas of poorly drained London Clay where cultivation was difficult and usually left to pasture and woodland. The gravel areas often provided easier routes for travel and as a result, many of today's Hertfordshire towns are built upon these deposits. Gravel has been extensively extracted in many places around the county; one site was by the river in Hicks Road, Markyate, now an industrial estate. In 1992 it was reported that around 30 million tonnes of gravel were being extracted in the region annually with an increase of 60% within the following decade. Often these extraction sites, once depleted, were turned into fishing lakes or wildlife areas, for example Frogmore 'pits', in Park Street.

In parts of the county there are almost parallel lines of low undulating hills, divided by wide valleys. The valley of the Ver is typical of this.

Swallow holes and springs are caused when the chalk is traversed by numerous cracks or joints allowing water to permeate. As chalk is slightly soluble in water containing carbon dioxide the rain, which sinks into the chalk, dissolves some of it and enlarges the cracks. Over thousands of years the chalk becomes full of holes and crevices, which convey water to springs and swallow holes at the bottom of valleys and into the rivers.

Kensworth and Flamstead have subsoil chiefly of chalk with an outlier of Reading Beds to the south of the village. Flamstead is also known for the great depth of its wells.

Chalk has been utilized in many ways over the centuries. Medieval armies heated the chalk to produce the highly corrosive calcium oxide or quicklime, a powerful irritant used against the enemy causing scalding, burning and blindness. It can also be used as a fertiliser and a kiln was used for this purpose in Redbourn near the former Punchbowl Inn. It was also a component in whitewash and mortar.

In Markyate, the village is mostly covered by Batcombe – brown earth with flints. On the west-facing sides of the valley close to the Ver is found a well drained brown calcareous soil, chalky, loamy and flinty called Coombe. The valley bottom is covered in a well drained loamy flinty earth called Charity. The Upper Cretaceous chalk is 89 million years old, and contains many fossils including brachiopods, ammonites and sea urchins. On top of the hills in some areas are layers of clay and flint up to 6 metres thick. Dry valley deposits of sand and gravel were extracted in the nineteenth and twentieth centuries and many puddingstones have been found in the area.

The Ver is one of a number of small river valleys flowing from northwest to southeast. It lies on the southeastern fringe of the Chiltern dip slope, which forms a chalk plateau sloping towards the east. St Albans is built mainly on glacial and river terrace gravel with areas of heavy, acidic clay and flint on the west of the town and more fertile heavy and badly drained boulder clay to the east. Park Street lies in the valley of the River Ver and is built on a mix of sand, gravel and clay deposited by Ice Age glaciers.

The gently undulating plateau of Bricket Wood is situated on a spur that juts out from a glacial drift deposited 30,000 years ago during the Anglian Ice Age. The terrace along the edge of the spur provided some protection from the lower boggier ground overlooking the Colne Valley for earlier settlers. Jack Williams Wood near the confluence sits on a terminal moraine – a ridge like accumulation of glacial material pushed forward by the front of the advancing glacier. Areas of gravel have been worked including those near Moor Mill and Drop Lane.

Hertfordshire puddingstones rarely found and very heavy for their size are remarkable objects. The large plum puddingstone on the bank of a lane from the village of Thorley to Bishops Stortford was said in the past to turn round when it heard the town clock at Bishops Stortford strike midnight. These stones can be found in sizes ranging from 10cm to over 2m in Hertfordshire and surrounding Home Counties.

Although types of puddingstone exist globally the strange anomaly about Hertfordshire pudding-stone is that the bonding matrix is generally a much harder substance than the rolled flint pebbles it contains and will often crack through the pebbles rather than pass around them. It is made from mainly oval flint pebbles bound by silica.

Occasionally Hertfordshire puddingstone can be found with no pebbles in at all. Stones called sarsens not unlike this matrix but without the pebbles can be found elsewhere in southern England, most famously used for the Triliths at Stonehenge. It has also been used in the walls of Windsor Castle and more locally the St Albans churches of St Michael's and St Stephen's.

This conglomerate of flint pebbles, which themselves can be as old as 80 million years, in a silica matrix at the base of the Reading Beds, was deposited in the Eocene period, around 56 million years ago when the climate in Britain was tropical. The pebbles were eroded from the chalk and rounded and sorted as they were carried along in water, the same process that makes the pebbles of the seashore smooth. During a brief period when the sea retreated in a semi-arid climate, capillary action brought dissolved silica from underlying rocks. The water evaporated leaving the silica, which hardened around the pebbles. The different colours are due to mineral impurities within the puddingstone and the red staining sometimes seen is due to the presence of iron oxide.

Hertfordshire puddingstone, sometimes called 'Hertfordshire plum puddingstone', because of its resemblance to an old-fashioned plum pudding, has always been an intrinsic part of Hertfordshire folklore. In AD 601, Pope Gregory instructed his missionaries to sanctify pagan idols and myths and include them in the fabric and teaching of the church. This is why the puddingstone was commonly placed in the foundations of churches as seen at the Holy Cross church at Sarratt, village greens, porches, boundary wall bases and buttresses, some which can still be seen today. Also in Sarratt there is a memorial to those lost during the two World Wars topped with a large puddingstone.

Through the ages it has been known by several names including 'breeding stone' and 'mother stone' and was thought to be continuously growing and collecting more pebbles or 'children'. There was also a belief that the stones were alive, had feelings and could move! Redbourn locals believed that these mysterious stones could walk!

The name 'growing stone' was a name often used by superstitious farmers who believed the stones 'grew' on their land and damaged ploughs and crops although soil erosion and ploughing would have caused this exposure.

'Woe Stone' was so called because when there was very heavy rain or floods, the puddingstone would be exposed as the rain washed away the soil from around it, associating the stones with misfortunes such as extreme weather conditions.

Pieces of puddingstone and also flint were known as 'witch' or 'hag' stones and were said to hold extra powers if found with a hole in, often being threaded onto horse harnesses to protect against disease. These stones would commonly be left on the doorsteps of houses or small pieces carried around with a person to ward off evil.

In a parish record of 1662 it recommends that a hag stone should be placed in a coffin of a dead woman as it was thought her body was bewitched and the stone would stop her from escaping.

It has had several uses throughout the centuries including building, an alternative to flint for making tools in the Stone Age, querns to grind corn, whetstones to sharpen knives, tools and jewellery – it is particularly spectacular when polished. A Stone Age puddingstone and flint quarry was discovered during the building of the A10 extension (formerly the Roman Ermine Street) at Puckeridge. Large pieces were used as parish boundary and track markers at strategic sites for example on hills and beside streams, especially at crossing points such as fords.

Substantial puddingstones can be found along the Ver outside Kingsbury Mill and by the village sign on the Redbourn/Harpenden Lane roundabout – both these stones originally pulled from the Ver, and at the water's edge near the old cress beds in Waterend Lane, Redbourn.

Part of an old puddingstone quern. (JBT)

Chapter Two
Archaeology

The Past! The dark, unfathom'd retrospect!
The teeming gulf! The sleepers and the shadows!
The past! The infinite greatness of the past!
For what is the present, after all, but a growth out of the past?

(Walt Whitman 1900)

Palaeolithic	c450,000-10,000BC
Mesolithic Period	c10,000-4500BC
Neolithic	c4500-2500BC
Bronze Age	c2500-700BC
Iron Age	c700BC-43AD
Roman Occupation	43AD-c410AD
Dark Ages/Anglo Saxon	c410AD-1066AD
Middle Ages	1066AD-1485AD

This chapter looks at just a very small sample of the archaeological finds discovered in and around the River Ver.

The past lives on beneath our feet and the archaeological finds of an area are the clues our ancestors left behind showing us how they spent their everyday lives, fragments of the past preserved by chance giving us an understanding of and a connection to their environment.

The presence of a water source, such as a spring or river brings life to everywhere it flows and has always been a natural and fundamental attraction for settlers and travellers and an important avenue for trade throughout time. The River Ver is no exception.

The original course of the river cannot be certain; its route has been altered many times in its history and for a myriad of reasons including the building of mills, watercress beds, ponds and roads, changes in agriculture and fluctuating water table levels. Geological and archaeological evidence of earlier river channels has been found as well as clues in written works, maps and photos. The river would have originally been larger with natural banks surrounded by reedy swampland and marshes with thick woodland beyond.

The fact that archaeological evidence hasn't so far been plentiful in parts of the Ver Valley does not necessarily mean it is completely devoid of any proof of our past. Very early samples may have been deposited far from their original location by Ice Age glaciers and it is thought many sites are under villages and towns making them impossible to excavate or they are simply waiting to be discovered! Unfortunately, many finds would also have been destroyed by the heavy gravel extraction in and

around the valley of the Ver.

The Palaeolithic time-span was vast, spanning hundreds of thousands of years and parts of it were devoid of human occupation, but during the time man was present he would have found much of his food around the rivers and valleys of the area, living in rough makeshift camps on the drier land away from the marshy areas near the river. Early hunting would have been with large stone hand implements adapted for other uses such as scraping, digging and chopping. Over time these weapons were refined and improved producing items such as spears tipped with microliths – small flaked sharp-edged stone tools usually made of flint or chert and later used for arrows fired by bows.

Mesolithic man began to live in larger more permanent sites not far from the river surrounded by woodland which had sprung from the tundra of the previous glaciations. Hunters would spend short periods of time away on expeditions finding food and setting up temporary camps. Large numbers of microliths from this era have been found. It was during the Mesolithic period that water levels continued to rise and Britain became an island, cut off from the rest of the continent.

Although little evidence of Neolithic tribes has been found in the area so far, they were the first farmers to spread further from the river, settling on areas of gravel, chalk escarpments and other drier places along the river valley where they cleared woodland for growing crops and keeping animals. Domesticating cattle, goats and pigs but still foraging for food and hunting wild animals, the bones of wild beasts such as deer and ox have been found in pits along with those of domesticated animals. The first people to produce pottery and more advanced weapons and tools, they were also thought to be the first to build religious structures such as henges, although little evidence has been found near the Ver to date.

Early Bronze Age man, known for his metal work tools and implements, lived in more permanent and larger communities although the population surrounding the river remained low. Burial burrows, often found with 'grave goods' have been found near the confluence at Bricket Wood and are found throughout Hertfordshire. As the population grew in the late Bronze Age, more land was cleared for farming and settlements, which were often surrounded by dykes with defensive hill forts on higher ground. With the beginnings of water deity worship, burials began to take place in and around rivers and marshy land.

The Iron Age saw Hertfordshire become an important part of Britain, with the Catuvellaunni based in the county and controlling a large part of southeast England by the time the Romans arrived. Some of the archaeological finds from this time are internationally important, including a royal burial from Verulamium, a town that became the third largest in Roman Britain.

Plenty of objects showing human activity have been found at the area now considered the source of the Ver around Kensworth and underlines the importance of the river to local tribes.

Gravel extraction in the river's flood plains along with the digging of local brick and chalk pits and quarries have uncovered many finds. Remains of Palaeolithic man were discovered on high ground, just beyond the source of the Ver at Kensworth by local archaeologist Worthington George Smith (1835-1917). Found mostly in pits that had been worked for brick earth, a flint workshop was discovered consisting of broken and unfinished implements, un-worked flints and leftover chips and flakes from manufacture. The amount of debris found at this site suggests that Stone Age man must have lived and worked here near the river over a long period of time. He also discovered four Neolithic axes in fields near Church End in 1892 and Neolithic and Bronze Age items at Kensworth quarry before it was extended including blades, an arrowhead, flints, a knife and axe.

Quantities of Romano-British artefacts have been found again close to the source of the river suggesting a possible settlement near the spring. In the nineteenth century during brick earth digging items found included millstones, cremated bones within urns, pans and amphorae – a vase-shaped ceramic container with two handles and a long neck used for storing and transporting food and liquids.

Much of the area would have been densely wooded with tracks and the river the main throughway. Evidence of early human settlement in Markyate is uncommon before Roman times.

Nearby the twentieth century Caddington brick pits are an area of great importance producing many finds including flint flakes and hand axes plus bones of large animals such as elephant and rhinos hunted by early man. Flint working sites found are thought to be over 70,000 years old. Also at Caddington Common a Stone Age puddingstone hand axe weighing 1lb 6oz was found by Worthington George Smith who also believed a Roman temple was located in Markyate. A brass tablet found at Markyate Street with the inscription 'TES DEI MAR SEDIARVM' (Tablet of the god Mars of Sediae) is thought to have allowed officials to collect contributions from the locals to sacrifice to their various gods. Despite this rare find there is not a huge amount of archaeological evidence from between 10,000BC and Roman times although burial urns containing human bones have been found in fields behind Markyate Cell and a Hibernia-Saxon bronze mounting from a horse harness was found in the garden of the old vicarage in 1955 dating from c.eighth-ninth century.

In the summer of 2008, Channel Four's popular *Time Team* programme, fronted by the actor and presenter Tony Robinson, chose a field just outside Redbourn at Friars Wash to carry out a three day archaeological dig. This local farmland lies in a gently undulating valley of chalk and clay with flints overlain locally by river gravels. The site was first noticed in 1965 when ploughing revealed building foundations and was chosen in response to aerial photos taken in the hot, dry summer of 1976 which showed outlines of possible Romano-British buildings. In a unique discovery for the programme, an amazing four Roman temples were uncovered. Tony Robinson was quoted as saying *'It's like a London bus. You wait for years for one to come along, and then you get not one, not two, not even three but four at the same time.'*

Although nothing specifically relating to the river was found, it does seem the ditches surrounding the temple complex did respect the river's course and were bounded to the southwest by the Ver, and it's possible the site was deliberately chosen for its proximity to the river. It is thought that these temples, which were in use from around the first century AD, may have been a place to worship water gods, in many cultures these deities were believed to live in springs, wells and streams, particularly apt as the River Ver is close by along with several springs.

It is likely the river would have been a source of fish and rolled lead sheets found in one of the trenches are thought to have been fishing weights.

The cella was a shrine housing cult objects and the ambulatory was used to display curses or inscriptions recording offerings. Interestingly, a wall of one of these cellas was constructed of flint and local Hertfordshire puddingstone bonded by pale grey sandy mortar.

Amongst the artefacts found in the trenches were pottery ranging from Iron Age through to Roman including items from the local Verulamium kilns, ceramic building material, flint-including a Bronze-Age blade core, two medieval buttons, bones of animals and birds, charred plant remains and small quantities of glass and red-painted wall plaster.

Of the forty-eight coins found, all but one (a 1835, William IV farthing) were Roman, dating from the first-fourth centuries AD, including a rare find in England – a silver siliqua of the Emperor Eugenius who ruled between AD 392 and his death after the battle of Frigidus in AD 394.

Jewellery finds include an unusual enamelled brooch from around the first half of the second century AD and a small ring

A large piece of red stone was found, seen in the photo below, in what seems to be roughly the shape of a human head and could have been a cult object. It is not thought to have originated from the area as reported in the Archaeological Evaluation and Assessment of Results:

'The object is in a fine, red, extremely hard rock with banding, quartz-rich and extremely dense. The rock type is very old and is unlikely to outcrop in the district of Hertfordshire where the oldest sediments are Jurassic. It could, however, be an erratic brought into the district or near to it by glaciation. If so it could possibly be a Norwegian metamorphic or igneous rock'.

The three day dig only uncovered 1% of the entire site. At the time of writing no further work is planned at the site for the foreseeable future.

Separate archaeological finds discovered near the river in the Friars Wash area include medieval gritty ware and Mesolithic, Neolithic and Bronze Age flints and worked stones.

Many archaeological discoveries have been found near the River Ver in Redbourn showing, as with much of the river, its importance to the local population as they carried out their day to day life. The Mesolithic people were the first to be born, live and die in the same area rather than hunter-gathering nomads. They lived close to nature and took all they needed from their local environment. They survived on foods including wild animals trapped and killed with spears tipped with flint arrow heads and early bows and arrows together with roots, wild fruits, berries and nuts, wild vegetables and herbs and fish caught in the river by spear, traps and hand-line with hooks made of bone. Pollen samples analysed from the river valley deposits show the species of trees in the area have changed little over time.

Palaeolithic and Mesolithic flints in their hundreds have been found and many of these would have been made for fishing and hunting the animals that used the river to quench their thirst.

Aerial photography shows crop marks near the river and these may be areas of Bronze Age burials.

Roman finds include a 750m linear crop mark between Watling Street and the river at Redbournbury which is thought to be an aqueduct carrying water from the river to Verulamium.

During the laying of a gas pipeline in the 1960s near Dolittle Mill, a collection of Mesolithic worked flints and flakes were found.

The archaeological finds at St Albans are understandably vast considering the area's history of habitation and a visit to its museums is highly recommended.

It was during the excavation of a large Roman villa at Gorhambury, northwest of Verulamium, that an early Neolithic site was discovered producing two rare Neolithic oblong structures thought to be building foundations along with pottery and charcoal deposits dating from around 2500BC.

The villa is thought to have been at least partially destroyed by Boudicca around 61AD in her revolt against the treatment of her family and the native people by the Roman conquerors.

Verlamion was the Catavaulani tribe's capital stretching between Prae Wood and along the Ver Valley to the south-west bank of the river, occupying the same site as the Roman city which followed it. Built on an important trade route, their chief wealth came from farming cattle and to accommodate this a large area near the Ver was used and fortified with earthworks. The town was an oppidum (from Latin ob-pedum, enclosed space) – the main settlement in an administrative area of ancient Rome – and defended on three sides by wide deep ditches and on the remaining northeast side the Ver flooded a considerable area forming a wide morass which was

The iron ring above has several possible functions, but one of the most likely is as part of a bridle bit, probably a snaffle-bit – it would have been one of two rings. This is a form of bridle bit which was commonly used during the Roman period. (©Channel 4)

Unusual head-shaped stone. (© Channel 4)

Bronze plaque possibly denoting a river deity from peat deposits near Verulamium. (MoS)

Iron Age linch pin used to secure carriage wheel to axle from fields at Gorhambury. (MoS)

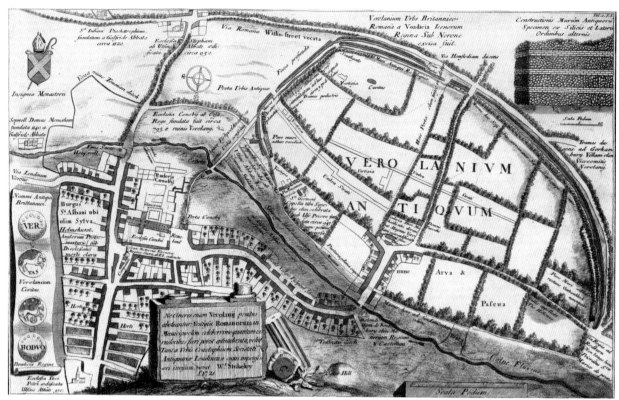

Stukley plan of Roman Verulamium. (MoS)

constrained by an embankment across the river in the east forming a causeway which led to a great cattle enclosure. The trackway led towards the marshy river which may have been the origin of the name Verulamion thought to mean 'the place above the pool' or 'settlement above the marsh'.

Various types and ages of coins have been found along the river's course many with names of a place or leader on them. Tasciovanus, chief of the local Celtic Catuvellauni tribe and his son Cunobelin minted coins with the inscription Ver, Verl, Vir, Cam and Verlamio dating from around 10BC -10AD. Mints have been found near the river including at Gorhambury.

It is thought that throughout time people considered much of the Ver religiously significant with many objects found in and around the river thought to be cult offerings thrown in by people as a gift to the water gods; these included coins, jewellery, river deities and plates. Roman river deities included Fontus, god of wells and springs and Volturnus, god of the waters. These offerings continued until at least the fourth century AD.

In the first century a flint and mortar conduit took water from the river north of the Roman theatre. This came as the population increased and the number of settlements along the Ver Valley grew with estates and farmsteads being built on both sides of the river, making Verulamium a major local centre from the early Iron Age onwards.

It is thought the river was canalised on the north side of St Albans c230-50AD. In the park the current river, north of the lakes is believed to run along similar lines and could have been used to help drain the marshy land and build up a head of water for the mills.

The causeway leading to it from near the Roman theatre was possibly already in existence when the Romans strengthened it and built bridges across the river and again marshy areas would have been used for burials and were crossed by raised tracks. These wetland and open air burials along with extensive river and water cults during the late Bronze Age onwards often left little archaeological evidence.

To be able to supply water and remove waste, a number of underground water systems were built running to and from the river at various places. The area around Verulamium being marshy and slow flowing would have required water to be piped through an aqueduct from further upstream near Redbourn as mentioned previously, where the flow and clarity of the water is thought to have been better.

In *Albans Buried Town* by R. Niblett and I. Thompson it is suggested that a second supply would have been needed for the higher areas SW of the town and suggests the possible presence of a streamlet fed by springs which would have run through a small valley, since silted up, near the south forum of the Ver. Evidence of a small muddy stream was also uncovered in 1955 several metres under what is now the car park of the Verulamium Museum. It is also thought that the baths at Branch Road were fed by a stream which ran through a now filled valley from around Normandy Road to join the Ver northwest of Branch Road.

On the southwest side of the river stood the two chapels of St Germain and St Mary Magdalen both dwellings of medieval hermits.

St Germain's chapel was built by Wulfa, a Danish monk who was prior at the Abbey in the early tenth century. According to Gesta Abbatum it was on the traditional site of a house used by St Germanus in the fifth century which was on the boundary of the Roman town, in the bottom of the uninhabitable marshy valley. It was still in existence up until the eighteenth century when it was used as a barn. The site lies close to the modern toilet block in the park at Verulamium.

St Mary Magdalen chapel was already old when the Bishop of Norwich dedicated it in the late eleventh century. There was a hermit living here in 1530 and it was still in use as a house and orchard in the seventeenth century and is shown on maps from this time together with Washing Lane leading to the river. The site lies between the modern lake and tennis courts on what is now known as St Mary Magdalen's Meadow.

During the construction of the park at Verulamium in the 1930s archaeologists discovered many finds ranging from pottery fragments to a number of human skeletons showing that this was likely to have been a third or fourth century cemetery. In fact many burial sites, including stone and lead coffins and evidence of cremations have been found along the river.

Before the Victorian warehouses by the Abbey Mill were redeveloped archaeologists discovered a large barn and grain processing oven dating to between 1300-1450 which would have been part of the monastery's milling and brewing site.

Fowler's survey of the medieval Abbey precinct in 1875-6, showed archaeological evidence near the millstream of the site of a possible medieval bridge and pier near the Abbey Mill.

In 1968 the foundations of a large Roman building, thought to possibly be a mill, were found at the site of the old Mud Lane near Holywell Hill entrance to Verulam Park/Westminster Lodge Leisure Centre. A ditch nearby was thought to have been a leat or artificial aqueduct which fed the mill.

In 2010 an excavation was carried out before work began on the extension of Westminster Lodge Leisure Centre. Twelve trenches were dug on a 3.7Ha site overlooking the River Ver. The earliest finds were struck flints from around the early Bronze Age, but the majority of items were Romano-British including coarse wares mostly produced in the Verulamium area and local medieval sandy wares including jars and jugs and some glazed ware. A Roman roof tile and brick were found along with animal bones and

An illustration by A. Sorrell showing the River Ver included in a depiction of a reconstruction of Verulamium cAD275 following the construction of the town walls with the London Gate where Watling Street entered the town in the foreground. (MoS)

Medieval/post medieval iron/brass/copper /wood dagger. Central plate made of brass; copper rivets, wood handles. Believed to have been produced locally due to crude riveting. Found near the bank of River Ver near Prospect Road. (MoS)

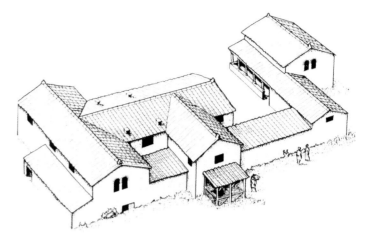

Above: *A reconstruction of Park Street Villa. (MoS)*

Below: *Some of the Park Street Villa finds on display at Verulamium Museum. (JBT)*

oyster shells.

One trench did reveal a flint and mortar foundation of a rectangular building from the Romano-British period along with a ditch, thought to be the same structure discovered in 1968. If it is indeed a mill, and so far there is no hard evidence to suggest this, the ditch could have been as thought in 1968 a leat.

Pondswick Close off Holywell Hill is named after a site in this area called 'Ponds Wicks', believed to date to at least the early seventeenth century and is thought to be on the site of a monastic fishpond. Archaeological digs at the river's edge here have uncovered wood and leather remains in the peat deposits.

Ten sherds of twelfth-sixteenth century pottery were found at the edge of the lakes of Verulam Angling Club at Riverside Road.

It is known that man has occupied the site of Park Street and Frogmore for many thousands of years with the earliest finds dating from around 50,000 years ago when hunters roamed the area. The Ver was an important and strategic route for settlers and navigable to the Colne and up the Thames to the sea with the river and its marshy surroundings confined and altered to suit the everyday needs of locals. The first real paths into this area were made around 50BC when the Catuvellauni tribe laid tracks between their settlements at Prae Wood to the Ver at Frogmore, near

where Hyde Lane and Burston Drive are today.

When the melt waters of the last Ice Age flowed into the valley much of the area became swamp and later impenetrable forest with the Ver the only navigable route. The Saxons built the first settlement of any size where Park Street now stands.

In 1943 a schoolboy was watching a bulldozer at work in a gravel pit at Park Street. The boy gave a shout, frantically signalling the driver to stop. With a dubious shrug the driver switched his bulldozer to another part of the pit. It is said the boy ran post haste to the Verulamium Museum, a considerable distance if true, where he asked if someone would come at once to look at a bit of Roman wall that had just been exposed. Thus was brought to light a Roman villa, built on a terrace of glacial gravel on chalk 230 yards west of the Ver. The villa had a wharf built alongside it on the old course of the river which would have been used for loading and unloading boats.

The excavations that followed showed that there had been occupation on this site for around 350 years beginning with a Belgic hut in wattle and daub, with earth floors and storage pits; it was rebuilt in stone during the first century AD when it consisted of only three rooms. About a century later several more rooms were added, all joined by an open corridor. In the fourth century, it was again rebuilt and a bathroom with hypocaust was added; but part of the structure appears to have been used, not as a dwelling house but for agricultural purposes. It was burned down and abandoned around AD 370.

Evidential finds relating to its use and the occupants were discovered including Bronze Age food vessels, jewellery, coins, a small silver mirror, part of a quern made of puddingstone, fragments of glass, bones and shells but perhaps the most curious object was a Belgic slave chain, uncomfortably short and very heavy with a ring at one end for attachment to a post and at the other a most efficient manacle. Two stone coffins were also found nearby. In the urgent need for gravel in wartime, the whole site, having been excavated, was again delivered to the bulldozer but not before the Germans dropped two incendiary bombs into one of the rooms!

Field walking can be a rich source of archaeological finds if you know what to look for. Items found by this method include a collection of scrapers, knives and flint implements found near a bend in the Ver not far from the former Radlett Aerodrome.

Bricket Wood is thought to have been occupied since at least the Bronze Age, but man would have passed through this remote and heavily wooded area whilst hunting and gathering his food long before.

Aerial photos of an area near the confluence in the fields near Jack Williams Wood show possible Bronze Age circular crop marks where huts may have been.

Also found near these woods not far from the confluence was a kiln from around the first century AD of one of the numerous potters working in the region, Oastrivs. Excavated in 1974 finds included a mortaria – a container for grinding and pounding food, stamped 'OASTRIVS LVGDF'. LVGDF is a place name thought to be an abbreviation of Lugdunum, by which this site may have been known in Roman times.

In 1941 Roman tiles were discovered near the Ver-Colne confluence, leading to extensive excavations in the early 1960s where finds were unearthed dating between 275-330AD including a bathhouse, villa, and two kilns.

Anglo Saxons settlers named the area Heanhamstede 'the place of the High Heath', settling on the terrace that overlooked the river. Gravel extraction close to the confluence at Drop Lane resulted in finds of a hearth and pits containing pottery and bronze objects.

The following are photos of just a few of the various items found in and around the Ver.

Brass hand decorated cow bell, believed to be nineteenth century European, possibly Swiss. Found in the river Ver at Park Street in the 1960's by the author's husband, Bruce who stubbed his toe on the top of the bell sticking out of the river bed whilst paddling!

Bowl with flower decoration. (JBT/MoS)

Bracelet found in river bog mud. (JBT/MoS)

Iron Age coin of Tasciovanus pre 43AD. (JBT/MoS)

Penannular brooch found in bog mud. (JBT/MoS)

Pointed hand axe. (JBT/MoS)

Chapter Three
Kensworth to Harpendenbury

He sendeth the springs into the rivers
Which run among the hills.
All beasts of the field drink thereof
And the wild asses quench their thirst.
Besides them shall the fowls of the air have their habitation
And sing among the branches.
He watereth the hills from above -
The earth is filled with the fruit of thy works.

'He Sendeth the Springs into the Rivers' From the Psalms

Each chapter has a simple map at the beginning of it explaining the area covered together with highlighted points of interest. They are not to scale, nor do they contain detailed descriptions of the land, there are maps and walks a plenty out there should the reader wish to pursue further information to accompany the book, which I greatly encourage you to do in your quest to explore the River Ver and its surrounding valley.

Our journey begins where a dry valley joins that of the River Ver at the place of its ever fluctuating source at Kensworth Lynch Bedfordshire, just outside the Hertfordshire boundary at Corner Farm and

Lynch House – Lynch from the old English 'hlinc' meaning a hill or projection and also a 'lynchet' – a ridge or series of 'steps' ploughed on the downhill side of land.

Situated at a point west of Watling Street or the modern day A5, this was the first Roman road to be built in England and runs for about 270 miles from London to Holyhead following sections of a route thought to have been built along an ancient way in the Ver valley creating six fords through the river at various points. Here the river rises from the underlying chalk aquifer below the eastern escarpment of the Chiltern Hills 180m above sea level and flows intermittently south-eastwards on its 24 km journey to the confluence with the River Colne at Bricket Wood. In the seventeenth century Chauncy writes of the source rising at Row Beech, in the Highway called Watline-Street. This is shown on an early map as a small field next to the river and along with larger fields and meadows covers the lower end of Kensworth Lynch.

The sixteenth century English chronicler Raphael Holinshed (1529–1580) writes the following about the source of the river, here calling it the Cole (Colne):

The Cole riseth néere vnto Flamsted, frõ whence it goeth to Redburn, S. Mighels, S. Albons, Aldham, Watford, and so by More to Richemansworth, where there is a confluence of thrée waters, of which this Cole is the first.

Being winterbourne the upper stretches of the Ver often only flow during the wetter winter months and at times of heavy prolonged rainfall.

The river tends to lose water from its upper reaches in drought or low rainfall situations winding along the valley base with the gradual gradient and saturation level in the aquifer altering the point of the source considerably.

Kensworth (Enclosure of a man called Cægin), recorded in the Domesday Book as Canesworde extends to the Chiltern Hills, approximately 600 feet above sea-level and has a long history of human habitation.

Before the Norman Conquest Leofwine, a thane

The gulley on the west side of the road as it emerges by Lynch House, 2011. (JBT)

Originally part of the Hundred of Dacorum in Hertfordshire, 1897 saw the parish which is divided into Church End, Kensworth Common and The Lynch, transferred to Bedfordshire. Past industries included brick making – producing a plum and grey coloured type called 'Kensworth Greys' and straw plaiting. Today farming and chalk quarrying are its largest activities.

Pitchering Pond in Beech Road was reported to 'always have water in it'. Pitchins were an old Hertfordshire name for rounded flint pebbles, used for paving and often found in river-gravels so the name of this pond may originate from this. Running as an occasional stream beside Church Lane, the flow was increased by springs near Studham Road junction and Church Lane and the waters from the spring pond as the stream neared Kensworth Lynch.

The village was renowned for its deep wells, sunk through the chalk, and had several donkey wheels to draw water including those at Nash Farm and Bury (stead) Farm. The donkeys would walk,

A donkey wheel in action. (JBT)

treadmill-like, encased within the large wooden wheel fixed on a horizontal axle. When water was required, the wheel would wind up the rope attached to a bucket containing up to thirty gallons of water. Even the Abbey at St Albans had a donkey wheel built in at least one of its mills for when there was less water available during hot, dry summers.

One of these wheels is thought to have been in use since at least the seventeenth century as a date of 1688 was carved upon it. In 1932, the wheel at Nash Farm was taken to Luton Museum for restoration and put on display. Before being removed the well depth was measured at 242 feet and the water level within the well was 39 feet 8 inches. The wheel itself measures 15ft by 3ft 11 inches and can be seen today, enclosed in the restored well-house behind Wardown Park Museum in Luton.

Kensworth pumping station was developed by the Luton Water Company and opened in 1945 to replace the wells at Kensworth, Caddington, Markyate and Flamstead and supply Luton. It is currently licensed to abstract six million litres of water per day from the aquifer leaving this part of the river almost permanently dry.

Brick culverts bridged the stream on the north side allowing access and it was said that lower down the lane the Ver flowed on the northwest side of the lane to the old pond opposite Corner Farm where today it has been made into a garden feature in the grounds of a bungalow.

The 1826 sale map of Kensworth Lynch Estate

of King Edward, owned Canesworde which had been passed down to him by his father Eadwine of Caddington but by 1086 the estate was owned by the Canons of St Paul's Cathedral, London, given to them by King William.

No mills are recorded in the Domesday Book at the estates or manors of Kensworth due largely to the dry chalk valleys the village stands upon and it's unlikely that the river's flow would have been powerful enough to support a mill. However locally grown grain would need to be ground and this would have been carried out using hand querns or at local windmills, one which was situated on the high ground at Church End.

In the fourteenth century, at the time of the Great Plague, the village moved to higher ground. It was thought by many that the disease could be carried by water, thus encouraging the movement of villagers away from the river. This had some truth in it. Rivers and disease have been linked for many thousands of years, with drinking water often taken from the same river used to deposit human and animal waste, so it didn't take the disease long to spread once it reached an area.

Some of Kensworth's Previous Names
Ceagnesworthe – tenth century
Canesworde – eleventh century
Keneswurda – twelfth century
Ikenesworth – thirteenth century
Kenisworye & Keynesworth – fourteenth century
Kneysorth – sixteenth century

Kensworth hostel land girls c1940s, with house in the background. (SA)

shows the source as a pond in front of the Mansion House but by 1973 a conservation area map of Kensworth Lynch shows it in the grounds of Lynch Lodge.

Kensworth Lynch was the home of Geoffrey ate Linch and was built around 1294. Four buildings on the east side of the road are on the statutory list of buildings of architectural or historic interest.

Kensworth House is a late nineteenth century Grade II listed building, white and prominent on the hillside and approached by a curving drive. Some of the windows and the staircase were fitted in the early twentieth century, from a house in Ealing where, as a small child, Queen Victoria lived.

From 1942, the house was altered to create more bedrooms and bathrooms to allow it to be used as a hostel accommodating up to fifty women of the Bedfordshire Women's Land Army. To camouflage the house from enemy bombings it was painted green. Women were employed by the Bedfordshire War Agricultural Executive Committee who subcontracted them as paid civilian workers to local farms and market gardens. Many dances and concerts were held at the house and American airmen from Chicksands were invited along. The hostel was

eventually closed in 1949. It was for some time the home of a religious teaching community, the Order of the Ancient Heart before becoming a private residence. A legend attached to the house was that a headless huntsman would ride by at night!

The three other buildings – Lynch House, Lynch Farm Cottage and Lynch Lodge, share the valley where the Ver has its source. They were all Grade II listed in 1967.

The former mansion house, Lynch House was built for the Howard family who had been adding to their estate in Kensworth since the seventeenth century. The present house is an early eighteenth century two storey building. In 1827 when it was sold to Charles Hamilton it was known as Lynch Mansion.

The sale details for the mansion and farm inform us that:

The situation is truly picturesque and romantic, rendering it a desirable residence at an agreeable remove from the great Chester Road with coaches passing almost every hour in the day.

As with many properties along the lane, its front boundary wall contains large white grills which would have helped drain past flood waters out into the culvert by the road, but very rarely needed today!

The river then flows in front of Lynch Farm a timber-framed seventeenth century cottage with an old clay tiled roof. The farm was once home to a steam corn mill and the nineteenth century sale details show it consisting of:

Mill House fitted with 2 pairs of stones, with storage and hopper Loft over; Engine house with horizontal Fixed Engine, Boiler house adjoining with…tanks, well, 2-throw pumps and well house.

There were also several springs in the grounds

Kensworth House. (JBT)

Lynch Farm Cottage. (JBT)

Lynch Lodge mid 1980s. (JBT)

and mention of a 'Reding Brook'.

Lynch Lodge dates from the early eighteenth century. It has roughcast walls and a slate roof. Opposite is the seventeenth century Chequers Cottage which was once a public house called The Chequer at the beginning of the nineteenth century but was reported in 1903 as being dirty and run down, closing soon after.

The Ver then passes under Kensworth Road where once the water from a line of springs on the north side regularly lifted the surface. seventeenth century coaches were often delayed here because of the flooding at Kensworth ford. Where the pumping station now stands there used to be a pond where the former gravel works were, said to be thirty foot deep!

Early postcard of Packhorse Inn. (JBT)

The stream passes west of the eighteenth century Grade II listed Packhorse Inn, once called The Orange Tree and in the early twentieth century The Old Pack Horse. An inn has stood on this site for at least 300 years and has had various uses throughout its history including a mortuary and up until the early twentieth century manor courts were held here triennially. It is reputedly haunted by a cricket player and the Wicked Lady! From 1723 a tollgate stood near the inn on the road from Dunstable to St Albans.

A newspaper article of 1837 reported that Benjamin Looker, a farm worker was on his way home from the Packhorse Inn after celebrating the birth of his first-born son, when he fell off the footbridge near Red Cow Field and was drowned. His body was found the next day in the river near Flamstead.

The river in front of Old Red Cow Cottages 1980s. (JBT)

As it runs along Watling Street the Ver disappears into an underground culvert below a petrol station and industrial buildings before reappearing in front of the little Old Red Cow Cottages and crossing to the east under Watling Street.

A 1987 letter in the VVS archive from Norah King records her memories of this area:

I am now seventy and when a very little girl…my grandparents farmed Red Cow Farm, on what was properly then known as the A5, and I have many happy memories of walking through the stream that was the Ver, in front of Red Cow Cottages, where grandfather's farm hands lived. It was then a sparkling living stream and its source was in the area of Kensworth Lynch. I recall that the river ran beneath the road and revealed itself again in Cell Park – near to the spot where the nun Christina of Markyate lived with the hermit Roger. I recall when slightly older sliding on the lake in the park with my cousins: it was I always thought from this lake that Roger fished. That lovely lake no longer exists; there was a bridge under which the river flowed just below Cell Dene and Markyate parish church.

The name Markyate originates from two old English words – 'mearc' and 'geat', signifying a gate at the boundary, the boundary in this case being the Bedfordshire/Hertfordshire border. The first settlers would have been attracted by the river and its supply of fresh water and food. In the twelfth century Markyate was a hamlet in the parish of Flamstead.

There have been various spellings throughout time, sometimes several changes during a single century including the examples below:

Markzate – twelfth Century
Mercyate/Marchiate – thirteenth century
Markeyghate – fourteenth century
Margate – fifteenth century
Marget – sixteenth century

Between the sixteenth and twentieth century 'street' and 'end' in its various spellings was often used:

Merkeyatestret – 1535
Market (t) Street, Markiatt Street,
 Markiate End, Markyatt End – 1660-1852
Marget Street – 1748, 1751, 1763
Markyate Street – 1845-early twentieth century

The Ver was once known as the holy river because at least half a dozen religious establishments were found along its banks, the largest being St Albans Abbey. It is said that the bodies of monks that had died at Redbourn Priory were brought to the Abbey along the River Ver, a journey that would be somewhat challenging today!

One of these settlements built overlooking the Ver was the Benedictine "Prioratum sancte Trinitatis de Bosco" or the Priory of Holy Trinity in the Wood. Founded in 1145 by Abbot Geoffrey of St Albans, its church was dedicated to St Mary. It was near here that a pilgrim named Roger settled after his return from Jerusalem and whilst sitting by the river had a vision of three angels carrying brilliantly lit candles. They told him to follow the Ver northwards, which he did, arriving at the ruins of an old church in a nearby valley, where he built a cell, hoping to live the rest of his life in peace as a recluse. However, nearby there was a pool, where travellers along Watling Street would refresh themselves, and by doing so observed Roger in his cell. As word spread of these sightings many came to visit him some wishing to follow his example, thus forming cells themselves and making Roger the head of this religious community.

A rich guild merchant Autti and his wife Beatrix, a noble and devout Anglo-Saxon family from Huntingdon, often made pilgrimage to St Albans Abbey. Their daughter Christina, was born with the name of Theodora c1097 and it is said that she was so influenced by the ceremony at the shrine that she made a vow of celibacy. However, her parents went ahead with their plans for Christina to marry a neighbour, called Burhtred and refused to take the vow seriously. In 1118, shortly after they wed and despite several attempts by her husband to consummate the marriage and suffering persecution by her family, Christina escaped and with the help of 'Eadwin an ermite' fled to live in hiding with a nearby anchoress of Flamstead, Alfwen. She then took refuge at Markyate with the elderly recluse, Roger, who became her spiritual mentor. It was whilst here that she experienced her first visions of the Virgin Mary and Jesus.

For some time Christina lived a difficult life shut in a hut and begging the monk, who was a friend of the Archbishop of York, to take her vow seriously and help her live a life of meditation.

Roger arranged for her to have her own cell and supported her against all criticism. After some time a meeting took place at Redbournbury where he persuaded Thurstan, the Archbishop of York to annul her marriage so it would be possible for her to become a nun and finally her husband released

Christina from their marriage vows.

Roger died c1122 and his tomb can be found at St Albans Abbey.

In 1130 Thurstan invited Christina to become abbess of his nunnery of St Clement at York. She also received offers from other nunneries but was persuaded to start a small priory and church by Abbot Geoffry de Gorham of St Albans and so became the first prioress at Markyate.

Around this time a house was built to give homes to the many women who gathered around Christina drawn by her visions and holiness. However, throughout its history the priory was often a place of rumours, scandal and disputes including the breaking of vows especially that of chastity and committing acts of immorality. Often in debt, in 1442, an area of woodland had to be felled to pay their creditors.

The River Ver and the fishing ponds fed by it were near to the priory and amongst the numerous disputes that occurred was one involving a sixteenth century prioress called Joan Zouche, who was accused of interfering with fishing rights belonging to the Manorial tenants. She was ordered not to obstruct fishing in the surrounding waters again.

It is not known exactly when Christina died but it is thought to be around 1155 and it is said she was buried in a special grave overlooking the River Ver, as yet undiscovered. In 1805, Thomas Fisher unearthed the cemetery of the priory on the north side of the Cell containing stone coffins and human remains. The priory existed until Henry VIII dissolved it in 1537 becoming privately owned and eventually incorporated into Markyate Cell.

In 1892 a correspondent of a Hertfordshire newspaper wrote 'It is an article of faith in Markyate Street, that a subterranean passage connects the cell with St Albans Abbey, some four miles distant, and that in this underground retreat the restless spirits of departed monks "patter their aves" in the dead of the night.'

In 1539 the priory was leased to Humphrey Bourchier by King Henry VIII but a year later he died. His widow, Elizabeth, married a barrister called George Ferrers who was granted the property which became the Manor of Markyate, later Markyate Cell. By 1596 his grandson, Sir John Ferrers lived at the Cell which had been converted into a grand manor house, where his daughter Katherine was born.

When Sir John died, the estate passed to Katherine. She was married at a young age to Sir Thomas Fanshaw and lived for some time at Ware Park. Upon their marriage the Cell became the property of Sir Thomas who sold it in 1655. At this time the area was notorious for highwaymen and Katherine witnessed one being caught and his body nailed to a tree on the spot where he was trying to rob the London to Chester mail coach. Sometime after this incident, two young men on Nomansland Common shot and wounded a highwayman and reported the incident. A party from St Albans looked for the body but found no trace. The next morning Katherine was not in her room and her bed was not slept in. At the end of the hall, the housekeeper found an open secret door leading to a flight of steps where the body of Katherine, soaked in blood and wearing highwayman's clothes was found. Her husband hushed up the story and had the passage blocked. She was buried in Ware Church.

Despite little evidence that Katherine was indeed the legendary 'Wicked Lady', the ghost of Katherine Ferrers has reputedly been seen by various owners of Markyate Cell and the spectral vision of a highwayman on a black horse galloping along Watling Street has been reported by terrified onlookers. Local people believed that there was a hidden stash of stolen treasure, described in this local rhyme:

Near the Cell there is a well,
Near the well there is a tree,
And 'neath the tree the treasure be.

It was a famous enough tale to lead to the making of the 1945 film *The Wicked Lady* starring Margaret Lockwood and attracted one of the biggest cinema audiences of the period. The Wicked Lady pub and restaurant named after her can be found at Wheathampstead, near Nomansland Common.

In 1657 Thomas Coppin bought the manor and its 60 acre parkland. By 1794 it was owned by Joseph Howell and the land surrounding the Cell was divided between walled gardens, pleasure grounds and its own farm. Today Markyate Cell lies surrounded by parkland just north of the village. The magnificent trees could have been saplings when Humphrey Bourchier pulled down the nunnery and set up the Tudor house. It has been rebuilt many times since then, but in the sixteenth century it was said there were stone mouldings on the kitchen walls from the church of the nuns.

In the mid eighteenth century extensive landscaping of the grounds included the widening of the Ver creating a lake. This had been carried out in previous centuries when it once flowed through two lakes said to have been fishponds for first the priory then throughout the centuries the great house. The 1834 OS map shows the Ver rising just north of Markyate with the river and its valley running into the grounds of Markyate Cell to the southwest. In the mid nineteenth century the mansion was rebuilt after a fire, one of many throughout its history, by Daniel Goodson Adey incorporating the remains of the house built by Humphrey Bourchier and the priory.

Looking down from the churchyard of St John the Baptist, built in 1734, in the corner of the grounds of Markyate Cell, the depression can still be seen where the lakes existed and which during wet periods still fill with water.

Sir Henry Chauncy wrote in his history of Hertfordshire:

This county is pleasantly watered with many small brooks and rivers which do greatly accommodate the houses of the nobility and gentry, increase the grass in the meadows...and produce variety of fish as eels, millers thumbs, cray fish, trouts, gudgeon, bream, carps, tench, perch, roach...

Cell Park, the Ver and small lake beyond. 1994 (DH)

Markyate Cell, 1805 by T. Fisher. (MoS)

The parish church of St John. Markyate Cell, river and lake in background c1830. (JBT)

The Second World War saw two high explosive bombs fall near Markyate Cell; luckily there was no report of any damage or injuries. Every house in the village that was able took in London children and for many this was their first experience of the countryside! On VE day at the end of WWII, locals, some in fancy dress, paraded through the village to Cell Park where they joined in a celebratory fête.

Many people have inhabited the Cell over the centuries and amongst its famous twentieth century owners were the conductor Sir Thomas Beecham and MP Sir John De Fonblanque Pennefather.

Now Grade II listed, it currently stands in 79 acres of parkland and gardens (which occasionally the river Ver trickles through) and has 18 bedrooms, four reception rooms and six bathrooms and in 2011 it was put up for sale for offers in excess of £10,000,000!

Nearby, a row of giant limes leads down an avenue from Luton Road to the eighteenth century church of St John with a handsome gallery and a carved pulpit. The tower and nave date from 1734 when the church was built by John Coppin for the villagers who up until then had had no local church of their own. The chancel was added in 1892 and has a stone cut with a floral cross, which came from the nunnery and a tabernacle with painted saints from Italy.

In his 1899 book *South Country Trout Streams*, George Dewar writes the following about the Ver and it's fish:

The Ver, or Verlam, rises north of Redbourne…almost as high as Markyat Street, in Bedfordshire. In its upper reaches it is not a very bright trout stream, and I have more than once noted a kind of curious and most objectionable scum constantly rising to the surface, and covering the fly and hook. It contains some good trout, though dace and other coarse fish are rather too plentiful, and restocking has been successfully carried on by several owners and renters of water. The evening is, as a rule, the best time for fly fishing, but the trout do not often rise in the upper parts very well to the natural fly. The small dry fly is not nearly so good, as a rule, as a large fancy artificial. I have never myself seen the May-fly on the river above St Albans, though I have heard of it there. About the mills some very heavy trout may occasionally be seen in the summer evenings, and the average weight of the fish killed will scarcely be under 1 1/2lbs. Below St Albans, and at Park Street, and near its junction with the Colne, the Ver is a much more taking looking trout stream, reminding one in parts of the genuine south country chalk stream.

Even before Kathleen Ferrers was the lady of the manor, Markyate, had its superstitions and for many hundreds of years the River Ver has been the centre of local folklore. It has often been recorded that the river had a strange tendency to flood during periods of prolonged drought and from this mystery superstition arose that it was an omen of disaster.

In *A Chronicle of the First Thirteen Years of the Reign of King Edward Fourth* by John Warkworth, the following is written about the Ver or "Wemere" in 1472, a year which saw a very hot summer:

Also in the same yere Womere watere ranne hugely with suche abundaunce of watere, that nevyr manne sawe it renne so moche afore this tyme. Womere is called the Woo Watere: for Englysch-men, whenne thei dyd fyrst inhabyde this lond, also sone as thei see this watere renne they knewe wele it was a tokene of derthe, or of pestilence, or of grete batayle; wherefor thei called it Womere; (forwe as in Englysche tonge woo, and mere is called watere, which signyfieth woo-watere) for all that tyme thei sawe it renne, thei knewe well and that woo was comynge to Englonde. And this wemere is vij myle frome Sent Albons, at a place called Markayate;and this Wemere ranne at every felde afore specifyede, and revere so hugely as it did this yere, and ran style to the xiij day of June next yere folowynge.

The sixteenth century topographer John Norden (1548–1625) in his *Description of Hartfordshire*, published in 1598, referred to the Ver when it suddenly rose near Markyate as *"a Womere' – a water*

presaging sorrowe to come", concluding that *"For these kind of waters some yield natural reasons of the cause, but for my part I will not deny but some devine mystery may be hidden therein…foregoing (as hath beneobserved) some dismall accident as yielding teares from the evils to come."*

But by the time he wrote *Surveiors Dialogue*, some twenty years later, he had come to the strange conclusion that the river was *"only fed with springs, which run only when they are at the highest, namely in the summer when the sun is highest."*

At the end of the seventeenth century the Hertfordshire historian Sir Henry Chauncy (1632-1719) also wrote the following about the Womer, this time including the River Red at Redbourn:

…the Ver was joined by a small brook called Wenmer or Womer, which sometimes breaks forth, and 'tis observed forerunneth a Dearth, or some Extremity of dangerous Import, thence streaming by the Ruins of Old Verulam, did heretofore feed a great Fishpool, between that Place and St Albans, afterwards watering the Nunnery at Sopwell.

In the eighteenth century the antiquary Richard Gough (1735-1809), wrote in his topographical work on Hertfordshire that the river rose above Flamstead and was called, "Woborne Mere the brook or mere of woe" and that it…"presages calamity."

The lowering of the water table largely halted these deluges but until relatively recent times traffic encountered problems at a ford on the Kensworth turn at Watling Street. Old coaching records refer to long delays and also reveal that Markyate High Street often flooded. This flooding not only caused problems for the traffic and local people, they also feared this strange phenomenon. It is easy to mock what seems like ignorance in the people of the past for not understanding the reasons behind their folklore but they did not have the technology to discover why the river flooded in dry periods or dried up in periods of wet weather.

It is now known why the river rose with such great speed and subsided almost as quickly; a massive natural underground reservoir holding millions of gallons of water existed in the Chiltern Hills. When full even light rain or a heavy dew on the hills above could cause a great torrent into the valley of the River Ver, quickly flooding the area and causing great alarm among the superstitious people of the area.

Another old belief concerning chalk hills, mentioned in *The Folklore of Hertfordshire* by Doris Jones Baker says that *"…when it rains on the chalk hills in Hertfordshire it rains milk, which can be seen running down them in torrents in bad storms when the ground is saturated."*

In 1555 an Act of Parliament made it the responsibility of the local parishes to ensure the roads in the area were in good condition, the local community would be ordered to work on the roads when required, not something they relished as it was unpaid work and often the roads would look little different than before the maintenance had started! Gravel from in and around the river was often used for these improvements.

Over a 150 year period from 1663, all major roads in Britain were covered by the Turnpike Act which enabled a toll to be charged to travellers and the money used for the upkeep of the major roads, although the smaller byways were still expected to be maintained by the locals.

In 1723 the main road between what is now the Bull Public House in Dunstable and Shafford House was turnpiked by what was known as the Pondyards Trust. It is noted in an Act of Parliament that between these two points…"*is very ruinous and almost impassable…*" The river Ver would have added to these problems, especially in areas where it was known to flood the roads as it was inclined to do in wet winters or heavy periods of rain around areas such as Friars Wash, leaving mud and detritus in its wake. To help alleviate this problem a bridge was built at the southern end of the village. Again gravel was taken from the river and gravel pits owned by the trust near the Pack Horse Inn to repair the roads.

Toll gates were placed at Turnpike Farm near Dunstable, The Packhorse Inn at Kensworth and Friars Wash and each mile of the road had a post showing the distances to local villages and London. Two of these mileposts still exist not far from the river at the west side of London Road and northwest of Markyate. From 1877 responsibility of the roads was handed over to district Highway Boards.

In 1908 a Water Scheme Enquiry held at Markyate investigated the need to provide a clean water supply to the village, a subject that had been of concern to locals for some time. Water was obtained from shallow wells situated near cesspits and the River Ver which the Sanitary Inspector described as "one elongated cesspool". An epidemic of diphtheria in 1918 convinced the authorities that action had to be taken and a waterworks was built in Pickford Hill along with a sewerage works in Holybush Lane.

In 1808 the first Wesleyan Methodist chapel was built by the river and could be reached by an alley from the High Street. It continued to be used as a Sunday school until 1879.

For the people of Markyate, the ghost of the Wicked Lady remained as real as the flooding of the River Ver. There is an event that many Markyate people know of and is typical of the long lasting superstitions of villagers. This incident was subject to a coroner's enquiry and reported in a local newspaper.

In the summer of 1925, despite some local objection, primarily because Hicks Lane was part of an undeveloped area much favoured by the ghost, council workmen were extending the sewers from Markyate High Street to Hicks Lane. A Markyate man giving evidence at the coroner's enquiry stated that he was the night watchman and had set his red warning lamps along the trench that had been dug to lay the pipes. As the night was cold, he retired into his hut. In the early hours of the morning, he became aware of a figure staring into the trench, the watchman challenged him but there was no reply. He described the intruder as young, slim with long dark hair wearing a dark knee length cloak, with several

ornate buckles and long leather boots. The watchman challenged again with no response became very frightened and ran to fetch the village constable along with some local men. They searched the site but found no sign of the stranger. The next day, after work resumed, the constable was called upon again. The workman had uncovered two skeletons lying head to toe just below the road surface. The mystery of their death has never been solved but at the time there were many thoughts on the identity of the skeletons including casualties of the civil war and victims of the highwayman Dick Turpin. Some claimed it was the ghost of the Wicked Lady seen peering into the hole and this was an omen of impending evil, this turned out to be tragically prophetic and within days Markyate suffered a great tragedy. A terrible outbreak of typhoid, often carried in water infected with human faeces, struck the village and many Markyate families lost loved ones. So bitter were the memories of that summer that some locals avoided Hicks Lane for many years. Today the river flows on the south side of the road in front of factories through an open culvert.

Local folklore also claims that the River Ver only flows through Markyate on the shortest day every seven years.

From Markyate Cell the river travels under the old and new roads by St John's church, east of the High Street and through private gardens, occasionally going underground through pipes below buildings. The land on which the buildings on the east side of the High Street were developed was once divided into strips stretching down to the River Ver and beyond its banks on the opposite side. These long strips of land, laid out in medieval times, with accompanying buildings were called 'tofts' meaning homestead and 'crofts' – an enclosed farm used for pasture or tillage often attached to a dwelling and worked by the occupier.

Long Meadow is now a road of modern houses with the river moved and contained in a ditch crossed by a wooden plank, but before being built this was the area of an Anglo Saxon water meadow called Longmede through which the Ver flowed and sometimes flooded. To enable the estate to be built a firmer foundation had to be established and this was done by raising the ground several feet.

For hundreds of years flooding was a frequent problem at River Hill. In May 1824 a commissioner's report recommended that a new stretch of road be built avoiding River Hill, commenting: "*At Flywash more culverts are wanting across the road to carry off the floodwaters*". This was completed in 1838. In the early twentieth century, the Ver at River Hill ford was said to be 30 feet wide and 4 foot deep with the water used to replenish the tanks of traction engines. This is a sight that could be seen on many parts of the river at this time and indeed still happens today. On the stretch of Ver between River Hill and the Chequers inn at Flamstead, Ashby's and Pug Coote had three watercress beds.

The river leaves the village near the sewage works, built on the former Molespitte Meadow, west of

Watling Street. In the mid 1980s, there were problems with pollution from the sewage works with the Ver often cloaked with a stinking white deposit, causing the disappearance of much of the wildlife along this stretch. This has thankfully improved over the years.

Pollution is always a threat to rivers, especially one as comparatively small as the Ver. The sources are many including riverside industries, farming and illegal dumping of substances. The run-off from road and industrial sites can also affect water quality. Even when cleared, contamination can remain in the river sediment and soak into the surrounding area. Unfortunately pollution is often not spotted until the damage is done with fish deaths one of the earliest indicators that there is a problem, although this can also be caused by ecological reasons such as deoxygenation of water due to lack of flow and depth.

River Hill early 1900s. (JBT)

Where the River Ver once rippled by the unbending Watling Street, lies Flamstead, one of the largest parishes in Hertfordshire. The first settlement by the river was abandoned and the village now sits upon a ridge, 480 feet above sea level, with its picturesque gabled seventeenth century almshouses and the Norman tower of its church, St Leonard's, crowned by a 'Hertfordshire spike'. A settlement has been here for well over a thousand years and although there was Roman occupation at Flamstead, one of the first records was in 1006 when it was mentioned in a charter granted by King Ethelred to the Abbey of St Albans.

At the time of Domesday the village was held by Ralph de Todeni who had inherited the lands from his father Roger granted them by William the Conqueror for his part in the Battle of Hastings. In the early fourteenth century the manor was in the hands of the Earls of Warwick before passing to the Crown until 1549 when it was granted to George Ferrers.

In medieval times a fair and market was held here. Today the village is home to a popular annual scarecrow festival.

The name Flamstead is thought to mean 'place of refuge', which is appropriate considering it is the site of an early hill fort. Suggestions of where the name of the village originated are varied, they include:

Fleomstead – Saxon for a place of fugitives, Stead (old English place)
Flamesteed – A place where the Abbey obtained its charcoal.
Fleamstede – A place of refuge and sanctuary

Other variations include:
Flamstede, Flamestede – eleventh century
Flamested – thirteenth century

As well as the above, there are also other variations such as stadt (Indo-European 'town') statt (German 'place') and stad (Dutch 'town').

But the most likely source is Verlamstead, the settlement standing on the Ver. In Eric Edwards *A New History of Flamstead* he writes:

The Celts had a word 'hamps' which has been translated to 'summer dry'. Now the flow of the River Ver has always been precarious in drought years, even before Friars Wash Pumping Station was built; it seems logical therefore that this aspect of the neighbourhood could have been incorporated into the settlement adjacent to the river to produce Verlam-hamps-stead (stead/stede/steed/stedt means place or site of a building or settlement). So the most likely source of the name of the village is a corruption of Verlamstead, a settlement by the River Verlam.

The original Beechwood National School was at School House Farm, in London Road where meadows ran down to the River Ver. It was built in 1844 and £2000 was bequeathed by Sir John Saunders Sebright in 1846 to help finance the establishment. The school log book records the punishment of children who were tempted to sneak out of the school grounds to play in the river! In 1866 the school moved to Cheverells Green.

In 1885, by the junction of London Road and Holybush Lane, the main access road to the village, the river was a dried-out ditch with the surrounding meadow – Horse Pit Field – also parched. A court case from this year is mentioned in Eric Edwards book:

Thomas Birdsey, from Markyate Street instructed William Parkins to take thirteen horses to Horse Pit Field, close by the junction of Holybush Lane with London Road. All the horses were weak, and they were neither fed nor watered for a week. The River Ver ran through the field, but that year it was a dry ditch and the meadow was described as impoverished. One horse got into a ditch and could not get out so it was pole-axed by Birdsey and left there. The RSPCA brought the case. Birdsey was found guilty and fined £5 with £4.9s costs.

This same area has been known to flood at the lowest point of the road where the Ver has been diverted for the building of the A5.

It is mentioned in *The Victoria History of The Counties of England*, Hertfordshire edition, printed in 1914, that *"this stream, which used to be the home of trout, is now almost entirely drained by the London Water Supply"*. The Ver was having water extraction problems even then!

The nave of the St Leonard's church, dedicated to an obscure sixth century French monk St Leonard of Noblat, was rebuilt in the thirteenth century and the chancel and vestry are fourteenth century. In the fifteenth century the high clerestory with its medieval frescoes and sculptured figures was added. It is however, believed to be built on the site of a ninth century Saxon chapel. There are also some original medieval wall paintings in the nave and north aisle and Elizabethan graffiti on the pillars. Elsewhere in the church we see apostles ten foot high, the last supper, the crucifixion and the raised Christ. Several of these once decorated a chantry chapel of the Beauchamps, one of whom was imprisoned in the Tower of London for conspiring against Richard II: the Beauchamp Tower in the Tower of London is named after him.

The little Benedictine priory of Flamstead was situated in River Hill about 200 yards from the river Ver until being demolished at the beginning of the twentieth century. Described as a 'hovel' in the 1838 Tithe Grant, there is a theory that it could have been where Christina of Markyate began her reclusive life.

The Old Priory, Flamstead early 1900s just before it was demolished. (JBT)

Several windmills once existed in the area including River Hill, Hicks Lane and near the Packhorse Inn and records exist as far back as the early fourteenth century. Three of these were destroyed one stormy night in the nineteenth century when despite the brakes being on the high winds caused the sails to turn, causing friction which set fire to the mainly wooden structures. It was said the fires could be seen for many miles.

There was once 4 feet of water at the former Chequers Inn, previously called The Halfway House, a seventeenth century coaching inn on the London Road at Friars Wash and the Ver often flooded the road here.

Records of its sale exist from 1657 when Francis Sells sold it to John Marshall. In 1699, 1766 and 1767 it is recorded in a survey of the Gorhambury Estates.

Up until his death in 1800 the landlord was John Leno, followed by his wife Elizabeth who ran it until 1826 when she died aged 87.

In 1817 Friars Wash Tollgate existed near the pub. That year 20,000 horse drawn vehicles, 12,500 single horse and riders and 118,000 animals passed through, which must have caused considerable wear to the road. A meadow and large pond could be found behind the house on common land used to hold and

water local cattle and horses using the toll gate and former major coaching route, the Holyhead Road that ran past the inn. The tollgate was closed in 1877 but traffic remained heavy and Edwin Burchmore who ran the Chequers was not only a licenced victualler but a hay and straw dealer who seemingly took full advantage of the many hungry animals passing his dwelling at the time!

Between 1876 and 1925 the Dunstable brewer Bennett's leased the property.

In 1880 during the breakup of the Manor of Flamstead, the Chequers and its land were described by Messrs Fox & Bousfield, the agents as:
Lot 8. Valuable freehold property situate at Fly's Wash on the Great North Road in the parish of Flamstead, comprising an old established tavern known as the Chequers and about 12 acres of meadow land intersected by a running stream in which are thriving watercress

Early photo of the Chequers. (WT)

Early advertising 'The Chequers Manns Beer' uncovered on the wall of the former pub in 2000. (JBT)

beds, *Let for a term expiring at Michaelmass 1884 @ £63 per annum.*

Part of the 1912 Beechwood sale catalogue states: *…There are 12 acres of rich pasture with the River Ver flowing through the meadows and there is a cartway approach from the western boundary to River Hill. At the rear of the house is a large pond, with rough grassland, kitchen garden and orchard.*

The pub was finally closed in the late 1950s and is now a private Grade II listed house.

Upstream from the Chequers, showing remains of wooden stumps which supported the centre board of the cress beds. Mid 1980s. (JBT)

Chequers Hill and the Moor 1920s. The watercress beds were further to the right. (JBT)

Chequers Inn from the Moor, Friars Wash. (JBT)

The river continues on the west side of Watling Street to the sewage works. In the mid 1980s, the river here was cleaned out from the east side of Watling Street where it continues past the nearby pumping station and under the M1 motorway, rebuilt in 1993 to accommodate an extra northbound lane.

Friars Wash is an area where the Ver is crossed by Old Watling Street, Chequers Hill (once known as Friars Wash Hill and Wellcut Hill) and Watery Lane. Up until the late eighteenth century it was known as Fly's Wash and is named so on some early maps. The area was once thought to have been named Friars Wash because long ago this is where the friars would stop to wash and refresh themselves on their journey to St Albans Abbey. However history often notes that most religious men were notorious for being unwashed and therefore it is unlikely this is the meaning behind the name!

In Eric Edwards *A New History of Flamstead*, he writes:

There used to be a ford on the Ver close to the junction with London Road and by it an ash tree known as Segam Ashe which was one time popular as a civic meeting place". (Secgham means a meadow where sedge grows.)

During WWII, Friars Wash was home to a REME unit (Royal Electrical and Mechanical Engineers) who were in charge of every aspect of looking after the equipment of the British Army. Flamstead didn't completely escape bombing when a low flying German plane dropped a string of bombs on the north of the village, one falling near River Hill, but thankfully there were no casualties.

Flamstead near Friars Wash, bridge, river, pump and old cottage June 1936. (SC/ HALS)

Friars Wash pumping station was opened in 1956 by the Luton Water Company and contained two pumps and wells of 150 feet sunk into the chalk. This water was used originally to supply the Vauxhall Car Plant at Luton. At its height the extraction rate reached 15 million litres per day from the same underground aquifer that fed the Ver and not surprisingly this contributed hugely to the disappearance of the river and water meadows through much of its course especially to the north of Redbourn and worsening even further during exceptionally dry years.

In 1987 a maiden speech was given by local Conservative MP Peter Lilley highlighting the problem of the disappearing river, commenting it had deteriorated to the level of a drainage ditch:

It is only in recent times it has declined because of excessive abstraction of water. As a result there has been substantial damage to the ecology and loss of leisure and amenity value…St Albans owes its existence to the Ver.

Between 1986 and 1989, the Thames Water Authority (TWA) and National Rivers Authority (NRA) commissioned consultant engineers Halcrow and Partners to compile a report on the management of six chalk streams of the Thames region suffering from low flow including the Ver which was cited as the most ecologically important. This concluded that one of the main contributing factors was over-abstraction – the legacy of many licences issued long ago and no longer able to sustain extraction levels. A later separate report dealt only with the River Ver laying out five options including the closure of Friars Wash pumping station and an alternative source of water for Luton.

After droughts in 1989 and '90, it was reported that the Ver was amongst the five most threatened rivers in the country. As a solution the then TWA suggested a borehole be sunk at the Ver-Colne confluence at Bricket Wood and the water pumped along a pipeline, this was rejected by local groups and the fight continued to close Friars Wash, although at the time this was considered too costly by the TWA.

In 1992, following a drought which started in spring 1988 – the longest on record at that time in southern England – *The Sunday Times* ran a piece 'Britain faces worse drought for centuries'. In his speech to the Royal Society for Nature Conservation the Prince of Wales *"demanded urgent action to conserve water and save those areas dying of thirst….and the drought bought to a head the problems of poor water management which threatens prolonged shortages for consumers"*. He went on to warn that *"dry river beds in many parts of the country are the result of a wasteful approach by households, farmers and industry…more than 95% of Britain's water meadows, fens and marshes – and the wildlife that thrives there-have been damaged by methods of modern drainage and abstraction…"* Alongside the article was a photo of a young boy in a canoe on the parched and cracked bed of the Ver.

In 1993 after decades of campaigning to restore the Ver and its valley by many individuals and groups including the VVS, Friars Wash pumping station was finally switched off only to be used in peak times and emergencies with a small amount flushed through the pipes daily to keep them clean and clear. Some notable attendees were the chairman of the then NRA Lord Crickhowell, VVS chairman Richard Thrale and Sir John Page Chairman of TVW. MP Peter Lilly who also attended said in his speech:

I am delighted to witness the switching off of Friars Wash pumps. The dwindling flow of the river over recent years has been of great concern to all who love the Ver, especially those who live in Redbourn and St Albans.

Unfortunately despite an initial rise in groundwater levels in the upper reaches of the river, with the source 8 kilometres further upstream than it had been for many years, this turned out to be insufficient to permanently re-establish the river's flow and populations of some species only recovered to half their previous numbers of the mid 1980s indicating that habitat had been completley lost or was taking longer to re-establish than previously thought.

In 1993 a pipeline was completed bringing 16 million gallons of water a day from Grafham Water in Cambridgeshire to the Luton area. The following year a survey of the country's waterways gave the river a clean bill of health with its water quality in the top one third of the country although its riverside and meadow habitats were still in poor condition.

By 2006 partly as a result of more houses being built in what is one of the driest parts of Europe, 23 million litres of water were being extracted from various boreholes (see abstraction table at front of book) at Redbournbury, opened 1960 for additional water supplies for the Luton area, St Albans opened 1865, H (St Albans) opened 1885 and ML (St Albans) opened 1948 (names of pumping stations abbreviated for security reasons). These are just a examples of the other boreholes and groundwater observation points along the Ver. As a country renowned for its rainfall it is an amazing yet worrying fact that by 2011 it was reported that there was less water in the southeast of Britain than in Egypt or Morocco with 13 trillion litres per year being used for homes, industry and

Two views showing the varying water levels of the river at Flamstead near Friars Wash, January 2004 and September 2005. (VWC)

agriculture, the vast majority from rivers.

This pumping of groundwater from under an area can create what is known as a cone of depletion or depression, this is when too much water is drawn from the water table without giving it time to recharge and the water table sinks in the region that has been heavily pumped, creating a large sunken area.

Before the development of the pumping station there were gravel pits worked by Rice's to the west and through the valley and beyond towards Trowley Bottom. These pits were 10 to 15 feet deep and needed pumping when in use. Gypsies would cut the surrounding willows for peg making and use the clear water for drinking. Later these pits were filled in and reclaimed for farmland.

Willow trees growing along the Ver had many uses for the local community. Baskets of all shapes and sizes were made especially for watercress transportation. The history of weaving willow by hand and especially the production of baskets for storage and transportation is thought to stretch back many thousands of years and the skill of the local hand weavers could be used to make many other useful items including fish and bird traps, fences, animal muzzles and chair seats. Straw and rush work was also produced along the Ver Valley from at least the fourteenth century onwards using the plentiful supply of materials found along the river. It was said that Hertfordshire straw was of superior quality. The craft gave employment to many thousands of women and children but had greatly declined by the beginning of the twentieth century mainly due to cheap imports from abroad.

From Friars Wash the valley extends westwards for 3 miles to Ballingdon Bottom and to the east, the valley runs almost parallel to the Ver as far as the west side of Caddington.

Where Friars Wash pumping station now stands there were once cress beds. In the winter of 1987/88 the river was visible at Friars Wash and the meadows towards Harpendenbury Farm which had been ploughed eliminating the riverbed became flooded. The river course had to be reclaimed by the TWA and quite a flow developed for some months.

At Verlam End beside an ancient tree is a hollow said locally to be the Friars washing place. There was often water here in the late 1960s and although the

riverbed has been ploughed down to the next hedge its course remained to Luton Lane.

From 1926 Verlam End to Luton Lane was the site of the Hertfordshire Hunt Friars Wash Point to Point Races, which were held, with several gaps, twice a year from 1890 until 1964. The 3¼ mile nine fence oval 'course' was often changed but generally started at Annabel's Cottages, where bookies took bets on the results of the races, going up by Watery Lane, parallel to Watling Street over to Northfield Spring and back to the start and included two 6-foot wide water jumps over the Ver which in 1904 caused problems for the jumpers as the river, swollen by rain was exceptionally wide. The time of year the races were staged often led to problems including mist, wind, ice and extreme boggy conditions. The local paper reported on one race saying:

A favourite watching point was the water jump positioned close to the starting line, having seen the mounts safely over, men, women and children ran 150 yards...to see the completion of the race.

Some years saw early drought conditions including 1898 when the Ver was a dry river bed and the ground very hard. Post WWII the usual local dignitaries were joined by national celebrities which helped attract television to the event for the first time in 1957.

In 1991, BBC *Countryfile* did a piece on the Ver as part of a 'Disappearing Rivers' slot, mainly concentrating on the stretch around Luton Lane and

Luton Lane – Minnie Hewett and daughters with Tom Fox c1930. (GW)

Pond and old cottage Near the Friars Wash Point to Point course. June 1936. The river flows under the bridge seen just beyond the pond. (SC/HALS)

The Friars washing place – dried out for many years until 1988. (JBT)

Left: *Friars Wash Point to Point Races taken in 1933 as riders jumped over the Ver. (JC)*

Right: *An original Point to Point Race Programme. (JBT)*

Luton Lane Bridge 1980s. (JBT)

Watercress in the river at Kensworth, an echo of a past industry seen through much of the Ver. (JBT)

the golf course.

The production of watercress in Britain was believed to have begun in Roman times although the first recorded commercial grower was Nicholas Meissner in sixteenth century Germany. Its use as a green vegetable can be traced back more than three millennia, to the Persians, Greeks and Romans. In 400BC, Hippocrates, the father of medicine, is said to have located his first hospital beside a stream on the Island of Kos so that he could grow watercress to help treat patients. It is noted for its health giving properties being rich in vitamin c and it became part of the ancient Greek soldier's diet believing it helped with stamina. The Romans valued it for its many medicinal properties especially as a cure for mental ailments and baldness. The Anglo Saxons used it in a potage which helped to clean the blood and the famous herbalist Culpepper praised its use against lethargy and "the gross humours of winter". Sir Francis Bacon (1561-1626) believed it restored a youthful bloom in women!

In 1808 the first British watercress farm was opened at Springhead in Northfleet, Kent by William Bradbury. Its success lay with the purity, temperature and abundance of the water supply, especially that of chalk streams such as the Ver which are slightly alkaline, and its geographic position with good road and rail links meant it could be shipped in wicker 'flats' easily to London and other parts of the country where it could be bought for a ha'penny a bunch.

By the 1940s there were more than 1000 acres of watercress beds. During WWII it was championed as

a healthy home-grown food and a traditional British Sunday-night tea was watercress and vinegar, with bread and butter. By the end of the twentieth century there were only around 150 acres of commercial beds left.

My own grandparents told me that not only was local watercress a staple of the war but to accompany it they also caught minnows from the river at St Albans and ate them coated in a simple batter and fried as a local version of 'whitebait'! One of my Grandmother's old cook-books actually has a recipe for 'battered minnow'! And of course any trout they managed to 'tickle' were a much welcomed addition to the meagre war-time rations.

The VVS archives contain the following memories of R.S. Dew, who came to Redbourn in 1937 to work with his father-in-law Bill Simpson in the watercress beds.

In watercress growing…

There were gravel bottom beds and mud bottom beds. The latter needed a runner platform down the centre of the bed to support a plank from the bank, this was worked along the bank of the bed and the cutter knelt on it to cut the cress, as he finished cutting within reach so he moved the plank to a fresh area. The mud in the beds could be as much as 4 ft deep. The river from Luton Lane ran by the side of our main watercress bed, it was about 2ft deep and 5ft wide, with 4ft banks.

The water from beds flowed into the river making it deeper and wide. Spring water was abundant until the pumping station started working at Friars Wash. Then the water started drying up and we had to abandon the beds…It also caused the drying up of our bed near Harpenden Lane. We had to keep the river free from weeds to allow the water to run away from the beds.

The watercress men wore thigh length waders that were so heavy and stiff that the men were unable to straighten up and walk away, so they walked with bent knees. These waders were completely water tight but very heavy.

Each bed produced around twelve crops annually and was cut during the summer approximately every twenty days. Once cut, the bed was manured and pressed down with a heavy wooden board to which a long handle was attached. Because of this regular manuring the level of the riverbed slowly rose throughout the year and had to be cleared annually.

Once cut the cress was packed for market in specially constructed shallow baskets called 'flats' often made from the willow that grew along the river, in double rows, with leaves towards the interior. The greater proportion was sent to Covent Garden in London. Although there were no published returns at this time showing the extent of acreage under cultivation for watercress in Hertfordshire, it was generally considered by those engaged in the industry that more than a third of the total amount marketed in London was from the county of Hertfordshire.

There were once many watercress beds in this area with commercial growing starting around 1830. In 1900, Tommy Sansom was one of the main growers, buying up smaller cress beds until he had around 20 acres; they included Waterend Lane, Luton Lane, Harpenden Lane and by the Pré. Once picked, cress does not have a long shelf life and therefore it was sold locally and sent to markets in towns where there was a good rail or road link, thus a quicker delivery. When he died his son, Tommy junior, took over until his death, when his widow sold the business to Walter Vise and John Simpson, both from Redbourn. From 1949 Walter ran it alone and employed many local people. The watercress beds grew in meadows that ran along the Ver from Markyate to Bricket Wood. But as the spring water supply dried up only the upper beds were left until eventually, only Bobby Vise was producing cress until the 1980s.

The head spring of Mr Dew's number two cress bed 1980s. (JBT)

The watercress in Flamstead seemed to be particularly susceptible to theft and it was recorded in March 1897 that two men were caught stealing cress from William Durrent at Flys Wash by the local bobby. One of the men, William Clark, was fined seven shillings; his accomplice, Edward Batchelor was let off with a warning.

The river beyond Verlam End, which was just visible as a ditch, was cleared allowing a decent flow down to Luton Lane by Redbourn golf course. The photo above shows where the head spring of Mr Dew's number two cress bed had once been, just south of Luton Lane with the golf course seen in the background. Unfortunately in the late 1980s, where the land had been landscaped near the river to create hazards for the golfers, flooding occurred and these hazards had to be cleared by the local water authority to allow drainage.

Mrs King lived in New Cottages, Harpendenbury with her family as a child during the 1920s and '30s and remembers the following:

There were watercress beds in front of the house as far as Luton Lane. At the footbridge downstream where the path from Harpendenbury to Flint Cottages crossed the river, we watched trout under the bridge. We skated on the pond nearby and caught newts although the ponds dried out sometimes. In the Osiers, which was forbidden ground to us, there were kingfishers…. kingcups grew among the willows.

Once part of the parish of Kinsbourne, Harpendenbury was the home to a large medieval demesne farm once owned by Benedictine Abbey of Westminster. After the Dissolution of the Monasteries it passed through many hands eventually being bought in 1649 by Sir John Wittwronge of Rothamsted, who served as an MP for Hertfordshire on several occasions, for the substantial sum of £76 14s 10d. Nearby is the Grade II listed tithe barn, built in 1398 on an earlier structure, it was used for the storage of produce supplied to the church as tax or tithe by the parish. Much of the original farmland was used as part of Redbourn Golf Course. The farm house is now in private hands and the barn and a nearby early dairy have been converted to offices.

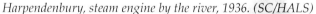

Harpendenbury, steam engine by the river, 1936. (SC/HALS)

Chapter Four
Harpendenbury to Dolittle Mill

...while from the valley up the hillside stealing,
The gentle rippling of the stream is heard,
Refreshing every better thought and feeling,
Till from the soul a glad response is stirred.

From 'Morning' – Rev. A.J. Treloar

At Harpendenbury the river when in existence flows through a large meadow to a bridge under the Redbourn bypass. This bridge has been built large enough to take the river if ever the full flow is restored. In the laying of the bypass, the route chosen was through the least productive land north of Harpenden Lane.

The Osiers was the haunt of naturalists albeit private land. Notes in Ted Banfield's archive from David Scott record the Ver in this area from the 1930s:

The Osiers for the benefit for those who have never visited it, was an area from 'Taylors Lane' westwards,

including the river, about 150 yards by 200 yards plus, up and down the river. Sloping down from Taylor's Lane hedge, it was a self set spinney and thicket with a small fenced clearing for beehives. Towards the lower river level the spinney thinned to more open wet ground with many alder trees... quite a few had fallen over but were still growing. Through this ran a skein of ponds of varying sizes and depths, all overgrown and linked by the meandering stream.

At the northern end were the dark red abutments to an earlier footbridge and the southern end opened out with shallower ponds and fewer trees. One could stand with the Osiers behind looking southwest to Harpenden Lane seeing the straight parallel ditches of the river and the cress bed and in front, the hedge, Taylors Lane and the hill to the left and on the open rising ground to the right stood three or four straggling Scot's pines.

In 1959 the course of the river was altered near Long Meadow and its new position close to the bypass was two metres below the level of the Osiers in order to allow a farm track culvert under the new road which because of a lip downstream often caused a build-up of road surface runoff and cattle dung.

Local conservationists asked that an ancient hedge be preserved during road works and the county council obliged. In the excavations the contractors dug a huge Hertfordshire puddingstone from the riverbed which now lies near the Harpenden Lane roundabout. There were other large

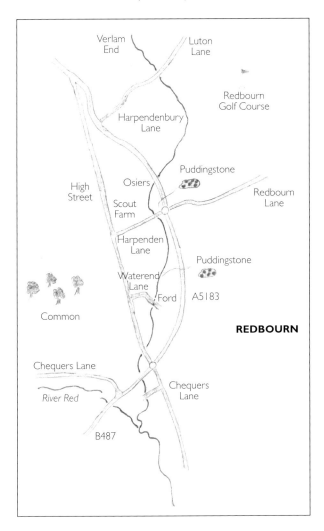

The Osiers, mid 1980s. (JBT)

Puddingstone and village sign next to the roundabout, Harpenden Lane 2008. (JBT)

Harpenden Lane, Redbourn.

Harpenden Lane (formerly New Mills Lane), Redbourn, early 1900s, the field on the right of this picture is "New Mills Field" possibly the site of another water or wind mill. (JBT)

examples around the village in the early twentieth century including behind the Chequers Inn and at the north end of the common. These may have been way markers on ancient routes.

Mr Dunkley was bought up at Scout Farm between Watling Street and the river; his recorded memories are part of the VVS archives:

My first recollection of the River Ver would be of the drying up in 1927, and of the trout splashing about in the remaining puddles, one in particular of 3-4 pounds. This was in the Osiers near the footbridge. The Osiers at that time did not come under Scout Farm but was in Major Sidebottom's 'Shoot' who I learned later had stocked the river once but never repeated. One thing I recall was the crystal clear water, many a time have we quenched our thirst directly from the springs.

Cress packers, the ford at Waterend Lane 1870. (JBT)

We made two swimming spots in the river meadows, the first being close to Harpendenbury Farm; we had to dam the river to get a depth of 4-5 feet, in this one we learned to swim. About 1935 we moved our pool lower down just above the Osiers, the first pool had become very muddy, the second being a bed of sand, I remember rushes making a good changing room, of course we had to dam the river again.

Below the Osiers a watercress bed was producing during the war.

In the river meadows, there were for several seasons, curlews and sandpipers, although their nests were never seen. In the Osiers there were plenty of moorhens and kingfishers. In the rushes below the Osiers was found mallard, teal, snipe and reed tit. Cranes were also frequent visitors.

At the bottom of Harpenden Lane the Ver crossed the road and was known locally as the Watersplash. At the beginning of the twentieth century, the river was an open ford and during heavy rain the road would be closed due to flooding. The winter months often saw the old Hempstead Road as a running stream that had to be crossed by stepping stones.

The river passes under Harpenden Lane, in a culvert, where there were once disused nurseries to upper and lower ponds and then onwards to the ford at Waterend Lane.

In the High Street, The Grade II listed Bull Public House, once known as the Black Bull and a popular

Watercress beds, Waterend Lane early 1900s (JBT)

May Walker riding through the Ver 1910. (GW)

Below: The river as it approaches Waterend Lane 1980s. (JBT)

Ford at Watery Lane Redbourn 1953. (MR) The lady is Mrs Yemm who lived at number 40 Harpenden Lane, the smaller boy is her son Martin, the little girl is Mike Richardson's sister Carol, and the older boy is Mike Richardson.

eighteenth century coaching inn, has been on this site since at least 1586. Manor courts were once held here and a Tithe Award Map of 1843 shows its land stretching down as far as the river.

Waterend Lane off the main High Street is crossed by the river at a ford near the old cress beds that once bordered the rear of Redbourn House.

The large red brick building of Redbourn House on the east side of the High Street was built in the early 1700s by the Carpenter family and passed to the Strathmore family; in the nineteenth century it was occupied by Lady Glamis. The tithe map of 1843 shows the grounds of the house stretching down to the Ver and ford at the end of Waterend Lane with a lake and island in the garden created from the river. WWII saw evacuees from Plymouth living here with the men employed at a local printer. It was demolished in 1955 due to escalating restoration costs and the portico can be seen in the grounds of the Museum of St Albans. Today Pondsmeade and Gertrude Peake House occupy the site.

Mike Richardson, who is seen as a boy in the above photo, lived with his family in Harpenden Lane and the river played a major part in his future career:

Behind the industrial estate off the High Street 2011. (JBT)

Mr Quick who worked the watercress beds from Harpenden Lane northwards to the Osiers. His thigh-high leggings would have been leather soaked in animal fat to keep the water out. (GW)

I lived in Harpenden Lane, Redbourn; only about 400m from the river, until I was 18, and the river played a major part in my becoming a biologist in later life. We were taken to the river to study its wildlife by a student teacher from the primary school in the 1940s. That led to me keeping a freshwater aquarium for many years, until I went to university to study botany. A favourite haunt was where the river crossed under what is now the A5183 (it was then the A5) just south of The Elms, where there were the remains of a mill and easy access to the beautiful chalk stream, with sticklebacks and miller's thumbs, freshwater shrimps and hydra, mayfly nymphs and caddis fly larvae, water snails and water crowfoot. I would take them home in an old accumulator jar – ideal, that had a secure handle and could be managed on my bicycle – which I got from my grandma (no mains electricity on Lamb Lane where she lived, so the accumulator powered the wireless, and I coveted the old jars). That was the start of my love of natural history. I went to the grammar school, then university (one of the lucky ones in those days), became interested in fungi, did research on cereal crop diseases and their importance and control for the Department of Agriculture and Fisheries for Scotland, took early retirement in 1993 and since then I have been doing my own research on fungi, all started by the Ver! I also found one of the earliest occurrences in the area of the

The river just before it disappears under Redbourn High Street in spring and a beautiful explosion of wildflowers 2011. (JBT)

floating water fern (Azolla) on the river, in about 1954 when doing surveys for the new Atlas of the British Flora, at the site of that old mill, just north of Redbournbury, an introduced species that is in the news again now as one of the introduced and invasive water plants that is causing problems. I also recall the damp patch of woodland, with mainly willow and alder called the Osiers, which ran between the river and the road to Harpendenbury, where in times of shortage (probably late '40s-early '50s) I would take a saw, chopper, and a two-wheeled trolley to collect firewood, making sure that nobody saw me 'stealing' wood.

Watering Lane showing cress beds and river. (JBT)

1896 painting, artist signature illegible, of River Red. (JBT)

The Manor of Reodbune was given to the Abbey by the Saxon Lord Aegelwine le Swarte in the mid eleventh century. The village itself developed over many hundreds of years on a thick wooded area, gathering together a number of dispersed hamlets. The habitable areas of cleared woodlands were called 'ends' and can be seen today in place names such as Church End, thought to be the site of the original village.

Redbourn, the 'reedy bourn' or stream, lies northwest of St Albans and is named after the River Red – Red or road signifies an old English passage where people ride or travel, and burne a pretty rivulet.

The word 'Burn' has its origins in old English from the word 'burna' or 'burrn(e), burna being an early name for a small stream, over time this became 'bourne' which eventually became a word associated with chalk streams that only had an intermittent flow, such as the Ver.

Salmon in his *History of Hertfordshire* claims it is:

from the Saxon burne or borne, as we use it still in Hertfordshire for a rivulet running between deep banks and rode for a passage where men ride.

The English Place Name Society places the villages' old English origins in the name 'Hreod-Burna' or 'reedy stream'. Others have said that Redburne signifies red water and part of a letter from the Hertfordshire Natural History Society & Field Club in Ted Banfield's archive from 1987 states:

In Spring 1904, after a wet year, the river rose above Markyate Street…also a stream flowed for nearly a mile from above into the ponds at Church End Redbourn – the old Womer Brook, which was one of the Woe-Bournes, and tended to flow a bit red – hence Red – bourn.

It is also said to originate from the red reeds that grew along its banks for hundreds of years. The Red is the Ver's main tributary and has its source near Church End. Fed by groundwater it helps to keep the Ver flowing in the area joining it near the rear of the Chequers pub.

Again superstition attaches itself to the river, especially when in flood. Many locals remember floods before the outbreak of the two World Wars. In *A History of Britain* translated by P. Holland in the seventeenth century, it notes:

….Wenmer called also Womer, a brooke that never breaketh out and riseth but that it foretelleth dearth and scarcity of corne, or else some extremity of dangerous times as the vulgar people doe verily believe.

The village's many spelling variations over the centuries include –

Reodbune/Reedbune – eleventh century
Redburniam – thirteenth century
Radbourne – fourteenth century
Ridibowne – fifteenth century
Rydburn – sixteenth century

In 1650 Redbourn was described as "a great streete in London Rode, of innes, ale houses and tradesmen."

In Church End, opposite the Hollybush pub is the old workhouse with a Dutch gable roof and a plaque seen in the photograph adjacent. When it was sold in 1837 the particulars of sale included… "a pump of water;

Work House Plaque (JBT)

there is also a good garden, with a small running stream at the end of it". The building has now been converted into a row of cottages.

In the late 1850s, a steam-powered mill was built by John Woollam at Redbourn, facing the common. This recruited local labour and there survives a surgeon's certificate under the Factories Regulations Act, 1844 requiring children to be at least eleven years old before working there. A large bronze bell,

The Ver at Redbourn – Kitton 1887. (MoS)

made by J. Warner and Sons, London in 1858 was used to summon the workers to labour and during WWI it was used to warn the villagers of Zeppelin raids. Today it can be seen at Redbourn Museum.

Redbourn mill closed in 1938. It was demolished and in 1960 the Brooke Bond Tea Company built a factory on the site. In October 1999 Silk Mill House, a Grade II listed building, was transferred to Redbourn Parish Council by Brooke Bond Foods Ltd for use as the village museum which opened to the public in May 2000 and is well worth a visit.

The River Ver runs east of the village and is crossed in several places by Watling Street meandering from north to south through the parish which stands at between 300 and 400 feet above sea level.

The word 'rival' is a sixteenth century term originating from the Latin 'rivalis' or 'rivus' meaning stream and referred to one who uses the same river as another.

Throughout history issues of river rights became more common and complicated with authority to use a waterway for navigation, setting up nets and eel traps, fishing, milling, removing water, dumping rubbish including sewage, constructing weirs and bridges, drainage and the right of riparian owners to the use of their land without unnecessary flooding. Many of these rights conflicted, for example the dumping of sewage and rubbish often killed fish and caused epidemics amongst those who lived near the river. Despite these constant conflicts which often cost dearly in money, time and temper it did go some way to helping to preserve many rivers although to some extent these conflicts still occur today for example extraction, pollution and flooding.

The St Albans Court Rolls of 1736 show an indictment of George Carpenter the elder of Redbourne for:

Filling up a great part of the channel of an ancient

stream in Redbourne, which runs from a place called Row Beach…through several places…and so on through Redbourne 'till it falls into the river Ver, with a bank of earth and other materials and planting upon the bank a quick hedge.

The River Ver, which at times throughout its history has been abundant with fish, has also had abundant locals trying to poach them! The problem of poaching increased as the population expanded and the rivers deepened and widened along with the increase of mill lands. Generally anyone caught fishing in the Abbot's waters, would have had severe penalties issued against them.

In 1822, John Dixon, a miller and owner of a fishery on the Ver, *"which runneth between a place called the Chequer bridge and a mill called Little Mill"*, accused William Barnes a labourer of attempting to *"take, kill and destroy fish in that part of said river as aforesaid, contrary to the form of the statute"*.

In the mid nineteenth century James Feary was fined 13s 6d for poaching an eel from the Ver near Fish Street Farm and an 1870 edition of the *Herts Advertiser* reports that three men, William North, Joseph Stratton and George Warby were charged with poaching in the Ver in waters belonging to Charles Woolham Esq. and netting trout valued at five shillings. Stratton, who had offended up to thirty times before, was fined the full penalty of £5 with 9s 6d costs with the alternative of three months in prison with hard labour.

Grade I listed St Mary's church on the west side of the common is a real Norman antiquity with a large square tower and an original nave. The church was consecrated by Herbert Losinga, Bishop of Norwich (1094-1119) early in the twelfth century and rebuilt in 1445 by John de Whethampsted. Drawings still exist that illustrate the old box pews and three-decker pulpit, sadly removed in 1850. There is still a beautiful rood screen across the chancel arch of 1478, although the rood loft was destroyed in the Reformation. The church is still very much in use.

The priory was built on the spot, not far from the river, where the relics of St Amphibalus were found in 1178. St Amphibalus was the priest who was hidden by Alban, a Roman citizen. This merciful act resulted in his martyrdom. St Amphibalus was put to death soon after on Redbourn common. His shrine is in the north chancel aisle of St Albans Abbey. On Watling Street running through Redbourn near the site of the priory there is a plaque on the wall. "The Priory. Nearby this site stood

The Priory Plaque. (JBT)

The Sansom family, Ver House, High Street, Redbourn c.1886. Rear l. to r. Dr O'Malley, Charles, Nell, Tom. Front l. to r. Mary, Harry, Mr & Mrs John Sansom, Arthur. (JT)

Maurice 'Mo' Sansom (rear) Bill Simpson, Ron Smith surrounded by cress baskets – rear of Ver House c.1919. (GW) Note Mo seems to be pouring tea into Bills hat!

Redbourn Priory dedicated to St Amphibal in the thirteenth century. Several outbuildings to the priory of a later date still survive in the vicinity."

The earliest recorded watercress grower in Redbourn is William Payne born in 1816; he was a Master Grower, who lived at Watercress Hall, previously Water Cress Cottage and part of Redbournbury Farm, next to the Ver from before 1851, when he first appeared at this address on the census, to 1890 with his wife Harriet and family. In the 1851 census he is listed as a Watercress Cultivator. Tragedy struck the family when their son, also called William was accidently killed at one of their watercress beds as reported in the *Herts Mercury*, 13 September, 1851:

An inquest was held at the Punch Bowl public-house, near Redbourn, on Thursday last, to inquire respecting the death of a lad named William Payne born 1840, son of Mr Payne, the water-cress dealer, living near Redbourn. It appeared that deceased was at work, in company with two others, and a man named Thomas Slaughter, at the water-cress beds, in Common Meadow, and deceased was "chaffing" Slaughter, who struck him without any intention of seriously hurting him, but having a knife, with which he was cutting cresses, in his hand, it penetrated his thigh, and injured the femoral artery. Medical assistance was immediately procured, but after lingering for some days, death resulted from the injury. After a patient investigation, lasting some hours, the jury returned a verdict of Accidental Death.

John Sansom was born in 1841 (died 1906) and came to Redbourn in 1885 to grow watercress, living at Ver House in the High Street, built by William Burchmore in the early nineteenth century for his two sisters. The watercress beds ran from Friars Wash to Watercress Hall near Shafford Mill and the site is seen on some old maps.

The 1871 census shows him as a 'watercress planter' living with his wife Ann (died 1896) and six children. By 1881 he had another addition to the family and was a watercress grower and gardener. In 1891 he is listed as a watercress grower along with his son Henry aged 15.

His brother, Tom, used to collect the watercress with his nephew in a horse and wagon and bring it home where it was packed into baskets at the rear yard of Ver House and another building a few doors down the street. At that time there was a great flow of water in the Ver and the carrying ditches besides the cress beds. By 1927 3,359lbs of watercress were being sent every day by rail from Redbourn to as far away as Liverpool.

John Sansom started a watercress business at Ver House around 1868. Tom carried on the business after John's retirement. Charles and Harry started a watercress business at Croxley Green, Watford, and Arthur did the same at Whitwell, Herts. Nell Sansom married Dr O'Malley and produced nine daughters and four sons, while Mary married Gregory Webb and produced nine sons and four daughters!

One of the last local watercress growers was Walter Vise, who lived at Do-Little Mill House; his watercress beds were in the meadows next to the Ver and ran from Redbourn to Bow Bridge following the river and at its height employed many men. He continued to grow watercress until the early 1960s.

Chequers Lane, once known as Heybrigge Lane, lies between the Chequers pub and the Moor. Geoff Webb has many memories of a childhood spent on the Ver in this area:

The river was a constant attraction for our prying eyes…watervoles-water rats to us-just had to be chased, only to see them disappear under water to reach their nesting chambers, via a river-bank hole. One of the wider bends was used as a swimming pool…with nearby reeds acting as our changing room. We were able to run along the bank and dive into the deepest part, often to emerge draped in duckweed or some other river vegetation. Near the cress beds, where the water was shallow, our fishing beds captured minnows and sticklebacks, displayed proudly on the bank in water filled jam jars. Fish could clearly be seen through the crystal water, moving in small shoals over the river's smooth muddied bottom, but in the breeding season male sticklebacks acquired an iridescent sheen of silvery green on their upper bodies, in contrast to their upper tummies painted in a striking scarlet. If anyone was lucky to catch one of these giants he was the envy of all

Egyptian Geese on fields near Chequers Lane 2008. Introduced to this country as ornamentals, they have escaped and established a feral population in the central and eastern area of England. (JBT)

those "tiddler" anglers...for we watched goggle-eyed, as the "red-throats", or "fiery-cots", circled strands of water weed in their glass prisons.

The river then passes under the old Nicky Line railway which was built in 1877 for the Harpenden & Hemel Hempstead Railway, a connection between the two towns via Redbourn. No longer in use, it is part of the 9-mile long Nicky Line walk and cycle path.

After the river passes under the Hemel Road it crosses the water meadows to the Chequers Inn.

The earliest reference to the Chequers is when it was sold to John Marshall in 1657 and the front of the building dates from the late sixteenth century. In 1699 the Chequers Ale House was included in a survey as part of the Gorhambury Estate and in the eighteenth century the inn, together with an acre of land was part of Fish Street Farm owned by Lord Verulam. In the nineteenth century it was called the Old Chequers Inn to distinguish it from the Chequers in nearby Flamstead.

1908 saw the first fatal road accident in Redbourn on the road outside the inn when a bicycle ridden by local man Fred Allen sped out of Chequers Lane and hit the side of a Rolls Royce travelling from London to Hertfordshire, killing the cyclist instantly.

In the 1930s it was run, along with a small antiques business next door, by a Mr Bridge who kept a large stuffed black bear by the front door and a large stuffed rat above the bar that had reputedly eaten the cheese of Dick Turpin!

Traces of wattle and daub were found in the foundations during the building of an extension at the back of the pub in the 1970's.

After a fire badly damaged the pub in 2004 it was completely renovated. However, this was not the first time fire had struck as at the WWII VE day celebrations the thatched roof was ignited and destroyed by a 'Very Light' – a kind of flare fired from a pistol used for signalling or temporary illumination. Today it is still a pub and restaurant with the river flowing under a small bridge at the back of the car park.

Once past the Chequers Inn the river crosses the water meadows to the site of Dolittle Mill, which was sited on the east side of Watling Street. In the 1920s, the river here was said to be over 5 foot deep and nearly 14 foot wide!

Grain has been a foodstuff of animals and humans for many thousands of years and would have originally been crushed by a simple version of a pestle and mortar this developed into saddle stones where a stone roller or 'muller' was pushed and pulled over the grain using the backward and

Looking downstream towards the Chequers pub, the bridge carries the bypass around the south of Redbourn 1980s. (JBT)

Chequers public house, Redbourn. The small white X in the right of the photo marks the spot of the first fatal motor accident involving a cyclist. June 1908. (GW)

forward movement of a kneeling person, grinding it against a stone base with a concave surface resembling the seat of a saddle.

The Iron Age produced the first Rotary Quern using a semi-circular motion of a large flat stone upon another of a similar size, the forerunner of modern day millstones. Animal powered mills, sometimes powered by man, were larger and had a long pole attached to the top stone which was operated by continuously walking around the stones.

The idea of water power for grinding corn was bought to Britain by the Romans and would have consisted of a wooden building with a horizontal wheel fixed to the shaft along with the stones; this was replaced by peg and rung gearing which allowed the use of faster, vertical waterwheels. Despite these developments the use of manual querns continued throughout the middle ages, sometimes with undesirable consequences.

Over 5000 water or animal powered mills are recorded in the Domesday survey of 1086, 132 in Hertfordshire, although some were multiple stones in one building rather than separate mills. Milling was one of the first rural industries to be effectively mechanised and in the 1700s many technical improvements were made including more efficiently designed iron waterwheels, cast iron gearing and automatic governors which regulated the gap between millstones.

The eighteenth century agricultural writer William Ellis believed that the county of Hertfordshire was best furnished with watermills in the whole of Britain and the Ver has had many along its banks throughout history.

In the 1864 edition of Cassey's Directory, ninety-three millers were listed in Hertfordshire. By 1965, that number had fallen to fourteen, only eight milling flour.

Millwrights were skilled craftsmen and in the early days wood was used to build watermills. Shafts and wheels were usually made of oak with elm, which was more resistant to rot, used for the paddles. Later iron was used for the gears. Stonemasons cut grooves in the stones to grind the flour to the correct fineness. These had to be perfectly set so they only touched the corn and not the other stone or they would quickly wear. A mill once sited was rarely moved mainly due to the amount of work and funds needed to establish it in the first place. A good head of water was required to give adequate power to turn the wheel and at night the river was used to replenish the supply needed to work the mill the following day. To help with this process a leat, sometimes called a head race, or millstream was constructed by embanking a length of river to raise the normal level or a millpond built by damming the river. In early mills a causeway or fixed weir, sometimes referred to as 'low-shottes' were constructed. To control the flow and ensure the millstream or pond did not flood and to allow the river to carry past the mill to provide water for local people and areas, sluice gates and weirs were built which required the skill of the miller to ensure the correct water level was maintained.

Redbourn Road looking towards Redbourn where the road crosses the river at the site of the medieval Dolittle Mill on the right of the road and mill house and pond on the left. (MoS)

Another method was to build an embankment on either side of a stream creating a millpond using sluices to create a water-store of power to drive the mill.

Two mills are recorded in the Domesday Book at Redbourn: "Bettespool Mill" (Dolittle Mill) and "The Chamberlains's Mill" (Redbournbury Mill), both owned by the Abbot of St Albans and taxed at twenty-six shillings with only five other mills with a higher value in Hertfordshire. They were leased to William Horne in 1537 at a yearly rent of £8 by the Abbot. The Dissolution of the Monasteries in 1539 saw lands and buildings pass to King Henry VIII and in 1550 the mills and manor were granted to Princess Elizabeth, later to become Queen Elizabeth I. In 1609 her successor James I granted titles of the watermills to Edward Ferrers and Francis Philips in return for a fee paid to the King.

Bethlespole Mill, named after a nearby meadow, was the earliest known name of what was last known as Do-Little Mill. In 1350 a prior from Redbourn was forced to purchase a road from the mill of Betlespol to Heybrygge Lane to allow safe passage of food for his monks. The name of the mill and its pool is thought to have come from one of the prior's tenants, the Bedel family. Mentioned in the Domesday Book, it would originally have been a wooden structure on the east side of Watling Street standing where the road crossed the river over the mill dam. Its many names over the centuries have included Bethlespole (thirteenth century), Bettespoll (fourteenth century), Betylpole (sixteenth century) and Bettell Poole (seventeenth century). From the mid seventeenth century it had various names including the Malt Mill, Water Corn Mills, Redbourn Mill, Little Mill, and The Paper Mills and from the mid nineteenth century "Do-Little Mill". In Kenneth Reid's book *Watermills of the London Countryside* he suggests that the name 'Dolittle' was normally applied to mills that were the first to be built on a river. A 1352 act of parliament allowed the surveillance of weirs and causeways, or causeys as they were often called, which if found to be raised were required to be amended to the original level. The mill water was supplied by a large mill pond made by damming the river and controlled by

The Little Mill – the water wheel can just be seen on the right of building (JBT)

Little Mill, early twentieth century, showing the house and barn on the right which are still there. (JBT)

Dolittle Mill Pond and river, Redbourn. Bridge and road to the right. The millpond was a power-house and store of energy for the mill. (JBT)

Council Workers and Engine at Dolittle Mill 1924. (GW)

Dolittle Mill House and barn summer 2011. (JBT)

This image from the Ted Banfield collection is entitled 'Us paddling near Little Mill, summer'; the people are unknown. They are not from the Banfield family – maybe you recognise them? (JBT)

sluices. These dams were first mentioned in a 1532 Court Roll as "the way leading over the damn of ye Mault Mill". This large pool would have been crossed by a bridge and the miller would be expected to keep not only the bridge in good repair but the water at a controlled height to allow the locals to cross in safety, if not he could be fined.

A chronicler of the Abbey recorded in 1334 that a young local girl accidentally fell into the mill-leat. Those nearby watched in horror presuming she would either be killed by the wheel or by drowning. Unexpectedly, the wheel threw her clear, but unfortunately she was dead. The people who saw this event prayed to St Alban and the little girl came back to life, their prayers had been answered.

In 1381, the people of Redbourn tried to acquire a charter from the Abbot allowing them to freely fish and hunt without being punished for doing so, he agreed partly to their request but unsatisfied with his deliberations they destroyed an embankment that held back Bettespol which finally persuaded the Abbot to grant the required charter!

Following the execution of Charles I in 1649, the Commonwealth was established by Oliver Cromwell until the restoration of the monarchy in 1660. In 1650 a survey of the mill, along with Redbournbury was carried out. Redburne Little Mill was at the time occupied by William Weeden and valued at £13 it was described as situated *"…neare the highway called Watlinge Streate Waye, consisting of two small rooms and a little house…with a little Close of meadowe belonginge to the said mill North, and the lands belonging to Redburne Bury south, with all bancks, pooles, lakes, waters, water courses, fishinges and all ways passages…"* However the mill was reported as being *"very much out of repayer…"*, and William was made to *"repair, sett and amend the mill and all its bridges and floodgates"*.

A sixteenth century property deed records that the Lord of the Manor granted to Edward Abraham *"a croft and meadow called Batispol lying together between the highway called Watling Strat on the south and the river bank on north"*.

In 1532 Ralph Rowlatt was the tenant of *"a croft lying between the field now called Cummyn Millefield and heretofore called Betylpolfold of the one part…and the other head upon the way leading over the dam of the maltmill there to the said field called Cummyn Millefeld towards the North"*.

Around 1666 the mill was demolished by Sir Harbottle Grimston and the land used as a smallholding. By 1669 it had obviously been rebuilt in a slightly different place as it was leased to John Legge *"all that messuage….lying nigh Redbourn Mill between the field called Battlepoolfield, alias Millfield and the King's highway called Watling Street, and abutteth*

upon the way called Beaumontlane towards the south and the river towards the north…and one close of meadow ground called Water Mead containing one acre and a half, one piece of ground where a mill or millhouse stood and a meadoe thereunto adjoining…for 15 years from Michaelmas 1669 paying £11 per annum".

The mechanical principles of the watermill were easily adapted for other purposes if the need arose. The appearance of paper makers in every Redbourn militia list between 1758 and 1783 was explained when a lease of Dolittle Mill was discovered. A 'water grist mill, which is intended to be converted into a paper mill', was leased in 1753 to John Vowell, a stationer from London. Destroyed by fire in 1783 a year later the newly built mill was leased to a new tenant, Richard Flintham and had been reverted to its original use as a corn mill.

There was enough water to run two breast mills – struck by the water at axle level – and at Dolittle Mill there was a 12-foot head of water now only lawn.

The Census of 1881 shows Arthur Dixon as a miller and farmer at Little Mill with 160 acres. By the end of the nineteenth century William Penny lived at the mill from where he ran a watercress business, but it seems it was still owned by the Dixons as in 1927 the mill was shut down by A.J. Dixon of St Albans. Up until then it had been milling every day. The building was used for engineering work during WWII. Due to the widening of Watling Street in the 1950s, the mill was demolished and the seventeenth century restored house, which was originally the home of the miller, and the barn are now situated on the west side of the road.

Mrs Ginger was born in Dolittle Mill Cottage on Watling Street and remembers salmon-trout in the pool below the old mill. Marigolds, kingcups and yellow iris grew along the river both up and downstream.

It is thought that a third mill possibly existed on the site of New Mill Field in the seventeenth century although no remains are known to exist and it could have been the site of a windmill.

On the west side of Watling Street stands part of the original building that for over 200 years between 1701 and 1917 was an inn called the Running Horses, also known around the 1780s as the Green Man. Owned for many years by the local Kingsbury Brewery Company, in 1898 it was bought by Benskins and was eventually sold in 1910 to become the private house we see today, called "The Runners".

Local 'lad' Roy Cutler was born at The Runners and remembers their cellar flooding every two to three years, the worst, during the war, was 5 to 6 feet. He also spent many happy hours swimming and diving with his friends in the Ver.

Chapter Five
Dolittle Mill to Kingsbury Mill

Can you tell me of a country, full of streams, and fords, and mills,
Where silver waters flow within the hollows of its hills;
A land of meadows green, and lanes, which please the traveller's eye,
And make him lengthen out his way, nor wish to hurry by?

'Between the Roman Roads of Herts' by Rev Albert J. Treloar

After passing Dolittle Mill House the river flows under Watling Street. In Barlies "Travellers Tales", it states that large boats had to be dragged across the fords at Frogmore End and the ford between Kingsbury and Redbourn; this could be where the river crosses Watling Street near Dolittle Mill or at Shafford. It is not known if these large boats were propelled by oarsman or towed from the banks. But it raises the question of how big our river was in the past.

The river in this area of Redbourn was described by Sir William Beach Thomas in his 1950 book on Hertfordshire as:

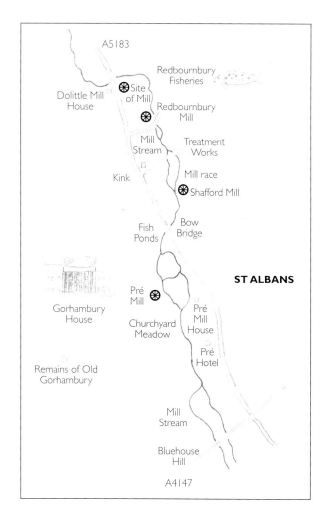

One of the few streams that remain pure, keeps much of its old charms and exercises its old attractions, is the Ver which runs through the valley from which St Albans climbs up the steep northern slope. It is a beautiful trout stream, in which the fish grow to four pounds or more, and along its course, not least within the confines of Verulam or ex-Verulam property, are to be seen at intervals birds that one would not expect in such surroundings. Both a stint and an oyster catcher have been shot thereabouts by sportsmen in search of snipe and duck, which rejoice in the valley. Those shy birds the golden plover come almost into the suburbs of St Albans.

Many people are drawn to the banks of our rivers by angling and Redbournbury Fisheries situated by the river off Beesonend Lane is no exception. Founded in 1987, it covers 7 acres of land on the site of the old watercress beds and includes well stocked lakes with course and game fish and a stretch of the river which has been improved with the help of English Nature and the Environment Agency. These improvements include narrowing channels to improve water flow and movement of sediment which in turn will benefit water life including conditions for spawning.

Several types of fish have already been seen in the river including brown trout, rudd and millers thumb and species such as snails, freshwater shrimp, hoglouse, leech and numerous dragonflies.

Many birds also frequent the area including the tufted duck, migrating bitterns, green woodpeckers, barn owls and the beautiful kingfisher.

Indeed Dame Juliana Berners in her 1496 book *Treatyse of Fysshynge wyth an Angle,* was well aware of the delights of angling and how close it brings man to nature and his surroundings:

And if the angler take fysshe....surely thenne is there no man merier than he is in his spyryte.

As an angler I wholeheartedly agree!

The kingfisher (Alcedo atthis) is one of the most beautiful birds of the British countryside with its brilliant blue and red plumage it is synonymous with our rivers and waterways and to see one is always a thrill. There is little difference between male and female – the colour of the lower mandible is all black on the male's bill and black with red on the female

The river after passing under Watling Street 2009. (JBT)

The mill stream behind Redbournbury Mill. (JBT)

and they both make a shrill whistle "chi-keeeee".

With 5000-8000 breeding pairs in the UK, in late April they usually excavate a tunnel in a bank next to slow flowing water where they both take turns incubating their six-seven eggs and feeding the young which fledge in around twenty-five days.

Their fast and low flight means they are often gone in a colourful flash. Hunting from riverside perches and occasionally hovering over water they feed mainly on fish and aquatic insects. They are currently amber listed and are at risk from habitat degradation, pollution and hard winters.

The following memories of the area around Redbournbury are from Geoff Webb:

Reaching the turning point of my ramble I cross the river by a rickety plank, acting as a footbridge... frequently water voles swim away in silent escape, only visible by a broad bow wave, but one soft brown little chap is sitting at his front door loudly nibbling a freshly gathered reed – beaver fashion. The bed of a shallow stretch of water is a mosaic of cleanly washed stones in many shades...small shoals of minnows, their tails fanning gently, hang stationary against the current. Fresh water shrimps or "toe biters", swim with an awkward sideways motion, while a brown and white mottled fish, a miller's thumb, or..."bull-head", lies

motionless between two stones, depending on its amazing camouflage for protection. Anaemic-looking snails cling to swaying underwater trusses of water crowfoot, whose yellow-centred, snow-white flowers stand out brightly, barely above the water's surface.

Redbournbury Mill early 1900s. The newly installed steam engine is housed in the shed on the right with the enclosed belt drive crossing the tail-race to the mill. (GW)

After passing under Watling Street the river goes many ways as it snakes across the water meadows until coming to Watersmeet by Crowhill Wood above Redbournbury Mill.

*I love the brimming wave that swam
Thro' quiet meadows round the mill,
The sleepy pool above the dam,
The pool beneath it never still,*

Tommy Sansom, local cress grower with Tom Burchmore one of his workers near the cress beds rear of Redbournbury Farm – now Redbournbury Fisheries 1928. (GW)

Redbournbury Mill mid 1980s. (JBT)

The meal-racks on the whitened floor,
The dark round of the dripping wheel…
(The Millers Daughter, Tennyson)

Few scenes are as quintessentially British as an old watermill set beside a stream. Currently the only working mill on the River Ver and surrounded by just a few old cottages and a farm, Redbournbury Mill, situated south of Redbourn, is a small red brick building of four floors with a welsh slate roof. The mill and surrounding buildings date back to the sixteenth century, although a mill belonging to the Abbey was documented on the site in the Domesday Book of 1086. The book recorded mills by the value of their rental and only five other mills in Hertfordshire are recorded as equal or greater value than Redbournbury. As with all early mills, the original would have been timber framed.

The earliest record of the mill after the Domesday Book is in the early 1300s when during the Abbacy of John de Wheathampstead the mill was razed to the ground and local people would have tried to put out the fire by filling buckets and containers from the river.

Between the eleventh and fourteenth centuries the mill was called the Chamberlain's Mill after the Abbot of St Albans' Chamberlain who managed the Manor of Redbourn from a house nearby. Between 1511 and 1609 it was named, as were many mills, after what it produced – the Corn Mill, Wheat Mill and Flour Mill. The earliest record of its current name is 1559, when it was known as Redborn Burie, burie or bury meaning a fortified or moated site. The moat here was caused by the Ver looping naturally around the house. From the mid seventeenth century to 1764 it was called the Grist Mill, grist being a general name given to animal feed.

It is thought that the mill once used a breast-shot wheel where the water strikes the wheel at axle level, but only produces around a third of the power of an overshot wheel. The current iron overshot wheel, measuring 9" 6' in diameter by 7" 6' wide, is powered by the weight of water passing over the top and onto its thirty buckets.

Overshot is the more efficient type of water wheel and more commonly used in a hilly landscape as the mechanical power derived is determined by the wheel's physical size and the available head of water. Once the water reaches the top of the wheel it hits the plashers, forcing the wheel to rotate. This gains a double gravitational advantage, firstly forcing the flow of water partially transferred to the wheel whilst the weight of the water descending in the wheel's buckets imparts additional energy. They were also generally more expensive to build as they required precise engineering and a significant head of water.

However due to its many shallow rivers, the historically older undershot wheel, where water strikes the paddles or blades below the axle of the wheel, is more commonplace in Hertfordshire. More inefficient than overshot wheels, they generate less power and can only be used where the flow, often supplied by a millstream or pond, is sufficient to provide torque.

To give a good head of water at Redbournbury a narrow elongated leat was created by hand, embanking the river and diverting it along the side of the valley with the river bed made waterproof with local clay and chalk; this kept it level for half a mile upstream and gave a good head of water to help work the mill with the control of the water level operated by sluices. This watercourse is believed to date back to Saxon times and was possibly built for an earlier watermill on the site. The mill is thought to have been part of the manor of Redbourn given to the Abbot at the time of Edward the Confessor (1003-1066).

View of the mill stream from the top of the mill. (RM)

As previously mentioned, Henry VIII left the Abbey lands, including the mill, in his will to his daughter Princess Elizabeth. It was then passed to James I, who leased the mill in trust through the treasury to various people. In 1651 owner Thomas Haydon leased a water grist mill called Redbourne Bury Mill to William Hickman for seven years with £100.5s down payment and 5s a year rent although the following year Sir Harbottle Grimston, bought the mill and its lands for £200. He was an ancestor of the present Earls of Verulam and therefore the mill became part of the Gorhambury Estate.

As with Dolittle Mill during the Commonwealth period in the mid seventeenth century, a survey was carried out of Redbournbury, then called "Redburne Great Mills" containing two pairs of millstones which was valued with its land at £23.6.8d. Peter Meadows who was miller in 1669 is recorded as being required to pay £8 from the rent of both mills to the poor of Brickhill in Northamptonshire; this payment was to continue for over 100 years. In 1694 the mill was leased to Samuel Clover:

Samuel Clover holdeth this mill and two meadows…from Michaelmas 1694 for 21 years also A massuege nere ye late Redbourne Mill (widow Legg holds this messuage with…one close of meadow land called water mead, a piece of ground where the mills and mill house stood…from Michaelmas 1684 for 21 years).

He also undertook:

At his own cost…shall new build the Mill and Mill House…mill pond, floodgates, banks, stankes…& to scour and clense the river as oft as shal require…

On one wall still exists a brick dated '1790', when much of the mill was extended and rebuilt.

For twenty years from 1841 the mill was occupied by Edward Hawkins senior then junior. There was one break in the 140 year running of Redbournbury Mill by the Hawkins family, between 1861 and 1881 when it was leased firstly by George Harrison and then Edward Arnold; this was because Edward junior died aged 37 leaving his sons too young to take over, but it was his youngest son Harry, who eventually took over the mill from Edward Arnold and continued to run it for over fifty years.

In 1846, after the repeal of the Corn Laws, grain and flour could be imported duty-free and abundant supplies of foreign wheat became available, giving a huge advantage to mills based near sea ports. Together with the development of the much more efficient steam powered steel roller mills around the same time many traditional mills began adding steam, gas or oil engines in an attempt to compete but despite their efforts many rural mills closed down at this time.

Redbournbury Mill also saw changes with a fourth floor added and the mill fitted with cast iron gearing and a wrought iron overshot wheel to replace the previous old oak fittings. At the end of the nineteenth century, and with the added problem of fluctuating river levels, a steam engine was introduced to operate the mill, but the machinery only lasted until 1915, when it was scrapped to help the war effort.

The 1901 Census names the mill as 'Bury' Mill and was occupied by Ivy, then aged four, father Henry, mother Julia, older brothers Hartley and Rex, older sister Elsie and younger brother Harry, all born at the mill.

Ivy, aged thirty-six helped by Julia took the mill over from her father when he died in 1932 and was reported by *The Times* Newspaper to be the only lady miller in England. By this time the mill was only used to produce animal feeds although flour was produced for a short period during WWII.

The following is an edited version of the memories of Redbournbury by Ralph Hawkins, nephew of Ivy.

My father, Harry Valentine Hawkins was the youngest of thirteen children born to the miller, Henry, and his wife, Julia. My mother, Doris, was the youngest child of Thomas Sansom's first marriage. Grandad Sansom owned the various watercress beds around Redbourn including one in the meadow upstream of the mill.

Henry's father, Edward had been the miller at Redbournbury but there was a gap in their tenancies because Henry was only 21 months old when his father died. Edward (1818-1855) was the youngest son of another Edward (1775-1849) also the miller at Redbournbury.

After this my grandmother was nominally the miller though in practice my Aunty Ivy was the miller. She was always known as 'I' to the family. The other occupant was Aunty Bertha…known as 'Bert'. Neither aunt was married. Many people of my generation had maiden aunts, the legacy of the First World War.

Ivy worked the mill and looked after the cows and pigs with the help of Old Harry. Now he was another legacy of the war having been one of the many survivors who did not find a world fit for heroes and became tramps. Old Harry (Shouler) arrived one day looking for work and stayed. He lived in a hut just the other side of the river. He also had a bunk in the office just inside the mill and counted in the sacks of grain by keeping a tally on the office door – four vertical stripes with the fifth a horizontal line through them – unfortunately the door was lost in the fire of 1987. His weekday garb included the traditional binder twine round his trouser legs below the knee to stop the rats running up. On Saturday evenings he shaved and dressed up to go along to the Punchbowl just along the main road towards St Albans.

One of his jobs was to operate a hand pump which supplied water from the river for the heat exchanger in a small room on the end of the cow shed where the milk was cooled. It did depend on the wheel being in use to drive it.

There was usually a couple of cats, the most memorable being a ginger one, 'Ginge'. He was one big, lean, fit cat as big as a small dog and we weighed him on the mill scales – 16lb. He came via the vet and so I very much doubt that he left any descendants. Generations of cats had sharpened their claws on the legs of the long table in the kitchen/dining room so that the legs tapered down almost to a point.

Later in the year the swallows arrived to make their nest in the roof timbers of the top floor of the mill. A broken pane in the window overlooking the wheel was never mended. The swallows would fly at full speed at the window and just fold their wings to zoom through. They felt quite safe on their nest and were not at all bothered by people watching them.

The other inhabitants were unwelcome, the rats. When the flour came down to the ground floor from the three mills it went in to a long horizontal box which contained a screw to feed it along and had several side openings which could be closed with shutters and hooks on which to hang sacks. This enabled an empty sack to be in position to take over when the other one was full. The drive to the screw would be disconnected and it would be turned by hand until the rat emerged to its fate.

A Stone Dresser at Work. (JBT)

In the cog-pit at the end where the shaft from the wheel comes in there is a remnant of a curved wall which could be the relic of a much earlier mill wheel of the type which revolved round a vertical axis.

I got my Miller's Baptism very early on. Aunt Ivy had been rinsing some crockery in the river and had left the end of the footbridge rather wet and there was no wire netting on it in those days. I went running out there in my wellingtons and fortunately went in the water on the side towards the wheel from where Mum fished me out after I had been under a couple of times. This was before Luton extracted Ver water upstream at Flamstead and there was a lot of surplus water going out through the sluice the other side of the footbridge. I would have had no chance if I had gone in on that side.

One of my delights was a ride on the chain sack hoist up through the trap doors.

Having mentioned the sluice taking excess water round the bypass, the rate of flow meant that the water just below it was quite deep and it quickly became shallower just further on. Big fish could get trapped in the deep part and one day Dad saw a tempting one. He got a stick with some string and on the end of the string a rabbit snare – a flexible wire with a running noose. The fish was keeping stationary facing the current; noose goes gently over from the tail end and a quick flick of the wrist – fish for tea.

During the war with all the millwrights doing more essential war work my father used to dress the stones. Although the stones run with a small clearance they do wear and eventually the furrows have to be re-cut. The tool used is known as a mill bill, a double ended piece of steel held in a wooden handle. Dad was himself on war work in a factory making electrical equipment so he cycled over to the mill in the evenings and at weekends to do the stone dressing. At the weekends I was able to go along and watch and 'help'. There was no nice crane to lift the runner stones in those days and the stone had to be raised using a crow bar and some wedges in order to get a rope round it through the central hole and then it was lifted using a chain block and tackle. The dodgy bit was when it went over centre before being lowered on to some straw-filled sacks. Essential equipment

included two laths. The narrow one was the width of the furrows and the wide one the width of the land between furrows. Guide lines were marked with red lead using a wing feather to transfer it from an earthenware jam jar to the stone. Another straw-filled sack provided an arm rest for the job. Health and Safety considerations did go so far as the use of goggles. Sometimes the stones were so worn that Dad would have to go down to the ground floor, where there was a big picture of a stone stuck on the door to the cog pit, in order to check the pattern of the furrows. When both stones had been done the runner stone replaced it had to be balanced and then the running clearance had to be set and this is where another essential piece of equipment came in – a postcard is just the right thickness.

In hot weather a thick green scum formed on the water in the leat and it was prevented from clogging the mill wheel by being held behind a floating wooden pole held in position by a chain at each end. When there was quite a build up the barrier was lifted and the wheel allowed to run free to send the scum on its way downstream.

Auntie Ivy hit the headlines when she became trapped inside the wheel. She had gone inside it, I don't know why but perhaps to mend a leak, when a surge of water from a storm upstream came over the control sluice and the wheel started to turn. She got part of the way out but became trapped between a spoke and the wall which supports the outer end of the axel and was held there by the weight of the water in the wheel. Someone from the farm eventually heard her crying for help. She ended up quite badly bruised. When people hear or read about her being trapped in the wheel they often imagine that she was running round inside it like a hamster. Her rescuers were unable to turn the wheel backwards directly and Ivy had to explain to them which way to turn the gears inside the mill in order to free her. She and they had to get it right first time.

A happier fifteen minutes of fame was when she was the subject of an article in The Times in 1959 as the only lady miller in the country. Though, thinking of it, she was probably not much in favour of all the fuss.

From 1958 onwards, Ivy continued to use the

Ivy Hawkins, working at the mill 1950s. (GW)

Horses drinking from the Ver at Redbournbury.
(Unknown)

Family tiddling at Redbournbury 1930s. (JBT)

Crown Commissioners bought Gorhambury Estate
from the 4th Earl and returned the mill to the Crown.
Some years later it was then sold to Redbournbury
Mill's present owners, the James family.

In August 1987, a devastating fire destroyed the
inside of the mill and part of the house. Thankfully
the main gearing was rescued by the fire brigade,
which was vital in the rebuilding of the mill.

Photographs and previous architectural drawings
helped the builders reconstruct the mill. Fire-

waterwheel to power a saw to cut her firewood. In
1959 she was interviewed by Trevor Phillpott for the
BBC *Tonight* Programme. Forty-four years later the
current owner, Mandy James was interviewed by
Pam Rhodes for a documentary called *Country Days*,
about nostalgia in the British Countryside. Ivy retired
in 1985 and died in October 1987 aged ninety.

*The Ver is truly the very heart of Hertfordshire – slow
moving, quite lovely in many reaches and ever full of
pleasant memories for many dwellers in mid Herts. It is
a delight in summer to see the children busily employed
with their tiny nets in the ever new pursuit of the
elusive stickleback or tiddler.*

W. Branch Johnson

In 1931, after 350 years of private ownership, the

Redbournbury Mill workings after the fire showing the in-
line arrangement of three pairs of millstones. (JBT)

The river at Redbournbury Mill, early twentieth
century. (JBT)

After the fire 1987. (MoS)

Redbournbury Mill (being rebuilt after the fire) and spillway. (JBT)

One of the old mill stones dressed in its autumn glory, on display outside the mill 2009. (JBT)

damaged items were reused wherever possible. David Nicholls salvaged some of the equipment from derelict mills and rebuilt the machinery with almost 12 tons of oak and 6 tons of softwood also used. The original mill stones were cracked by the heat and replaced by two pairs of stones retrieved from a mill at Tring.

In November 1998, the late television personality and steeplejack Fred Dibnah opened the mill. On that day, the first stone-ground flour was produced for more than fifty years.

The mill is now Grade II listed and nationally unusual in that when it was modernised in Victorian times instead of the usual arrangement of stones around a central circular gear, it was given an in-line arrangement of three pairs of millstones which was the very best in milling and is unique in

Fred Dibnah at the opening of the mill in 1998. (RM)

Hertfordshire.

At the end of 2009, after a twenty-two year restoration project by a large group of dedicated volunteers, renovation of the mill was finally complete. A year later a successful attempt was made to increase the flow of the 200 yard channel of water between the tailrace – the section of the leat below the water wheel – downstream towards the Ver and onto the water meadows towards Shafford Mill. This allowed the wheel to turn at quite a pace for the first time in many years, driving the millstones which are normally driven by an alternative power source.

Currently producing 50 tonnes of flour a year, the mill sells its own organic flour and breads to visitors and local bakers, shops and farmers' markets. The mill is open to the public on limited days, as a working mill and museum.

Volunteers in the mill stream 'willow spilling' 2005. (JBT)

The above photo shows volunteers using the ancient craft of spilling, a method of weaving a natural looking screen from living willow through wooden stakes along a watercourse including riverbanks and leets. This eventually creates a mass of roots, protecting the soil on the banks from erosion.

The main advantages of this traditional craft over other bank protection methods includes cost saving as the willow is normally already growing along the water edge, the long life span of the willow, and the fact that a natural product is being used, which in turn provides a home for wildlife.

The willow is the tree most associated with our rivers and can be seen at many places along the Ver. The history of the use of all parts of this versatile tree is long and varied and the herbalist Culpepper recommended it for many ailments including the leaves, bark and seeds alleviating bleeding from nose and mouth, sickness and preventing consumption, the leaves rubbed with pepper and drunk in wine help the wind colic and if you are at all concerned about your virtue and temptations of the flesh he highly recommends *"the leaves bruised and boiled in wine, stayeth the heat of lust in man or woman, and quite extinguish it, if it be long used!"* Or one could cool down by simply jumping in the river!

Verford Cottages 1980s. (JBT)

A farm track comes down from Watling Street past the quaint Verford Cottages, and passes across the millrace bridge to Redbournbury House ford by a small footbridge, which puts the house and the farm on an island.

In the past the Ver would have been surrounded by marshland and riverine forests and supported many natural and manmade water meadows. The felling of trees and land drainage for building and farming often caused irreversible change to the landscape and its ecology, but some water meadows such as those at Redbournbury, do still remain along the river.

Part of the Crown Estate, the ancient Redbournbury Meadows are a Countryside Heritage site covering land surrounding the Ver between Watling Street and Shafford Mill. This ecologically important landscape is looked after sympathetically by the land owners to ensure it retains the wildlife and landscape the meadows support.

The Irish or Redbournbury Mill weir was installed at the upstream end of Shafford millstream during the 1990s when flows were very low and the river and meadow drying up. The weir allows water to pass down the old river bed through pipes set at a low level through the mill stream bank and creates a wetland habitat in the water meadows downstream. Higher flows pass over the reinforced bank which incorporates stepping stones for walkers.

A conventional ford allows a passage through the river; however the structure is termed an Irish weir as it emulates an Irish bridge – a piped ford or vented causeway which is dry during normal flow with water passing through the pipes. The Irish weir also dispenses with the need for a footbridge alongside the ford.

A common sight above the fields in this area, the buzzard is the commonest and most widespread bird of prey with around 40,000 breeding pairs. Buzzards and red kites are often confused with each other. Buzzards are slightly smaller and have a fan shaped tail as opposed to the forked one of the red kite, variable in colour from all dark brown to very pale, they have dark wing tips and feed on small mammals, birds and carrion, although like kites they will adapt their feeding habits to their surroundings.

The millstream and the main river join just south of the farm before winding across the water meadow to what is now the treatment works.

On the 1890 OS map, the fields and river between the former Punchbowl pub and where the old quarry stood are shown as a 'rifle range' including a 'markers hut target'. During WWII the local Home Guard Rifle Teams were still using it to practice with their .303 rifles.

Originally named the Gorhambury Chalk Works, the site of the treatment works was in use between 1943 and 1966 when the Anglo Roman Lime

A misty autumnal sunrise over the river 2011. (JBT)

Bridge between Redbournbury and Shafford with chalk works in background 1980s. (JBT)

Opposite Redbournbury Mill 2008. (JBT)

The Irish weir, Redbournbury 2009. (JBT)

River as it passes the chalk works on the right 2009. (JBT)

Looking towards Redbournbury Mill with green plastic covering building works at the mill after the fire, late 1980s. (JBT)

Company supplied lime for agricultural use helping to improve soil quality. This was especially important during WWII when many of the fields between Kensworth and Redbourn had been continuously used for many years to grow crops and hay depleting the soil of potassium and magnesium. There was a 50% subsidy on chalk and lime during the war and up to 30 tons an acre were spread on the fields supplied from local quarries and pits.

It is now an environmental treatment works and has been designated a Registered Important Geological Site (RIGS). Many fossils have been found amongst the chalk including shells, sponges, sea urchins, belemnites – a squid like animal – and the remains of a baby mammoth!

In the fields near the works are the remains of a former lime kiln where chalk would have been

Taken in the 1980s, the above photo shows the ruins of the old kiln, now demolished. (JBT)

The Punchbowl by Kitten 1900, before renovation and demolition of nearby cottages. (MoS)

Early twentieth century postcard of the Punchbowl. (AL)

Between Redbournbury and Shafford Mill 1980s. (JBT)

layered between coals, the heat from a fire at the bottom of the layers turning the chalk into lime to use for agriculture.

There has been an inn on the site of the current Kink premises, not far from the river, since at least the early 1600s. In the late seventeenth century it was known as The Bole or Bowl Alehouse and kept by Mary Peacock. In 1754 it was ran by George Grimston until his death when it was carried on by his wife. In 1851 it was taken over by William Seabrook and by 1871 it was known as the Punchbowl. 1901 saw it rebuilt and the date is seen above the original door commemorating this. It became Spritzers in the late 1980s before becoming Fudge in 2003 and Kink in 2010.

Just north of the quarry the river divides for the millstream of the picturesque Grade II listed Shafford Mill, also known in the past as Shawford from shallow ford. In the mid seventeenth century the owner of the mill also owned a flour shop, farmed cereal crops and leased the neighbouring Redbournbury Mill owned by Sir Harbottle Grimston along with Shafford and Dolittle Mill.

Once called Childwick Mill, a bhp steam engine was used to pump water to a tower supplying Childwick Bury Manor, a house that dates from the seventeenth century and where there was once an eleventh century Benedictine Abbey and monastic buildings of which nothing now remains. It was owned by Geoffrey de Childwyk, a bailiff of St Albans in the thirteenth century. The 1978 sale details printed in *The Times* newspaper advertised the estate as:

The Manor House, mainly eighteenth century has… a Victorian Dairy House with about 19 Acres, Two Coach House Cottages with Magnificent Stable Yard with Paddock and Woodland 16 Acres, Cheapside and Shafford Farms... Old Mill and other Buildings for conversion...and fishing in River Ver and Mill Race. Total 1,100 Acres.

It was the home of the late film producer Stanley Kubrick until his death in 1999 and he is buried in its grounds.

What we see of Shafford Mill today was mostly built over 170 years ago. Its millers include:
Jonathan Parsons, Miller and Baker (1840/50s)
along with his sons Jesse and Henry, also millers.

Silvester Bond (1860s)
James Ridgeway (1880s)
Another Jonathan Parsons (1930s, Pigot's *Directory*)

Milling ceased in 1933 and it is now a private house. In 1978 a fire destroyed all but the ground floor machinery. It retained its iron breast wheel and millrace and was converted to a house in 1980.

The river passes south across the water meadow between the millstream and Watling Street to where they join below Shafford Mill. This is the longest millstream on the River Ver.

In the early 1990s the national press and overseas media regularly mentioned the river, which was often dried up as were many rivers and streams in southeast England. The article bottom left was a result of a press conference and concerns of local groups and societies about the state of the river.

The river passes south of Shafford Mill under

A very wide river looking from Bow Bridge towards Shafford Summer 1980s. (JBT)

Shafford Mill & Millstream -The gentleman sitting on the grass is a good friend of dads, Geoff Standard. They walked the length of the river together taking photos and ensuring the local ale was up to scratch! The river flows to the left of the building, rejoining a little way along. (JBT)

This used to be a bubbling mill stream

A 1992 newspaper article showing Shafford Mill during drought. (JBT)

Watling Street (and it is here the old Watling Street was diverted) at Bow Bridge, a brick built, three-arched structure whose upstream side was widened in 1959, and continues through the grounds of Gorhambury.

It is reported in the 1950s that otters had been killed on the road here and they could still be seen along the river in winter months.

In the Watford Natural History Society *Transactions* of 1877 Henry Howard is quoted as saying:

…of the Ver…on the eighth of July, 1958, I killed one trout at Bowbridge, of 3lbs., and since then, about four years since, I have landed three fish in one day averaging 3 ½lbs., from the Ver, for Major Gape.

One of the most widespread of all freshwater fish, brown trout need clean unpolluted water, synonymous with chalk streams, to survive. They remain in fresh water throughout their life whereas the sea trout migrate to the oceans for much of its life returning to freshwater to spawn.

Their colour and size is varied depending on their habitat, size of the river they live in and the amount of food available. Their diet is varied ranging from small fish to small invertebrate such as caddis fly larvae and mayfly nymphs.

They require a stream with a clean gravel bottom to spawn between September and October as water temperatures start to cool. The female digs a shallow

Brown trout (Salmo Trutta) of around 2lb caught in the Ver near Redbournbury. (AB)

A family fishing for trout from Bow Bridge 2008. (JBT)

The river on the opposite side of the road at Bow Bridge spring 2009. (JBT)

Below: *The same view September 2010. (JBT)*

hole into the gravel where she lays her eggs which take approximately 150 days to hatch, the longest time of any British freshwater fish. The record for a British brown trout caught in a river is 28lb 5oz 4drm in 1992 on the River Test.

Along the Ver the brown trout is mainly found in those stretches of river that are still blessed with a clean, gravel bottom and decent flow along with protective plant cover.

The pumping station at Bow Bridge was opened in 1967 with a licence to extract five million gallons of water per day, later reduced to 2.5 million gallons. In 1997, following the driest eighteen months in 230 years, TVW resurrected an historic water order and released water from its borehole at Bow Bridge for the first time in decades helping the depleted river to flow again.

Following the Buncefield oil depot explosion in December 2005, Bow Bridge pumping station was turned off to reduce the possible risk of water table contamination from oil and PFOS (perfluorooctane sulfonate) a type of fire fighting foam. Abstraction began again in June 2009 at a third of the licensed abstraction figure along with continuous testing of

This local traction engine named 'Bertha' is owned by a Redbourn resident and had stopped at Bow Bridge in the summer of 2011 to refill its water tank from the river, a task carried out on many parts of the Ver in the past 150 years. (JBT)

the ground water. This is expected to have some effect on the Ver aquifer and at the time of writing this is being monitored by the Environment Agency and VVS.

Between 1629 and 1670, Sir Francis Bacon had his summer residence, Verulam House, just north of Bow Bridge. Unimpressed by the way water was fed to

Plan of Lord Bacon's fishponds at Verulam House. (MoS)

Gorhambury where he lived; he announced that if he were unable to carry water to his house, he would carry his house to the water, with plans to turn *"ye pond yard into a place of pleasure"*. It cost around £10,000 to build, three times the sum spent on the original construction of Gorhambury House by Sir Nicholas Bacon!

Therefore he built fishponds covering four acres nearby at Pond Meadow adjacent to Bow Bridge and called it 'Pondyards' which was built some years before nearby Verulam House. These geometric ponds had colourful mosaic bottoms with patterns of fish incorporated, and in the centre was a Roman style banqueting hall overlooking the ponds where carp and other coarse fish were bred for the table. It was said that *"if a poor bodie had bought his Lordship half a dozen pebbles of curious colour, he would give them a shilling so curious was he in perfecting his fishponds"*.

The grounds were enclosed by a square brick wall with a 25 foot high walk *"and under that waulke some 4 foote to have a fine litell stream rune upon gravell"*. It was to be surrounded by *"frute, birches and lyme trees"* with a profusion of plants and flowers including *"lylyes, violets and strawberries"* and the *"Iland had an arbour of musk roses sett al with double violets for scent in autumn"*.

In the late seventeenth century, Verulam house was sold for £400 to two carpenters who demolished it and reused the materials. However in the 1960s the old ponds, despite being very overgrown still had water and fish in them. The middle one had a depth of about ten feet with a landing stage and dilapidated boathouse.

In the first half of the twentieth century, the river here was over five foot deep and there was also a secondary stream along with extensive watercress beds and a large shed used for storing wicker baskets.

On the west bank was once a spinney of beech trees, devastated in the hurricane of October 1987, snapping most of them like matchsticks. These were replaced and beyond this spinney on the west side of the river is arable land and to the east water meadows. This is a most peaceful and tranquil stretch of river.

Britain's largest and heaviest amphibians, the

Beech Trees, devastated by the storms of 1987. (JBT)

*Common toad (*Bufo bufo*) spotted upstream from Pré sawmill spring 2009. (JBT)*

common toad can live up to forty years, but is not found in Ireland. Hibernating in October they breed in spring laying up to 4000 eggs in long double row strands of about 10 ft. Only around 5% are likely to survive into adulthood. Their main predators are grass snakes and hedgehogs and on the Ver, Herons, which aren't deterred by an irritant secreted from the toads' skin. Their slow crawl often leads to the death of thousands of toads on roads which they cross on ancient routes to their breeding spots and many villages and towns set up rescue parties to help them safely on their journey. Their decline has been put down mainly to habitat loss and road kill.

Along this stretch, just north of the Pré Hotel is the smallest mill on the River Ver, Pré Mill. A corn mill was recorded on the Gorhambury Estate in 1637 and by 1671 three watermills are listed. It is thought to be the site of the pump built by Nicholas Bacon to get water from the Ver to Gorhambury House. This would have involved laying pipes for about 1¼ miles with the pump supplying pressure. Although costly this was done at many large houses built above water courses.

Sometime later a series of reservoirs was constructed at Pré Wood where water was filtered through the gravel by natural drainage into deep tanks where a pump would have conveyed it through pipes ¾ mile up to the house.

After the death of Sir Nicholas, a law suit saw his widow Lady Anne take down the force *"not finding such need of the water"*.

In 1660 Lady Anne *"erected and built one other corn mill upon the said stream, brooke or river"*. Named locally as New Mill it was half a mile from the Abbey Mill on the site of the force used to bring water to Gorhambury in the past.

A deed of 1680 included Pray Mill:

William Francklyne holdeth all that massuage and three water corn mills for 19 years from Michaelmas.

The original corn mill is thought to have disappeared by the early nineteenth century and the building we see today is thought to be from around the same time. It was used as the Gorhambury Estate sawmill until the mid twentieth century.

There is believed to have been other mills close to

this site, including Butlers Mill. In Kenneth C. Reid's book *Watermills of the London Countryside* he writes:

The Ver, flowing southwards after Shafford Bridge, was reputed to have driven a mill of which no signs remain today. A witness in an Exchequer lawsuit said that it had been built by a Londoner and, though at first the property of the Bacons of Verulam, it was owned later by William Preston who, at that date, held Kingsbury Mill in St Albans. In the late sixteenth century it was worked by a miller named Butler from which it took its name.

Some remains of a medieval mill were found in the riverbed of the Ver in 1887 between Pré and Kingsbury, but no further records have been found.

The Saw mill (JBT)

The water meadows next to the saw mill 2009. (JBT)

Pré Mill House and Ver Meadows 2009. (JBT)

Old Tudor house at Gorhambury. (MoS)

There are also twelfth century records of a mill called Dichmulne or Ditchmill in this area belonging to the Manor of Kingsbury and in 1194 it is mentioned in the foundation charter of Prae, again no further evidence has to date been discovered.

The first Gorhambury House, named after Abbot Geoffrey de Gorham was built in the mid twelfth century near the river on the site where a Roman villa once stood in an area known in Saxon times as Westwick.

For two hundred years it was the home of the de Gorham's and then the de Vere family.

In 1541, after the Dissolution of the Monasteries, the estate along with the manor of Pre was granted to Sir Ralph Rowlatt a wealthy London Goldsmith. In the 1560s it was purchased by Sir Nicholas Bacon, whose second wife, Ann Cooke was sister-in-law to the son of the original owner of the estate, Ralph Rowlatt, who by this time had inherited.

Elizabethan Gorhambury was built between 1563-8 by Sir Nicholas Bacon, Lord Keeper and it was visited at least three times by Queen Elizabeth I. The cost to a household of a visit by a monarch was a massive outlay: her four day visit in 1577, cost £577 6s 7d farthing – around a third of what it had cost Sir Nicholas to build Gorhambury!

His youngest son, Sir Francis Bacon a lawyer, philosopher and writer, took over the estate in 1601 after the death of his brother Anthony becoming

Viscount St Alban in 1621. He bequeathed Gorhambury to his former secretary, Sir Thomas Meautys, who married Anne Bacon, the niece of Sir Francis.

In 1652 the estate passed to Anne's second husband Sir Harbottle Grimston. His son Samuel died childless and it was passed to his great nephew William Luckyn, who in 1719 became the first Viscount Grimston.

During WWII Gorhambury was requisitioned by the war office and used by branches of the intelligence services for transmitting messages to occupied countries in Europe. Prae Wood House was used to train secret agents and occupied by American officers with General Eisenhower rumoured to have held a meeting there before D-Day.

Towards the end of WWII, Gorhambury was one of several places in the area to house Italian and German prisoners of war. Dressed in tunics with recognisable yellow and green patches they helped with farm work and jobs for the council and despite being guarded by civilians wandered freely around the local area when not working.

The following is taken from an interview in 1998 by David Broom with Charles Cockell, born in 1901, as part of the St Albans Museums Oral History Project.

During WWII –

They tried to get Gorhambury Park...because it was the home of the Free French and they used to send their coded messages to the Maquis (French Resistance) out there.

We had to go up there one night, they'd built a big water tank up in case of fire... we had to go and fill it up, took all afternoon, next morning, it was empty, it had leaked! Oh it must have had about 10,000 gallons in it, huge thing it was! We had to bring a hose right from the River Ver, right up Gorhambury Drive.

Partially rebuilt in the late eighteenth century with a catchment basin dug at Pré Wood to supply water, this impressive Palladian style house was designed by Sir Robert Taylor who was commissioned by James Bucknall, 3rd Viscount Grimston and refaced with white Portland stone in

A view of Gorhambury, possibly during the war when much of the land would have been used for food production. (Unknown)

Looking towards the Pré Hotel with a line of old red pollarded willows on the right 2009. (JBT)

of Pré House now a hotel and restaurant.

St Mary de Pré church was to the west of the river at the other side of the original route of the Roman road. It was supposedly established on the site of a vision seen by a layman at a spot where the bones of St Amphibalus had met those of the relics of St Alban.

The similarities between hospitals and monasteries in the twelfth and thirteenth centuries were many and not only concerned the care of the body but also the soul. Prae Monastery, the monastery in the meadows, was founded near the church as a hospital of St Mary cia Fratis in 1190 by Abbot Warin of St Albans (1183-1195), later St Mary de Pré, hence Prae Monastry. (The spelling of Pré varies between documents and maps, I will use Pré from here on). It is thought it took its name from the Praetorian Gate of Verulamium just across the fields.

the 1950s. The ruins of the Tudor house built by the Bacon family lie in the grounds. It is still owned by the Grimston family today. A member of the Historic Houses Association the house is open to visitors for part of the year.

Cricket bats are produced from the willow *Salix Alba Caerulea*, which grow on the Gorhambury lands along the Ver. Around 25% of these are cut every seven years with each trunk producing between 30-40 cricket blades. Young trees are then planted which are cut in fifteen years and so the cycle continues.

The beautiful red kite (*Milvus Milvus*) can be identified by its deeply forked tail, yellow eyes with a grey head, red-brown streaked underneath and black wing tips with a white patch under the wings. Weighing between 4-5lb they can live in the wild up to their late twenties. From the mid sixteenth century they were seen as vermin and a threat to food production with an Act of Parliament putting them on a list of species to be shot or poisoned, there were even offers of one penny for every bird killed. They had been completely eradicated from mainland Great Britain except for a small number of breeding pairs in Wales by the end of the nineteenth century.

1989 saw red kite chicks from Spain introduced to the Chilterns and by 2008 there were around 500 breeding pairs.

As very opportunistic feeders they will take small mammals, insects and fish.

They are social birds and can be seen in groups, especially in winter when up to a hundred can often be found roosting in woodland.

Now protected by law, they can often be seen with wing tags which identify each bird along with its age and where it was hatched.

The track from Gorhambury to Pré House crosses over the millstream by a small bridge built of flint and stone, similar looking to the stonework on the Roman walls seen around the city. The river then flows through the grounds of a large private house and, after rejoining the millstream, passes to the west

Red kite. (HO)

The back of Pré Hotel across the Churchyard Meadows 2009. (JBT)

Originally for sick and leprous women described as *infirme femine*, some had previously been living at the nearby hospital of St Julian, eventually it became a wholly religious community.

It is recorded that those who lived here were allowed to use two mills, the Abbey Mill and the previously mentioned Dichmulne Mill which may have stood near the grounds of the monastery, but was destroyed before the fifteenth century.

Abbot Warin, who was a physician of high repute, had studied at Salerno and took a great deal of trouble to help leprous monks and nuns. He established the female leper hospital of St Mary de Pré in 1194 and made his monastery responsible for its maintenance. Warin permitted considerable latitude to those performing bloodletting and his sincere concern for the sick is apparent.

Warin's successor as Abbot was John of Cella (1195-1214), also a physician, who was compared to the prominent Roman physician and philosopher Galen. He appears to have been particularly skilled in the art of diagnosis from urine, even predicting his own death from such an examination.

It was perhaps in this field of caring for the afflicted with leprosy that the private benefactor or patron became most active. High status persons at the time made it their business to care for these people, including royalty, such as Queen Matilda, and great ecclesiastical figures including St Hugh of Lincoln and Archbishop Lanfranc.

During the twelfth century individual patrons of lesser degree, endowed and supported leper hospitals and ensured their maintenance by contributions while they lived and by provision in their wills when they died. Monasteries also established similar hospitals and in the case of St Albans Abbey, two houses were founded and maintained by it. The first, built in 1146 by Abbot Gregory (1119-1146) and named after St Julian, was intended to accommodate six brethren. However, it fell on hard times due to taxation by the crown and the inmates were not well cared for. The second was St Mary de Pré which around 1261 became a Benedictine nunnery.

It remained in use until 1528 and when the Kings' agents came to suppress the priory, there was nobody there. The last prioress, Eleanor Barnarde had died the year before and the remaining five nuns had simply walked away. It is said the money from the sale of the monastery was used by Cardinal Wolsey to go towards building Christ Church College Oxford.

The present day spelling is not found before the eighteenth century and is evidently an attempt to give a Latin appearance to a place name adjoining the site of ancient Verulamium.

In the thirteenth century pike were a highly valued commodity and when Edward I decided to regulate the cost of fish to stop sellers charging their own often random prices, pike was valued higher than salmon!

In his book *Thirteen Rivers to the Thames*, Brian Waters writes the following about pike in the river here:

There are also pike in the Ver, always a sign of a fertile stream, and some years ago, when ducklings were mysteriously disappearing from the river without trace at Pré, the river was dragged between there and Kingsbury Mill…not without result – a large pike was netted and several ducklings were found in his belly.

Some years later, another notorious 'monster' pike was caught in this stretch of the river that was so huge it was reported in a national angling journal!

In the seventeenth century a lease was given to William Oxton by Sir Harbottle Grimston allowing fishing in the river at the manors of Pré, Gorhambury and Kingsbury with certain trout to be given yearly.

Lady Francis Cook, the seventh of eight children of James 2nd Viscount Grimston, paid £4139 in 1838 to build a house at Pré, currently the present day restaurant. Pré Monastery would have originally stood in the meadows behind this house. She lived there for ten years before dying aged ninety-one.

In 1881, the Mayor of St Albans, Henry Toulmin and his family moved to Pré, enlarging the house and improving the gardens, they lived there from 1881-1911. In Constance Toulmin's 1960s' book *Happy Memories*, a chapter entitled 'Happy Childhood at the Pré', refers to a large hump backed trout caught in the Ver by her brother which was stuffed and put in a glass case on the wall. She also writes *"…and on the river we had a boat and could row from the sparkling waterfall (now covered by the sawmill) as far as the old mill at St Michael's".*

A ghost was also seen by her sister Isobel in the grounds by the river. She had gone out into the garden one evening to chase away a noisy cat and saw a large, shining motionless figure in a haze of gold light, but when she called her family and turned back it had gone. There is also reputed to be a 'shadow child', which occasionally appears in wedding photos and a room where a tapping noise emanates and footsteps can be heard walking down corridors!

In the 1930s the 4th Earl of Verulam sold the house to a local gentleman, Montague George Dashwood who lived there until his death in the early 1950s when it returned to the ownership of the Grimstons who rented it to hoteliers and it has remained a hotel and restaurant ever since.

The river then passes through a small spinney from which a picturesque view of St Albans Abbey can be seen at the top of the hill.

Running parallel to the site of the old Roman wall, the river divides for the millstream of Kingsbury Mill, flowing under Bluehouse Hill, by the gardens of Pre Close and on to the mill.

The city of St Albans is the largest town the River Ver passes through and has a long and well recorded history built around the martyrdom of a local pagan named Alban, the first British martyr, who according to Bede was believed to have been beheaded around AD 305, although modern scholars date it to around AD 209.

The story tells us that Alban allowed a Christian priest – Amphibalus – to shelter in his home, where he converted Alban to Christianity. When Roman

View of Abbey from river near Gorhambury late nineteenth century. (SKC/HALS)

The Ver flowing through Gorhambury Meadows with the Abbey in distance 1980s. (JBT)

The millstream Bluehouse Hill 2009. (JBT)

The River at Bluehouse Hill, a shadow of its former self, during drought in the 1990s. (JBT)

The Ver below St Albans. (MoS)

soldiers were sent to find Amphibalus, Alban exchanged cloaks with him and fled to Chantry Island in the grounds of All Saints' Pastoral Centre in London Colney, where the soldiers eventually found and arrested him. His deception was discovered and he was given the punishment that Amphibalus would have received. Tortured and condemned to death, he was taken to Holmhurst Hill via the ford at St Michael's, where several followers drowned in the deep, flowing waters. Here it is said the waters parted in reply to Alban's prayers to allow him and the vast crowd to cross safely. As the fourteenth century monk and poet John Lydgate described – *"sodeynly the river was made drye"*.

In medieval times and long before, it was reputed that springs would well up in holy places such as where saints were killed and once Alban reached his place of execution, a spring did indeed appear to allow him to quench his thirst. He was beheaded and it is said the eyes of his executioner fell out at the moment of Alban's death.

The site of his grave is still in some doubt. In 739 A.D. a Benedictine monastery was built on Holmhurst Hill on the opposite side of the river from the Roman town. The site of the medieval shrine behind the high altar, in the eastern apse of the Norman church, may mark the original site, but in 1257 during the demolition of the east end before its extension, a stone tomb was found with a leaden inscription indicating that this was the original grave of Alban. But there is no evidence for the date of this structure. It could have been built or moved to this spot when the east end of the Norman church was erected between 1077 and 1088 by the Abbot Paul de Caen, and the inscription, if genuine, might have been made then or even at the time of Offa's translation of relics in 1077-88, there is no certainty. The Cathedral and Abbey Church of St Alban, now stands on this spot. It became a cathedral in 1877 and is the second longest in the UK. The 22nd of June marks the feast of St Alban and he is the patron saint of converts, refugees and torture.

The present version of the town's name dates back to an act of parliament in 1879 which made the town an official city and removed the apostrophe between the 'n' and 's'.

Previous names include:

Verlamcester
Vaelingacester
Werlamceaster
Wæclingacaester
Watlingcester

The Catuvellauni oppidium and river. (JBT)

St Albans Bury
St Alboynes's
St Alban's

Matthew Paris said of the River Ver *"The Werlam River was once very large and flowed about the city"*, as clearly seen in the image opposite.

Before the Roman conquest a Belgic tribe of south-eastern Britain called the Catuvellauni, selected Werlamceaster as the most important town of their district. It was almost inaccessible to enemies, being surrounded by thick wood and marshy land. They further secured the area by digging huge ditches and banks on all sides of their territory, except the northeast; here they dammed the waters of the river, forming a huge artificial lake and swampland.

In 1956, four hundred yards to the east of the Ver, near Bluehouse Hill, evidence of a Belgic mint was discovered. A Belgic settlement was known to have stood at Pré Wood seven hundred yards to the northwest on level ground above the river valley.

The Romans built the first Verulamium around 43AD on the hillside from Pre Wood to the Ver, now Bluehouse Hill, where it protected the ford. It was destroyed by the Icenii led by Boudicca in 61AD. After which a second town was rebuilt to the west of the present city, along the slopes of the Ver Valley in about 78AD, this lasted over three hundred years. This is the Verulamium we know today with its hypocaust and theatre.

St Alban's origins are owed largely to its geological position on the River Ver. The river was once wide, deep and strong enough to supply drinking water to locals and power their mills. It became the market centre for the surrounding Roman villas, where farmers would bring their produce to sell and grind their corn.

Most Roman towns had their own aquaducts to bring water into the area. Wooden water mains have been found under the streets of St Albans, which imply an aquaduct in the area; this would have tapped the River Ver upstream to bring water to the city.

In Michael Drayton's superb seventeenth century work *Poly-Olbion* he writes of the country's topographical features, traditions and legends, describing the countryside, including elements of our history relevant to each region. He uses the 'Muse', which he compares to a falcon, throughout the text to view the country. It may not be a coincidence that the Ver was called the Muse in some documents around this time. It is divided into thirty 'Songs' or sections of which the 16th Song – The Argument – describes the conversation between a much bigger River Ver and the ancient Watling Street which cross paths near the ruins of the Monastery of St Albans. Below are just a few passages from this section, describing the river and some of its history.

That Ver of long esteem'd, a famous auncient Flood
(Upon whose aged Bank olde Verlamchester stood,
Before the Roman rule) here glorify'd of yore,
Unto her cleerer banks contributed his store;
Enlarging both her streame, and strengthening his
* renowne,*
Where the delicious Meads her through her course doe
* crown.*
This Ver (as I have said) Colnes tributary brook,
On Verlams ruin'd walles as sadly he doth look,
Neere Holy Albans Towne, where his rich shrine was
* set,*
Old Watling in his way the Flood doth over-get.

Thou sawest great-burthen'd ships through these
* valleys pass,*
Where now the sharp-edg'd Sithe sheeres up the
* spyring grasse:*
That where the ugly Seale and Porpse u'sd to play,
The Grashopper and Ant now lord it all the day:

To Verlam by her Streame, when Verlam famous was;
She planks and Anchors shews, her errour to
* maintaine;*
Which were, indeed, of boats, for pleasure there to
* rowe*
Upon her (then a Lake) the Roman Pompe to showe,
When Rome, her forces here did every yeere supply,
And at old Verlam kept a warlike Colony.

And Ver upon his course, now hasted to be gone
To accompany his Colne: which as she gently glides,
Doth kindly him imbrace: whom soon this hap betides;
As Colne come on along, and chanc't to cast he eye
Upon that neighbouring Hill where Harrow stands so
* hie.*

Bluehouse Hill was built in 1962. Previous to this, if a traveller wished to go to Hemel Hempstead, the road between St Michael's village and Branch Road had to be used. It is believed to have been named after a 'blue house' or 'brew house', which once stood nearby.

Chapter Six
Kingsbury Mill to the Old Cotton Mill

By the mill the little stream goes peacefully upon its way.
Willows stoop upon the bank where swallows skim and children play.
Through the cool dusk of the leaves the dappled gold of sunlight falls –
where the swan glides in the shadow of the ivy-covered walls.
Once the stream rushed loud and busy past this lattice window pane – full
of froth and self importance, turning wheels and grinding grain....
now unhurriedly it flows where green boughs trail amongst the reeds –
softly, slowly slipping out into the quiet water-meads.

The Mill Stream – Anon

Kingsbury village to the east of the modern day town was once completely separate from St Albans. It was described in the Abbey's ancient records 'Gesta Abbatum Monasterii S Albani', as being inhabited by the King's ministers who plied their trade in the fish pool south of Fishpool Street, known continuously by this name since the Norman Conquest, something few roads in St Albans can boast.

It is not known exactly when the castle was built but it may have been constructed by King Offa around 793AD when the Benedictine Abbey of St Albans was converted from an existing church. Abbey View Road, just off of Fishpool Street, marks the top of the hill where it is thought the castle once

stood and here its ramparts were marked by a black cross. The name 'Black Cross' appears in many local documents spanning several hundred years. In the fourteenth century a black cross was used to mark a section of the Ver where there was regular flooding and it was also used as a boundary marker. In 1491, Thomas Kylyngworth left a tenement in his will *"set to at Blake Crosse"*, and in a 1556 survey of St Albans a Robert Wenton was the tenant of a dwelling in Black Cross Close which would have been the same piece of land and name shown on the Hare map of

Rear of Kingsbury mill Early 1900s. (SKC /HALS)

Kingsbury Farm House from across the river early 1900s. (SKC /HALS)

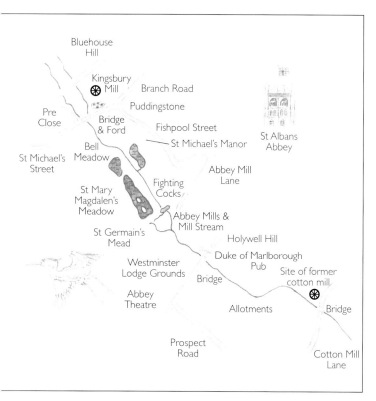

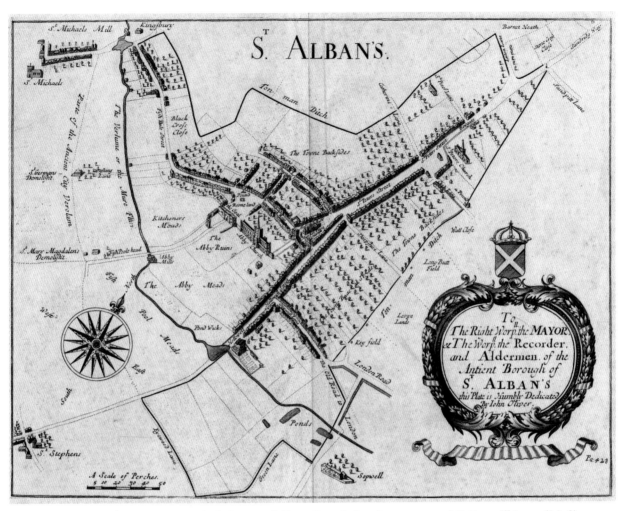

1700 map showing the Mure River, Black Cross and Green Lane before it was renamed Cottonmill Lane. (MoS)

1970s collage by the pupils of St Michael's School showing St Albans and the River Ver. (JBT/SMCES)

1634, an area of land with a single dwelling on the north side of Fishpool Street near the river. The same map shows the houses along Fishpool Street between Kingsbury and Black Cross Close some with land running down to the river, as 'The Towns Back Sides'.

In 851, King Bertulph of Mercia held council at the royal manor of Kingsbury, from the name Kings Burh (a burh was an early fortified settlement) or Kings Town. Mentioned as a Municipium at the end of the tenth century and in the Domesday Book, early spellings include Cyngesbyrig, Kengesbiri and Kyngsbury.

This Saxon stronghold covered Fishpool Street, Verulam Road and Branch Road. Representatives of the King, along with villagers would have lived there, with local people often earning their living selling the fish caught from the very large, deep royal fish pool which was separated into 'stews' or smaller ponds and stretched from the south of Fishpool Street to St Michael's and beyond to Holywell Bridge. Fishponds had been an indication of a land owner's status since Norman times.

In 955 A.D. Aelfric applied to King Ethelred to buy the fish pool, thought to have been on the same site as the current lakes at Verulamium and having done so drained them, keeping one stew for the monastery. The Gesta mentions that:

the inhabitants of Kingsbury oppressed the household of the Abbey because they were tenants of the King and proud.

Aelfric not only accused the locals of being Pagans but by emptying the pools he put an end to any fishing rights they may have had. Furthermore his actions put paid to any future costly visits by Royalty who would come not just to feast on the plentiful supply of fish but also to sample the pleasures of boating on the ponds.

It has been said that when the ponds were drained of their water, the remains of a sizable Roman ship and anchor were discovered.

The sixteenth century English chronicler Raphael Holinshed (1529–1580) writes the following about the river and the great fish pool:

Furthermore, whereas manie are not afraid to saie that the Thames came sometimes by this citie, indeed it is nothing so; but that the Uerlume (afterward called Uere and the Mure) did and dooth so still. For albeit that the riuer be now growne to be verie small by reason of the ground about it, which is higher than it was in old time; yet it kéepeth in maner the old course, and runneth betwéene the old citie that was, and the new towne that is standing on Holmehirst crag, as I beheld of late. Those places also which now are medow beneath the abbaie, were sometimes a great lake, mere, or poole, through which the said riuer ran, and with a verie swift and violent course, wheras at this present it is verie slow, and of no such deapth as of ancient times it hath beene.

As those aforsaid workemen digged in these ruines, they happened oftentimes vpon Lempet shels, péeces of rustie anchors, and kéeles of great vessels, wherevpon some by and by gathered that either the Thames or some arme of the sea did beat vpon that towne, not vnderstanding that these things might aswell happen in great lakes and meres, wherof there was one adioining to the north side of the citie, which laie then vnwalled, but that also is false.

This mere at the first belonged to the king, and thereby Offa in his time did reape no small commoditie. It continued also vntill the time of Alfrijc the seuenth abbat of that house, who bought it outright of the king then liuing, and by excessiue charges drained it so narrowlie, that within a while he left it drie (sauing that he reserued a chanell for the riuer to haue hir vsuall course, which he held vp with high bankes) bicause there was alwaies contention betwéene the moonks and the kings seruants, which fished on that water vnto the kings behoofe.

Although a pond was retained to provide food for the monastery, fish would also have been caught from the river, especially the much favoured eels. There would have been a large variety of fish including tench, bream, perch, roach and pike; up until the sixteenth century carp were usually only eaten by kings. Sea fish were also common. In fact this was one of only a handful of fish ponds mentioned in the Domesday Book along with a vivarium or zoo for keeping wild animals which existed at Kingsbury during the reign of William the Conqueror.

Fish was a significant part of the diet for hundreds of years with Benedictine law only allowing meat for the ill and infirm, as time passed fish was eaten on Fridays, Saturdays and certain religious days with meat being allowed more regularly but with penalties for those caught eating it on forbidden days.

The mid twelfth century saw King Stephen using the land for crops. In 1553 Edward VI granted the manor to Thomas Wendye and in 1657 his descendent another Thomas Wendy sold the manor to Sir Harbottle Grimston for £5, 700.

Its eventful history includes narrowly escaping ruin during the rebellion of Wat Tyler in the fourteenth century. It remained the property of the Abbey until its dissolution when it was passed to the Crown.

Today all that can be seen of the castle once here is the plateau on which it is thought to have stood.

One of the first maps of St Albans produced around 1634 shows a small pond below the bridge where the Ver still widens to this day, but there is no 'Fishpool' shown. However, the map does show fields either side of the Ver described as "A meadow sometimes the King's Fishpoole".

The course of the river has been altered over the centuries to help create a good flow for the working mills in the area including the three-storey Kingsbury Mill, once known as Malt Mylle and for many years St Michael's Mill, belonging to the Abbey until the dissolution.

The current mill has been here since the sixteenth century, but a mill on or near this spot was mentioned in the Domesday Book named as the Abbot's Malt Mill. The mill was in existence in 1194 and work was carried out on it by John Whitby for the Abbot of Wheathampstead.

It was one of the mills involved in occasional disputes between the Abbot and townsfolk, more often than not over the obligation of grinding corn at the mills.

One Water Corn Mill called the Abbey Mylle situated upon a certain stream, brook, or river there, and all custom, suit, token, and tol there unto belonging…the inhabitants of St Albones towne had ever been wont to grind their corn at this mill.

Originally most mills would have been owned by the Church or the Lord of the Manor and flour could only be ground at their mills. A law known as the 'Right of Soke' meant the tenants of the manor had little choice but to use the manorial mill paying a fee called a 'Multure', which could be in money, flour or more usually a fixed percentage of the tenants grain and often the landlord took a further cut, with the rent or profit used to increase the manorial receipts. A multer bowl was used by some millers to take one bowlful from every two bushels of grain. Many corn dealers, millers and bakers were deemed corrupt by the locals with the more dishonest miller taking more than his due resulting in many court cases. In 1386, Chaucer describes the miller of Trumpington in Cambridgeshire as

A thief as well of corn and meal
And sly at that; his habit was to steal.

And an early rhyme describes a miller with:

One hand in his pocket and other in his bag;
As the wheel went round, he made his grab.

The Lord of the Manor was usually the only person with adequate finances to build the mills and to help recoup this outlay his tenants had to obey this customary law to take their corn to his mill. This was often a bone of contention among the local people who would prefer to grind corn with their own hand-mills which were treasured possessions often handed down through several generations and there are records as early as 1237 showing refusal to use the Abbey's mills, resulting in the Abbot Roger de Norton sending his men to seize the mills and arrest the ring-leaders. In 1327 Richard de Wallingford became Abbot and in 1332 after many problems with the townspeople, he ordered them to surrender 80 hand-querns found when their homes were searched, which he had set in the floor of the Abbey Chapter House. He also required them to once again pay for the privilege of using the Abbey's mills. Milling and fulling rights were two of the major issues of feudal obligations that led to the Peasant's Revolt in 1381.

However, it has to be remembered that a mill was a major investment for its builder and not just of benefit to him but also to the community whose existence relied on a good crop of corn and a steady supply of water, that often came with the building and maintenance of a mill and the river which had to be used efficiently to enable a return on this investment.

In 1568 the ownership of Kingsbury *"A watermill and free fishery in St Michael's"* was transferred from John Machell to Sir Nicolas Bacon.

A document in the Gorhambury Records shows that in 1637 when Gorhambury and the mill was owned by Sir Thomas Meautys, he leased the *"water corn Mill in St Michael's now in his possession and the buildings, gear, orchards and meadows....for 21 years at £20. 6s. 8d rent to John Raven of St Michaels, miller, and Alice his wife."*

The process of producing malt from barley allows the grain to ferment before being dried and ground into powder. It is then boiled producing 'wort' which is used in beer and whisky making.

The mill was described in 1658 as St Michael's Mill "formerly a Mault Mill."

The mill and the attached miller's house was modernized in the eighteenth century with a Georgian brick facade being added and little has changed since that time. Lava millstones found at the rear of the nearby Black Lion pub are thought to have

belonged to Kingsbury. In the 1880s Cornelius Waller ran a steam and water mill here.

The last millers to use the power of water to run the mill were brothers Arthur and William Fisher who leased the mill from Lord Verulam and operated it for thirty years until the early 1960s. During restoration in the 1970s and before being removed because of disrepair, there was a bakery containing two beehive-shaped ovens with an old tiled floor, attached to the mill along the river bank. In fact St Albans is said to have had its own bread in the middle ages called 'Peyne de Seynt Albon'.

It is recorded that a ghost of a singing miller can be heard at Kingsbury Mill!

In an early edition of *The Hertfordshire Illustrated Review* there is an amusing fictional tale based on the mills and rivers around this area. Called 'Three Men in a Boat, with apologies to Mr Jerome K Jerome', it takes place in the thirteenth century and involves a group of notorious robbers called "Ye Guylde of ye Bllacke Sainnttes" and three local monks who set out to catch them, plotting their scheme 'under the shadow of the weeping willow, whose drooping boughs sank deep into the river'. It involves a local fictional inn called the' Black Crow' which supposedly harboured the Bllacke Sainnttes and the tale of how the baddies including a wicked monk called Friar Cuthbert are caught after a fight in the muddy river under the 'rudely constructed bridge' by the corn mill at St Michael's and hung in the nearby woods for their crimes!

Today it is a museum and popular waffle house restaurant.

Most of its

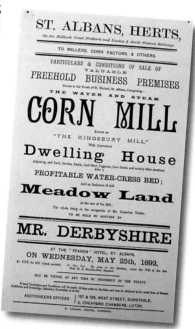

Kingsbury Mill sale poster showing that the mill also had a thriving watercress business at the time. (JBT)

The ford, bridge and Kingsbury Mill 1880-1900. (AL)

gearing is modern and its iron undershot wheel, 12 foot in diameter and 6 foot in width, lies idle.

A curiosity is its' sack hoist on the top floor, in which the wheel of the hoist rises to the brake instead of the brake descending to the wheel.

Standing outside the mill is a large Hertfordshire pudding stone, which was once used as a stepping stone in the Ver at a point where the 1635 St Albans boundary changed. It was taken from the bank of the river in the late nineteenth century and placed outside the mill to mark the jubilee of Queen Victoria by a local man, Mr Aldridge.

In Charles Swift's 1930 book *Historic St Albans* he describes St Michael's Street as follows:

Words cannot adequately describe the quiet, dignified beauty and real charm of peaceful loveliness of this village street, with the tower of its ancient church standing out against a background of trees flecked with the gold of sunlight, which is reflected in the blue and silver crystal water flowing beneath the bridge spanning the Ver in the foreground.

By Kingsbury Mill is the former Abbots Grange of Kingsbury now known as Kingsbury Manor. Once owned by Alfric, King Ethelred's chancellor, the manor was confirmed by King John to the Abbey in 1199. Thought once to have been the home of the Abbey cook, it passed to Henry VIII at the Dissolution. Afterwards it was rented to various people including members of the previously mentioned Wendye family.

A rambling eighteenth century building built on medieval foundations its land once extended to Verulam Road and beyond Batchwood to the north, Everlasting Lane to the east and near the Gorhambury Estate to the west. Built over the old roman road to Colchester, it is believed the remains of a bridge beneath the front garden once spanned the Ver before it was rerouted long ago.

Behind the manor house is the recently restored Kingsbury Barn, a Grade II listed timber-framed grange barn, dating from the late fourteenth century when it was built by the Abbey. It is the oldest secular building in St Albans. The back road that once went behind the barns and manor included a 300 foot ford on the river.

Each year, starting outside Kingsbury Mill, the annual event of 'Beating the Bounds' takes place. The origins of this tradition are thought to go back to the thirteenth century when city boundaries were established to control unruly locals by the Abbot of St Albans. In 1913, the bounds included Sopwell Mill where the group were pelted with flour and to maintain traditions the mayor carried out his privilege to fish the mill stream with rod and line.

Held on Rogantide, the third Sunday after Easter, the Mayor, a mace bearer, the Town Crier and the Mayor's Chaplain plus a group of locally invited people go to four local points on the medieval bounds of the city, the river marking the southern boundary. Willow wands are used to carry out the beating and a prayer is said – these bounds which are as near as possible to the original boundary of 1327 are the puddingstone outside Kingsbury, Kingsbury

The millstream alongside Kingsbury Mill (JBT)

Bridge next to Kingsbury Mill 2008 (JBT)

St Michaels Bridge & River (SKC /HALS)

Mill, a boundary mark near the Jolly Sailor pub, Keyfield car park in Old London Road and the bridge over the Ver next to the Fighting Cocks pub. A chosen person is also 'bumped' at each bound. Those who complete the whole 4 mile circuit receive a certificate of attendance.

The river then passes behind Fishpool Street, one of the oldest roads in the city. First mentioned in 1250, its lower part was known as Salipath, from the old English word for willows, which are still in evidence behind the Blue Anchor public house. Until the nineteenth century, it had been part of the main route to the northwest of England. Among those who had land in this area were the nuns of St Mary de Pré, holding a meadow of 55 perches (perch = 16.5 feet).

In 1334, work was carried out here by Andrew the Tanner to improve the flow of the river to the Abbey Mill.

Boys in the river at St Michael's. (SKC /HALS)

St Michael's Bridge and Ford with artist on left 1920s. (AL)

In 1659, the first stagecoach ran between London and Chester through Fishpool Street and as the coaches became more frequent it was necessary to build a bridge over the river at St Michael's. This three arch Grade II listed bridge was erected in 1765 at a cost of £280 by the Turnpike Trust who were founded in 1715 and is thought to be the earliest surviving bridge in Hertfordshire; the old ford by the bridge is still there today and is thought to have existed for 2000 years reputedly being the crossing point for Alban on the way to his execution. However, this was not the first bridge to be built here, it is thought the Romans built a bridge c300AD and one was also recorded in 1505 as "pons de la Maltemyll" or Malt Mill Bridge in an account of the Second Battle of St Albans which took place in 1461. A bridge also appears on Saxon's map of 1577, although earlier structures would have been wooden footbridges with other traffic using the ford.

In a 1688 article of agreement between John Bressie on behalf of Sir Samuel Grimston and John Turner, miller, Turner is covenanted to build a new bridge at St Michael's River and *"was allowed £13 and the old shiff of the old bridge, and to keep the bridge in repair for 60 years"*.

However in the 1689 Session Rolls it mentions that the *"Abbey Bridge being an aintchant bridge, which lies partly in St Michael's Parish and partly in the Abbey Parish is very much out of repair"*.

In 1678 1d a year was paid to the Corporation by a local market gardener Henry Townsend to divert the river in Fishpool Sreet into "Pittocks".

The meadow next to the river between the lake and St Michael's village is called Bell Meadow, thought to be named after the Bell Inn. However, in the unpublished *Memories of St Albans* by Charles Chapman (1914-1998) he writes the following:

I wondered where Bell Meadow's name derived from and it happened in conversation with Les Pritchard, the foundry foreman at the Sphere Works that I found the answer. He had worked at a foundry which made castings in bronze for sculptors and was knowledgeable about such things. He said that in medieval and even later times bell founders travelled to wherever their work took them and worked in any convenient open space. Thus Bell Meadows up and down the country got their name.

He also remembered…

Walking past Bell Meadow one crossed the Ver and the water meadows on the right. The lake and so on did not exist. Kingcups and forget-me-nots grew in the meadow and a little off-shoot of the Ver flowed through the meadows, under the Causeway and through Verulam Hill Farm.

This meadow is prone to flooding and there have been small lakes of water in the past.

A civil case bought before Judge Whigham at St Albans County Court in March 1871, accused Mr Payne, a watercress grower of St Michael's of accidental damage to a neighbouring watercress bed owned by Mr Sansum, he was made to pay the sum of 10 shillings.

The English Civil War of 1642-1649 between King Charles I and the Parliamentarians led by Oliver Cromwell ended in the Royalists being defeated at the Battle of Naseby in 1645 where Charles I was caught, imprisoned and eventually executed in January 1649.

His eldest surviving son Charles, evaded capture after the Battle of Worcester was lost to Cromwell in 1651, by hiding in an oak tree, he then escaped into exile.

On 29 of May 1660 he was restored as King Charles II and crowned. Oakapple Day commemorates the entry of the King into London and the restoration of the British monarchy. An act of parliament made 29 May an official holiday and until 1859 services of thanksgiving were held in churches with the rest of the day given over to fêtes and other merry making. Pepys recorded in his diary on 1 June 1660:

Parliament had ordered the 29th of May, the King's birthday, to be forever kept as a day of thanksgiving for our redemption from tyranny and the King's return to his Government, he returning to London that day.

From miles around people went to the Mayor's Pageant and Fair at St Michael's attracted by an almost continuous line of stalls, booths and proprietors placed between Gorhambury Lodge to St Michael's Bridge, and the celebrations that were an annual occurrence in St Michael's on Oakapple Day.

A greasy pole was set up in a spacious yard attached to the Angel Inn, which stood at the junction of Verulam and Branch Road. Substantial prizes were given to those who succeeded to the summit of the pole!

During these festive occasions the village streets were decorated with flags and branches of oak, the inn signs receiving special attention at the hands of the loyal inhabitants. Boats on the river were also decorated and used during the celebrations. People marked the day by wearing oak apples or a sprig of oak. It also became known as 'Pinch Bum' Day – because anyone not sporting an oak sprig had their bottom pinched or could be kicked or punched. In some areas it was called 'Nettle Day' as whipping with nettles was a favourite punishment!

The river then flows past the grounds of St Michael's Manor. Situated at the foot of Fishpool Street, the house as it currently stands was built by John Gape in 1585 with foundations going back to the eleventh century. The Gape family owned the manor until the current owners took it over in the 1950s. Much of the manor's land was split up into plots and sold for housing with gardens running down to the river.

The original track or Sali path as it was once known, which the street followed, meandered between marshy lands next to the Ver on the south side, which is now partly incorporated into the manor gardens, with the Saxon stronghold of Kingsbury on the north side.

The manor house is Tudor in origin and the date of 1586 can be seen carved into the oak of one of the ceilings. It was home to one of St Alban's oldest families, the Gapes, who held the office of mayor of St Albans on sixteen occasions in a period of three hundred years. In 1556, after the Dissolution of the Monasteries, there was mention of a Henry Gape who had a house in Romeland and in 1895, the manor house was owned by the Misses Gapes.

The tanning industry in St Albans was established

Boating on the fishpond in the grounds of St Michael's Manor c1920. (MoS)

on the south side of Fishpool Street as early as the mid fifteenth century. In 1538 Henry Gape bequeathed his son John his property in St Michael's and *"all his other leather and hides in his yards and vats and bark"*, which in 1744 continued to be owned by the Gapes and helped make their fortune. The large pond in the grounds of the house was part of an eighteenth century garden scheme replacing the tannery when the manor was also given a new front. During 1941-49 regular St Albans Folk Dance Festivals were held in the grounds and from 1950 they were held at Gorhambury. The family finally sold the house in 1953 to pay death duties.

During the drought of 1976, the lake in the grounds dried up causing the thick layers of silt laid down over many years to crack and all flora and fauna to disappear. The lake and the River Ver had always shared the same water level so as the Ver dried up during the hot summer so did the lake.

It was decided to take advantage of this rare drying up and restore the lake. Many lorry loads of silt totalling 1400 tons were removed over a two week period and this extremely rich organic material was taken to Smallford fishing lakes as top soil. There had been a tannery in the grounds of St Michael's Manor since at least the sixteenth century with the River Ver providing the essential supply of water needed for the tanning process and evidence was discovered in the grounds, including the lake where local archaeologists taking advantage of the parched conditions found numerous pieces of leather including almost intact and preserved medieval leather shoes.

The previously shallow lake was now 6 feet at the centre with gently sloping edges and over several months after the drought ended filled with water and welcomed back flora and fauna. Two new sluices were constructed linking the lake to the Ver, which would conserve water for the lake and disperse it when necessary.

The house is now a four star hotel and restaurant standing in five acres of beautiful gardens sloping down to the River Ver with a one acre lake in the grounds.

St Albans Cathedral and Abbey Mills. Early print by Beck. (HALS)

The rear of St Michael's Manor House by JH Buckingham. There seem to be two separate streams here, one possibly a millstream? (MoS)

Lads by the river early 1900s. (JBT)

Looking towards St Michael's late nineteenth century. (JBT)

Note the above postcard spells the Ver with two 'r's. (JBT)

When Verulamium Park was part of St Germain's Farm 1900-1910. (DH)

Besides the River Ver before 1921. (SKC /HALS)

Long burgage plots run in narrow strips from Fishpool Street to the river as seen on a 1634 map and remain unchanged to this day. Burgage plots are long narrow sections of land running at right angles to the main street in medieval towns. They had narrow fronts and long thin courtyards with connecting alleyways at the back. The houses or shops would usually be at the front facing onto the street. Behind them would be workshops and yards. The traces of burgage plots can often be seen in towns that were laid out during medieval times.

During six beautiful summer days in July 1907 the meadows on the banks of the Ver, inside the walls of old Verulamium, were the site of the St Albans Pageant. Months of planning went into this magnificent event of eight episodes from the history of the town, written by Charles Ashdown a master at St Albans School, on what were to become known locally as the Pageant fields. Over 3000 performers took part in the episodes including the martyrdom of St Alban, Boudicca's revolt, Queen Eleanor's funeral procession, the second battle of St Albans, and the visit of Queen Elizabeth I to Gorhambury. Two episodes mention the Ver. In Episode III The Martyrdom of St Alban, a citizen on a wall exclaims:

Early postcards of river, note how much better it looks with flora along the banks. (JBT)

The poster for the 1907 Pageant. (MoS)

Great Lords, a wonder hath befallen –
For when the crowd of citizens had come
Unto the narrow bridge that crosses o'er
The Ver; so great the personality
Of Alban, that they wept, and prayed, and held
Their little ones for him to bless, forthwith
They kiss the ground where he treads
They near the place, and now
And now (sinks to his knees and hides his face).

And in Episode VI the Peasants Revolt 1381 John Ball the Itinerant Preacher pronounces:

The nobles proud and arrogant are set
To hound you down the vilest of oppression.
The lawyers (howls of hatred from the crowd)
Make your life a living death,
And bind you to the soil with parchment rolls.
But you in Albans town have many wrongs
Against th' ecclesiastics. You're to take
Your cloth, forsooth, unto their mills to full,
Your corn, likewise unto their mills to grind;
You have no right to fish in yonder Ver,
No right to pasturage upon the sward
Which God has given to his faithful people.

Abbot. (Takes the charter and reads)
Know all that we
Do right of pasturage allow Kingsbury,
And Nodaissh, in Barnet Wood and Sopwell,
From Sissebourne to Del Pary. And we allow
The right to have hand-mills in your home.

In Charles Chapman's *Memories of St Albans*, he writes the following:
I have paddled in the stretch of the river in the photo-graph below. The water was deeper then and a lot of weed grew in it. We were quite sure that "blood-suckers" lay in wait for us under the weed and did not often venture far from the bank. The meadows beside the river where the lake is now were much more exciting. There was a

The River, St Albans.

small weir up near Bell Meadow and an overflow stream went through the Ver Meadow and the water returned to the river where the lake outlet is now.

The man in the photo on the bottom right may have been in trouble if he had been caught fishing a hundred years earlier as the Corporation minutes of 1764 explain:

The mayor having been lately informed that the river belonging to the corporation had recently fished by persons having no right to do so, it was ordered that a notice be affixed at the market cross warning people that anyone fishing without leave of the mayor would be prosecuted.

The above photo from 1923 shows the river and water meadows on farmland where the lakes now stand. (Unknown)

On the west of the river is Verulamium Park. In the 1820s the Ver flowed through marshy ground where the two lakes now stand and where there were once watercress beds.

The following is taken from an interview in 2000 with Bernard Smith, born in 1901, as part of the St Albans Museums Oral History Project.

Soon after WWI there was a lot of unemployment. I suppose it was the council authorities (who) decided to do something with a swamp that was alongside the river Ver. You know the Fighting Cocks, that was there in those days and opposite the Fighting Cocks there was a silk mill...and then a rickety wooden bridge over the Ver and then on the other side of the path alongside the Ver was a swamp with reeds, well the children used to paddle in the edges of it but it was a swamp covering quite a number of hundreds of square yards and the council decided to employ a lot of unemployed in turning that site into the lake with a couple of islands on it which is now in existence.

(Copyright St Albans Museums Service)

This land was turned into a leisure area by Sir Mortimer Wheeler with plans for a boating lake, paddling pool, football, cricket and hockey pitches and tennis courts. There were also plans to improve the path along the river, which had previously been separated from the water meadows by a fence as seen in some of the postcards in this book.

Built in the early 1930s, the work was often wrongly credited to the Jarrow Marchers; in fact it was constructed by local unemployed workers, 75%

of which had to be ex-servicemen. Built on over 140 acres of meadow and farmland bought by the city council from the Earl of Verulam in 1929 for a sum of £29, 996 equivalent today of over £300,000, £19,960 of the total sum was for labour alone. At the time the land was purchased it consisted of almost all of St Germain's and Verulam Hills Farm, including the 960 foot long frontage to the riverside walk (which had been bought previously for a sum of £1 from Captain Gape), through to King Harry Lane, the Causeway and the woods.

However, Bell Meadow, the land between the boating lake and St Michael's, which the city wished to buy to add to the park lands, was not purchased until some years later as the price asked at that time was almost double that offered of £400! It had already been used during WWI as allotments and Captain Gape had received £45 towards restoring it to its former glory!

In June 1929, the St Albans Chamber of Commerce wrote to the council –

...it is hoped that in due course a Boating Lake, as suggested by his Worship the Mayor, will be formed upon the Old Fish Pool and thus attract an additional number of visitors to the city.

Money was raised to allow archaeologists to carry out work at the site. Examples of Roman pottery and other items were uncovered along with several skeletons from a Roman cemetery which lies beneath the lakes; these were reburied in St Michaels churchyard.

The photos on page 88 are of the lakes and park during construction. Alan Malin tells us the following about his grandfather who worked as part of the team of men hired for this work.

My grandfather, Gordon Malin was born in St Albans in 1885. He was a trained carpenter and joiner and

'Sitting by the river's side is....the quietist and fittest place for contemplation' (Walton 1653) a lovely photo of a man fishing in the Ver, the Abbey just seen in background c1880. (AL/DH)

Construction of the lake. The hut shown in the bottom left image was the engine house that drove the lift along the tracks over the wooden bridge taking tons of spoil to the top of the hill. (JB/AM) Bottom right: Lake, island and Abbey just after being built – no toilet block yet! (JBT)

served in the trenches in France in the 1914-1918 war and returned to St Albans after the war ended. He would tell me about his work on the lakes when I was a boy.

When the lake was built, from 1929-1931, it was constructed mainly by previously unemployed people who were glad of the work. Some were local people, and others came from the north east and Wales. Taffy Green was the 'project manager' in charge of construction.

Initially materials were bought to the park up Mud Lane past where Westminster Lodge and the athletics track are now located. But it soon became impassable so a tramway track was constructed up Abbey Mill Lane. This worked on some sort of pulley system and my grandfather built the shed for the small engine. He also worked on the shuttering to the edges of the lake.

Earth from the excavations was moved towards King Harry Lane. If any artefacts were found, work stopped, and so did pay! Many of the men who found things said nothing as they were desperate for money – items were left in the ground where they were found. The pay was very poor (one shilling and four pence – 7p per day) but my grandfather and some of the men got two pence – 1p – extra if they bought their own tools and a wheelbarrow.

The following is taken from an interview in 2000 with Rachel King, born in 1911, as part of the St Albans Museums Oral History Project.

...another thing the King family did...The lake there is

manmade and John's brother Stephen – while they were making...the island, without anybody knowing anything about it, he got onto the island and he planted something like a hundred bulbs so that come spring – where did they come from! It was a great thing to have done!

(Copyright St Albans Museums Service)

With its two lakes connected by a weir under the central bridge, the park stretches over nine and a half acres with the lakes fed by the river which runs along the north-eastern edge of the park between St Michael's and Holywell Hill. To enable the area to be developed, the river was moved and straightened on the northern side and diverted at the top by St Michael's. Unfortunately little remains here of the original chalk stream, the sterile concrete edges and generally slow flow of water often result in a cloudy, silted mini canal with little natural fauna to create a diversity of habitats seen on other parts of the river. A faster flow created by weirs for example, would help to flush out sediment and thus reduce algae, creating a clearer, healthier and more attractive stream.

One of the first events to take place in the newly developed park was the Rotarians Fete in aid of St Albans Hospital and Nursing on Bank Holiday Monday, 7 August 1933.

Events included Review of the Fleet, pillow fights on rafts, Greasy Pole, Boat Race, the "Wallopers" a famous low rope act, life saving demonstrations,

This lovely old advert from the early 1930s, shows the newly constructed lake and its bridge and islands, with the Abbey on the hill, but note there is no river!

AT THE SIGN OF THE FISHER KNIGHT

THE HOUSE FOR FIRST CLASS PRINTING

COMPLETE BLOCK MAKING DEPT. ON THE PREMISES FOR HALF-TONE COLOUR & LINE WORK

FISHER, KNIGHT & CO. LTD.
GAINSBOROUGH PRESS ST. ALBANS
Telephone – 1111-1112

Cover of Rotarians Fête Programme. (JBT)

Cruises on the river for children on a 'fine model liner' and a reproduction of the 'Attack on Zeebrugge', which occurred in WWI with some of the men who took part in the real event assisting in the demonstration. Sideshows included Aunt Sally shies, darts, the motor car game and splash ball, plus many stalls selling everything from soap, scent and notepaper to cakes and ice-cream. The day culminated in a huge evening fireworks display.

Despite several signs positioned around the park asking the public not to swim in the lakes, this was often ignored, especially on hot summer days! There was also vandalism with trees being destroyed and the bulbs of spring flowers dug up and stolen!

Those of us who lived in St Albans used to spend a lot of our holidays down at the lake. We used to take salmon and shrimp paste sandwiches. You could swim in the lake then – it was beautifully clean and the River Ver was almost transparent.

Noel Godman.

During WWII, 22 acres of the park was cultivated for food production including allotments for local people who would often report finding Roman coins whilst digging. Verulamium Park was also used for regular events including fetes and concerts as part of the governments 'Holidays at Home' idea to help lift the spirits of war-torn Britain.

Water from the river and lake were used to fill a large emergency water tank near the clock tower for the use of extinguishing fires. Ian Howgate a local Air-Raid Warden remembers:

…after the German bombers had plastered London, they used to come out to the lake which was a good landmark for them and just circle around for a few minutes while they had their sandwiches then went back to have another go. And if they were feeling particularly resentful, they'd toss the odd one overboard!

My grandfather William Harris was a fireman during the war and part of a team that would sit on top of the square tower of the Abbey watching for enemy aircraft and 'doodlebugs' and reporting their direction and number. He also recalled the lakes being drained at one point to avoid reflecting the moonlight which could have been used by enemy bombers as a way marker to strategic points around the country and there was also a threat that the Abbey would be targeted. At the beginning of the war its twelve bells were removed to prevent the damage that could have been caused if it had been bombed.

St Albans was comparatively lucky during the war as far as bombing was concerned and although there were casualties, it is thought most of the bombs dropped on the area were surplus from raids elsewhere, these included ones dropped in or near the river at Bell Meadow, Bluehouse Hill, Cottonmill allotments, Hedges Farm, Park Street, Prospect Road, the Causeway, various watercress beds, Verulam Golf Course and Verulamium playing field.

When war ended in 1945 huge celebrations took place over much of the district with VE day declared a national holiday. Parties took place in streets and parks including Verulamium where some overzealous revellers ended up in the river! My grandfather remembered finding a man fully clothed sitting in the Ver his arms resting on the river bank, head in arms, smiling but fast asleep!

Today, many species of wildlife are found in and around the park and in 2010, 64 bird species were recorded including five types of birds of prey.

Our most common duck of ponds and rivers, the mallard's name is derived from the old French mallart meaning wild drake. The male as with most bird species is much more colourful than the light mottled brown of the female with his green head feathers, purple tinged breast, black tail and yellow bill. It feeds on a variety of foods including insects, invertebrates,

Female mallard (Anas platyrhynchos) and young on the river. (JBT)

crustaceans, seeds, plant matter, berries and tubers. The female lays a clutch of between 8–13 eggs, which are incubated for 27–28 days. The average life expectancy of the mallard is twenty years.

Male pochard duck (Aythya farina) (JBT)

With 472 breeding pairs in eastern England and lowland Scotland the attractive pochard duck is largely an over-wintering species with around 85,000 visitors a year. The number of UK residents is increasing slowly, thought to be partly due to the increase of gravel pits and reservoirs. They look for food by diving beneath the water.

Floods, early twenty-first century. (JBT)

The bridge between the two lakes 2010. (JBT)

Model boats being launched on the large lake during the 1950s. (JBT)

From the 1930s onwards the Model Powerboat Association (MPBA) has met frequently at the park, using the large lake where highly powered hydroplanes were anchored to stakes placed in the water between the islands. The competition involved boats in various classes speeding around the water trying to achieve the fastest time. Today St Albans hosts a two day MPBA international regatta during the August Bank Holiday. The local branch of the society meets throughout the year using the small lake to launch their boats powered by steam, electric and the more peaceful sail.

Ice skating on Verulamium Lake and river 1930's (JBT)

The lake was built in 1930-32. Most winters were cold enough for the lake at Verulamium to freeze and was used by the ice skaters.

Noel Godman.

…a wonderful sight, it was a misty morning and the lake was frozen and there was this one lone lady in Victorian costume….long, long coat, waisted and a little sort of bowler hat thing and she had a muff and she was going round and round the lake just like the Victorians, smooth and smooth, beautiful.

Taken from an interview in 2000 with Rachel King, born in 1911, as part of the St Albans Museums Oral History Project (Copyright St Albans Museums Service).

Between 21 and 26 of June 1948, The St Albans Millenary Pageant took place celebrating the thousandth anniversary (948-1948) of St Michael's, St Peter's and St Stephen's churches, St Albans School and the town's market. It was visited by the late Queen Mother, then Queen Elizabeth. The pageant was divided into a prologue, nine episodes and an epilogue.

The episodes were as follows:

The Millenary Pageant programme.

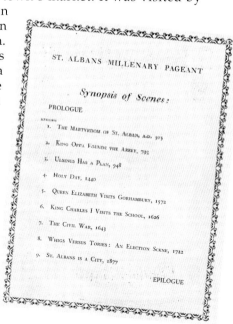

The Pageant on the field known as St Germain's Mead by the lake, 1948. (MoS)

Dead fish at Verulamium during the heat wave and drought of 1976. (MoS)

In June 1953, the year of the Queen's coronation, another pageant took place at Verulamium called the 'Masque of the Queens'.

The above photo shows the tragic scene of hundreds of dead fish in the lakes caused by the lack of water being supplied by the River Ver, and where there was water, a lack of oxygenation during the incredibly long, hot and dry summer of 1976. Other wildlife, especially wildfowl suffered as the water disappeared and the greenery that supplied their food withered and died.

By June the remaining water in the lakes became stagnant and polluted, causing further suffering to wildlife. A four inch pipe was used to circulate the remaining water in an effort to increase its oxygen content. More than 3000 live fish, including roach and carp were netted by members of the Verulam Angling Club and council workmen and taken to the healthier and deeper waters of Stanborough lakes in Welwyn Garden City.

Human kindness helped some of the local wildfowl survive with people putting out food and paddling pools and other containers filled with water in their back gardens.

However the fish deaths of 1976 were not an isolated incident, similar events had occurred on several occasions including the early 1970s and 1982. The water quality in the concrete-lined lakes has often been a problem, especially during the warmer months. As a result of the early fish deaths, St Albans City Council asked the then Hatfield Polytechnic to provide students, led by Dr Avis Hall, to undertake a survey of the lakes complete with suggested management.

The project looked at many areas of the park, lakes and river including algal and bacterial investigations, water flow, sediment analysis, animal and vegetation surveys, and a short visitor questionnaire. However no water samples were examined or tests carried out at the time of the more major fish deaths, so any results could only be speculative.

The amount of algae found was substantial and could act as a barrier halting oxygen to enter the water and increase transpiration leading to water loss. A high number of sulphur reducing bacteria were also found in the silt that can actively produce oxygen reducing hydrogen sulphide; both potentially deadly to fish.

For many years in the 1950s and '60s, local groups including angling clubs, would volunteer to help with the netting, recording and redistribution of fish from the lakes (dad and our little boat 'Heron 1' included). They would also help with dredging and cleaning of the lakes and river. The numbers of fish mainly roach and rudd, could be quite substantial up to 100,000. When in this number these fish would not generally become large specimens as a result of the size of the environment and limited food supplies.

The visitor questionnaire resulted in the following data kindly supplied by Dr Avis Hall.

When asked what aspects the people liked about the park:
1. Overall pleasantness
2. Ducks
3. Trees
4. Space to play
5. Convenient to home
6. Water
7. Wildlife
8. Roman ruins/history
9. Easy to park car
10. Only decent park in St Albans
11. Fish
12. Museum
13. Sport

The changes visitors would like to be made to the park:

Canada geese grazing in the evening light 2009. (JBT)

Geese and a frozen River Ver. (MH/JBT)

Right: *Eighteenth century painting of the river, Abbey and Fighting Cocks. (MoS)*

Adult heron feeding its chicks a small bream at the lake 2011. (JBT)

*Adult heron (*Ardea cinerea*) arriving to feed chicks at the lake 2011. (BBT)*

The Fighting Cocks and silk mill early twentieth century. (JBT)

1. Lake/river cleaned
2. Improve café
3. Boating on lake
4. Separate area for dogs
5. Less birds
6. Geese droppings
7. Improve flow
8. Enforce no cycling
9. More children's facilities
10. Free parking on Saturdays
11. Lights on Causeway
12. Too formal
13. More seats
14. More litter baskets
15. Change the green bridge
16. More concern for wildlife
17. More flowers

Many people had also voiced their concern about the number of dead fish and wildfowl seen.

Nearly thirty years later several of the above still cause concern especially enforcement of no cycling and the condition and flow of the River Ver and the lake.

Many man-made lakes benefit enormously by the oxygenation supplied by fountains, waterfalls, weirs and aquatic plants (plants and improved water flow were recommended as part of the management plan above), plants would also encourage invertebrates, a food source for wildfowl and fish, which to this day, the lakes at Verulamium lack. Although without a guaranteed and improved water supply, even these benefits would not always be of use.

The two islands in the large lake provide important nesting and roosting sites for wildfowl away from the public and predators and the importance of regular maintenance especially to halt flooding and ensuring continued healthy tree and plant cover is important to both wildlife and to maintain a pleasant view.

In recent years the islands on the lakes have become home to a heronry, now the largest in Hertfordshire.

Herons, with a wing-span of 185cm are one of the largest birds in Europe. Since the first nests appeared in 1990, the heronry has attracted many birdwatchers that are able to observe these usually shy birds at close quarters.

In 2008 it is reported that from 23 nests 48 chicks were successfully reared. The British Trust for Ornithology (BTO) fits many of the chicks with leg rings and they have been found in many parts of England. In the spring of 2009 a special viewing station was set up by the RSPB to enable the public to watch these fascinating birds at close quarters whilst raising their young, which are fully grown within three months. They feed in a fascinating way – silently so silently, stalking until...a sudden lunge – they seldom miss! And this can be observed along much of the upper Ver, something I never tire of watching.

In Geoff Webbs book *A Redbourn Commoner*, he describes dead herons being discovered many years ago "...*with eels, or the tails of water voles protruding*

from their dagger-like bills – instances where the size of the meal has caused the gourmet's death".

In 1947 on the opposite side of the river, the land known as the orchard was acquired by St Albans School. In 1634 this was still part of "Kitcheners Meade", referring to the Abbey official to which income from this land was assigned. The river passes the lake and where a small bridge now stands was once the main ford to the Abbey from Watling Street.

Early print – Fishing on the river. (HALS)

Below: *Abbey Mill Lane 1929. (JBT)*

Fishpool Street, the river and lake. (©English Heritage. NMR. Aerofilms Collection)

The two large hangars seen to the left of the photo above are in Miskin's Yard and were placed there during WWII resulting in many complaints from local residents. C. Miskin & Co were a local builder and contractors established in 1790.

The long thin building centre photo to the left of the school is the old straw plaiting factory, originally built by Munt, Brown & Co around 1860 which incorporated a three and a half acre meadow stretching down to the Ver. The factory, house and garden were bought by St Albans School in 1935 and eventually used for their science block with other buildings put to various uses. The meadow was purchased separately by a Miss Glossip to prevent it being built on but was also purchased by the school some years later.

Many ghostly sightings have been reported around this area.

One winter during the 1970s, the ghost of a cavalier carrying a sword, floating in a silver mist was sighted by two boys riding their bikes through the park.

Also one of St Albans' 'local characters' the late Ginger Mills, was reportedly startled by the sound of marching feet very early one morning, when walking near the lakes at Verulamium. On turning to see where the noise was coming from, he was shocked to see a ghostly army that caused an icy breeze as they passed!

The road we know as Abbey Mill Lane was once the passage through the Great Gateway of the monastery and to get to the area around the old mill

would have required permission from the Abbot.

On the east of the river in Abbey Mill Lane is the Fighting Cocks public house, arguably the oldest English inn. The cellar is built on an eighth century gatehouse to St Albans Abbey and has massive foundations to keep the damp out from the river whose level it is below and coursed with flints and tiles, some taken from the ruined Roman city with tunnels running from the cellars to the Abbey.

This was once the Prior's dovecote, an octagonal building situated in the Prior's garden thought to have been built by Abbot John Moote in the late fourteenth century.

In 1600 it was purchased and *"rebuilt since the flood"* which occurred during the previous year by Thomas Preston who *"pulled the same downe and*

The river near the Fighting Cocks, around 1900. (DH)

The Silk Mill, river and meadows around 1900. (DH)

A postcard with a similar view naming the Ver as the River Colne? (JBT)

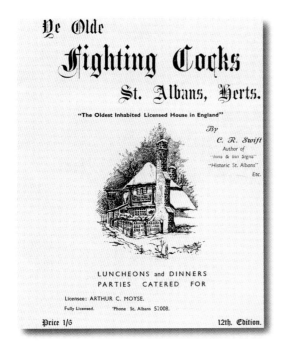

Local advertising card. (JBT)

erected it upon the said pightle and afterwards put up a chimney and made thereof a tenement which is now called the Rounde House". It remained the Round House until the nineteenth century.

Oliver Cromwell is said to have spent at least one night at the inn during the Civil War with his horse stabled in what is now the bar area!

When cock fighting was thankfully made illegal in the mid nineteenth century the name of the inn was changed for a short time from Ye Olde Fighting Cocks to The Fisherman, maybe in reference to its one time use as a store for the monks' angling equipment? In 1855, licensee Daniel Halsey was a witness in a poaching case and presented himself as landlord of the Fisherman beer house.

During restoration in the 1970s a very old fireplace was found behind the one being renovated and this is now an attractive feature of the pub, especially on a chilly winter's day.

It was reported by a member of staff in 2001 that two apparitions, dressed in brown monk-like habits emerged from the cellar, visible only to their knees, climbed the stairs from the cockpit and sat by the fireside before slowly fading away!

Part of the Fighting Cocks' long history and that of the millstream opposite includes a television appearance in 1989 as part of a scene from an episode called 'Sins of the Fathers' from the popular TV series *Morse* starring the late John Thaw and Kevin Whately. It included a boat being punted along the millrace between the bridge and mill. What the viewers didn't see was that each end of the 'river' was a dead end and the boat could only be punted backwards and forwards on a fifty-foot stretch of water! I was working at the local company Marconi Instruments at the time where part of the programme was filmed and I was lucky enough to sit and chat with John Thaw, a lovely, quiet and talented actor and have a much treasured photo of us together. He remarked how lucky we were to have such a lovely

The above photo taken outside the Fighting Cocks is on the album cover of a 1969 LP, Folk Songs Of Old England, Vol. 2 by Tim Hart & Maddy Prior, founder members of the group Steeleye Span. (JBT)

Morse and Lewis – John Thaw and Kevin Whately. (ITV/GI)

Boat scene on the Mill Stream. (ITV/GI)

park, asking questions about its history and that although filming could be somewhat longwinded at times, he enjoyed visiting some of the many different places used in the series.

The former Abbey Mill and millrace, opposite the Fighting Cocks, is a lineal descendent of the corn mill of the medieval Abbey, where the monastery obtained its flour and local people were obliged to grind their corn.

One Water Corn Mill called the Abbey Mylle situated upon a certain stream, brook or river there, and of all custom, suit, token, and tol thereunto belonging…and the inhabitants of St Albans towne had ever been wont to grind their corn at this mill.

The Romans first diverted the Ver to use as waterpower and nearly all St Albans mills had the river diverted to power them at some point in history. The mills are certainly Saxon or medieval in age, maybe earlier. During the middle ages the river was harnessed and powered the corn mill owned by the Abbot. Barley was also processed here to be used together with water from the Ver at the monastery's brewery which stood nearby.

Many centuries later in 2011 as part of a television programme on Roman archaeological finds presented by Rory McGrath, trenches were dug in the grounds of the Six Bells pub in St Michael's Street finding not only pottery and coins but the remains of what could be a large hotel. During the visit an attempt was made by a local brewer to reproduce two types of Roman ale, small beer used by peasants called Roman September Serf Ale and a stronger version Roman September Middle Class Ale both using local ingredients including water taken from the Ver near Bell Meadow and plants from the riverbank along with seasonal fruit and local honey.

Once used to drive the mill-wheel, the water would flow down the millrace and meet the river in Westminster Lodge meadows, the original flood plain, which in very wet weather still forms large pools of water.

In the thirteenth century, Abbot John de Hertford carried out urgent and costly repairs of the Abbey water mills and also built a horse-powered mill to compensate for low flows. In the fourteenth and fifteenth century the mill was used for fulling. There were further additions in the eighteenth century with the millstream containing the wheel running through the middle of the new building. Adjoining at right angles to its west end stood the mill house, a rambling affair dating from the seventeenth century which was added to in Regency days.

In 1804 the buildings were bought by silk thrower John Woollam who installed a silk-throwing machine thus changing its name to the Silk Mill. This process involved twisting the silkworm cocoon fibres ready for weaving into cloth. One of the largest employers in St Albans, many orphans previously kept by the local parish, were employed as cheap labour earning just enough to survive and releasing the parish of their responsibility. At the beginning of the twentieth century over 100 people worked at the mill.

The Silk Mill c1800 (illustration from Oldfield's book on St Albans).

Early twentieth century postcard of the Silk Mill. (JBT)

It was said in Brayley and Britton's 'Beauties of England and Wales' 1806 that *"This manufacture promises to become flourishing, and a new mill is now fitted up near the former one"*. It was also said that the mill machinery, which filled three rooms, was very ingeniously contrived, some of it constructed on a new and a much improved principle.

At least two generations of Woollams worked Abbey Mill using partly waterpower, partly steam.

Having established himself in St Albans, John Woollam expanded to Hatfield, where by 1818 he was employing pauper children. Around 1849 Abbey Mill which was at that time steam powered, closed down. As mentioned previously, in its place in the late 1850s, a steam-powered mill was built by Woollam at Redbourn, facing the common.

At this time the water supply for the area either came from the Ver or wells but the increasing population caused many problems including pollution of the water table and river. In 1877 Charles Woollam (1832-1915), angry at the continued pollution of the river, prosecuted the council for allowing sewage to contaminate the Ver. As a result in 1884, a sewerage scheme was set up for the town as part of the Public Health Act.

There still exists a red brick, two storey erection, dated 1810 alongside the old Silk Mill, and badly bonded onto it is a three storey mill house, built in

Early postcard of the Old British Causeway. The cottage is Verulam Hills farmhouse or Ver Cottage and was situated on the edge of the river near where the public lavatories are now. It was demolished in 1929 when the lake was built. (JBT)

Weir next to the Abbey Mill before the fish steps. (MoS)

the seventeenth century, designated on an Ordnance Survey town plan of 1880 as a school.

However, the two large buildings, one with what appears to originally have been a second wheel, described by C. H. Ashdown's *St Albans Historical & Picturesque*, 1893, as modern, makes the earlier position of the site difficult to follow. The Silk Mill was closed in 1938. Nothing is known of the fate of its equipment when it was sold to J. Maygrove and Co of London, who continued to operate there until c1955.

Owners Faith Craft Studios Ltd demolished the old mill around this time and leased most of the remaining buildings to other firms including Livingstone Organs, makers of classical electronic instruments.

The other buildings have now been converted into private flats.

In 1998, the Environmental Agency completed a project to restore flow and encourage habitation upstream of the River Ver at St Albans. In the 1600s, when the mill was rebuilt, a channel was dug above the natural watercourse in the side of the valley which helped to increase the flow of water to the mill. As time passed the flow of the original river fell putting a halt to any fish being able to swim upstream past the mill. The solution to this problem was to join the channel and the river using a 'pool and traverse' system including fish steps with a 30cm drop. A channel of approximately 1km was created along the original watercourse, part of the passage built in 1634, to encourage fish and wildlife to colonise the area, although fish are rarely spotted in the river below the fish steps and those seen would definitely be too small to scale it! This has been done at various sections of the Ver including Gorhambury. The pool below the fish steps, which can be crossed by stepping stones is affectionately known locally as the gudgeon pool as it was once full of these little fish.

The path on the earthwork running from the bottom of Abbey Mill Lane to King Harry Lane is known as the Causeway, which is believed to be part of the southern boundary of the Roman city and on the northern side was the ancient dam built to divide the great fishpools, now the site of the lakes. In Victorian times, as today, the Causeway and river walk were very popular.

Of the town's most infamous people none was more renowned than Mother Haggy, the local witch who lived during the reign of James I (1566 -1625). She married a yeoman and for a while lived in good repute. At the birth of their daughter there was much merry making during which Mother Haggy's high crowned hat seemed to take on a life of its own. It leapt into the baby's cradle, turned into a coronet then broke into a thousand pieces. Mother Haggy was quoted as saying "such will be the fortune of my daughter and such her fall". This occurrence was vouched for by clergy. Mother Haggy displayed a gift for fortune telling, discovering lost or stolen items and could reputedly turn herself into a lion, hare or cat.

After her death she was said to often be seen riding at full gallop on her broomstick at midday and sitting in a kettle drum floating down the Ver.

She survived several attempts to prove her sorcery by plunging her in the River Ver fastened to a ducking stool.

In Frederick Lane Williams 1822 book *The Historical & Topographical Description of the Municipium of Ancient Verulam* he calls the river the Ver, Mure and Meure and describes Verulamium as follows:

It is built upon a bold projecting knoll, or eminence, rising from the banks of the transparent little rivulet Ver, from its shores the abundant foliage of various majestic trees of many species rise in rural grandeur from its base up the acclivity of the hill, on which the town stands...without the aid of that universal component water, all landscapes are found to be defective, nor is this denied...in the picture before us: tasteful meandering of the little River Ver, fortunately, here are at intervals – affording relief to the eye, in search for all the contributive beauties of nature, heightened by the labours of art.

Walking along the banks of the river, visible across what were the flood plains of the Ver, at the bottom of Holywell Hill, is the Abbey Theatre. Designed by Michael Meacher it was built in 1967 for an amateur dramatics company that was originally founded in 1934, and which had to vacate its original 99 seat Abbey Mill Theatre at nearby Verulamium in the mid 1960s.

In 1968 the new theatre was opened and the late Queen Elizabeth the Queen Mother watched the opening performance of *The Recruiting Officer*, by George Farquhar performed by The Company of Ten, as the group named themselves. Each year over twenty thousand people are entertained at the theatre.

Stukleys map of 1721 suggests that the sewage of the monastery was conveyed to the river in this area by a large underground drain although it is also said this was once the location of the great garden of the monastery. On the opposite bank at one time was a large osier bed used for making hurdles to contain cattle.

Up until the early twentieth century, St Germain's and Verulam Hills Farms were situated near the Ver and with its water meadows covered many hundreds of acres between Holywell Hill, across where the lake now stands and up to St Michael's village. St Germain's farmhouse was on the site of the present Verulamium Museum. Both farms were bought in 1929 for the development of the park.

In the seventeenth century it was recorded that *"water is thrown up from the river for use of the town"*. This was through pipes that pumped water from the 'waterhouse' at the former Cotton Mill which was closed by the Duchess of Marlborough in the 1720s.

In 1838 there was an outbreak of typhus in St Albans caused by the lack of a public sewerage system. In 1866 a public meeting was held at the Town Hall where it was recorded:

The sewerage is clearly a question the Corporation ought to deal with; the river is being poisoned and the health of the inhabitants of the town will be affected by the malaria arising from the polluted stream unless a speedy alteration is made.

But it was not until eighteen years later that a main sewer and its connection to the towns houses had began!

It is near this site that a pump was sunk in 1945 at

Hay gathering at Verulam Hills Farm. (MoS)

a depth of about 100 feet. This pumping station works in tandem with two other nineteenth century pumping stations on Holywell Hill and at the top of St Peter's Street, which was the first pumping station to extract water from the area, set up in 1865. All these are used to remove water from the underlying chalk for the use of the public and businesses in St Albans.

In medieval times the production of woollen cloth was one of the main industries in St Albans with the town's textile industries located around what is now the Westminster Lodge/Prospect Road area. In the mid twelfth century there is mention of a tenterground in Fuller Street, which ran down to the Ver, where cloth was taken to be stretched and dried. The Abbot also owned a fulling mill on the Ver below Eywood on the east side of Holywell Hill. Fullers Street, now Mud Lane, ran from Holywell Hill near the bridge to the London Gate, now Westminster Lodge and had been there since medieval times.

Early photo showing cows grazing in Verulam Hills Farm meadows, river to right with mill and Abbey in background. (JBT)

Fulling techniques had been practised by the Romans but is thought to have been introduced to Britain around the twelfth century when King John demanded the local fullers not only use the Abbey fulling mill but also pay 2 marks (around £1.35) to renew cloth trading rights to boot! Already angry about having to take their corn to be ground at the Abbot's mills, this further demand did not go down well!

The fulling process would originally have been manual, using people called walkers to physically trample the cloth in tubs with their bare feet and then in streams such as the Ver. Fulling was the first part of the cloth-making process to become mechanised. These fulling mills processed the cloth made from wool belonging to the local monastery. However the Lord of the Manor usually obtained an income from tolls levied on non-monastic cloth, the tenants of his estate having to pay to use these mills to full their own cloth.

The fulling process was needed to remove dirt, natural grease and oil from the newly woven wool. It allowed the cloth to shrink and thicken with the pounding also helping to strengthen and smooth the cloth. At the fulling mill, the cloth was put into different solutions and pounded with mechanised trip-hammers, powered by the watermill. The process would usually involve three noisy and foul smelling poundings, each taking around two hours, but the exact timing would be down to the skill of the fuller.

The first pounding after the cloth had been washed, was done in a solution, mixed with urine in the early days, to loosen the grease. The urine would have been collected in casks from local houses, which would be paid for their offerings!

The second pounding used a solution of 'fuller's earth', and the final pounding was in a soapy solution. The cloth would then be rinsed and stretched out to dry on racks studded with tenterhooks. These were L-shaped nails used to secure the cloth in place. Cloth could shrink anything up to 12 yards in length and 5 yards in width while being fulled, an extra 2 yards or so could be obtained by stretching it. This process could be abused and the material over-stretched to produce inferior cloth; because of this an Act of Parliament was passed in 1550 to attempt to stop the actions of unscrupulous fullers! The phrase "on tenterhooks" has its origins from this process of being stretched like the cloth on the tenter, describing a state of uneasiness or suspense.

Once dry, the cloth would be finally brushed with teasels to raise the nap and sheared to create a shiny surface. The surnames Walker, Fuller and Tucker (tuckering was another term used for fulling) all have their origins from the fulling process.

Local references to fulling include a plot of land in Fuller Street belonging to Richard son of Robert attached to a tentorium where fulled cloth was hung to dry in the mid thirteenth century and in 1266 Emma Goldstob was granted by her father a messuage – from the Latin *manere* 'dwell' (a house with outbuildings and land) – and two tentoria in Fuller Street.

In the thirteenth century it is recorded that a glove-maker called Richard of Waltham had a messuage, with pasture land and a vineyard in Fuller Street near the river called Holystreme which ran towards Sopwell.

It is believed that the course of the Ver was canalised in the thirteenth century between the Causeway and Holywell Hill to allow ponds to be dug on the land for monastic use. Until 1684 the river's course was to the north of the area and the remains of a medieval timber water course have been found between 79-81 Holywell Hill. Kitcheners Ponds and Pondwick no longer exist but the river remains in its altered position.

The 1804 St Albans Petty Sessions Records mention the following:

Persons exposing themselves naked in a field within this Borough adjoining to…the river…for the purpose of bathing or washing in such River. Whereby persons particularly female passing and repassing…are continually annoyed…Bills and Indictments will be preferred against all persons who shall assemble together on the banks of the Holywell River and after stripping themselves naked, bathing in the said river.

The naming of the river here as Holywell River seems to go back some time as James Bennett was issued a licence in 1699 to supply water to the borough from the Holywell river.

The Pinnock family were well known local watercress growers with beds in St Albans and other parts of Hertfordshire. Here Claude Pinnock tells us of the watercress beds in this area:

We had Didlem Hall, that was down the bottom of Holywell Hill where the swimming pool is…they came out into the river just below the Duke of Marlborough and then we had up Gorhambury Drive, we had cress beds there, we was one of the biggest in the country in them days, oh yeah we got rid of some cress!

A family enjoying themselves late 1920s as described below. (NG).

Where the lake is now were fields with cows in. A stream used to run through the fields which I used to paddle in. I have a photo of my wife as a child paddling in this stream before the lake was built. Noel Godman.

The original Westminster Lodge was a beautiful large 13 bedroom house standing in 8 acres of land leased from the Gape family, just south of the river near Holywell Bridge. Built in the late 1800s by Isaac Newton Edward, a descendant of the brother of Sir Isaac Newton, it also had an entrance lodge, coach house and stables which still exist, the coach house now housing a veterinary surgery.

From the beginning of the war until 1955 the house was taken over as a head office by J. Evershed & Co, a printing firm. It then became the headquarters of the YHA who renamed it Trevelyan House in memory of their founder Dr George Trevelyan. Once they left, the building was divided into separate offices and many private homes were built on the grounds in roads called Westminster Court and Trevelyan Place.

In 1961 part of the site was acquired by the local council and developed into a sports area, indoor swimming baths and the Abbey Theatre.

During WWII, near to the modern day entrance to Westminster Lodge, stood a transit camp for prisoners of war. All that survives now are the

The original Westminster Lodge. (Unknown)

foundations of the buildings and a wooden hut within the grounds of the leisure centre.

The field next to the river at Westminster Lodge was used in May 1977 for an episode of a hugely popular television programme of the time called *It's a Knockout* presented by Stuart Hall and Eddie Waring. The three teams taking part were St Albans, Wandsworth and Southend.

At the end of the competition Southend and St Albans had tied with twenty-five points each. As a tiebreaker both teams took part in a sack race. St Albans got off to a bad start and Southend won. The final score Southend twenty-eight, St Albans twenty-seven points!

Fishpool Mead, now Westminster Lodge Field by the river, was an old hedge-lined route to Verulamium. Pondswick Close not far from the river is named after the fishponds that existed here in medieval times serving the monastic community.

A stall promoting The Heron and Verulam Angling Clubs and the Ver Valley Society at the St Albans Carnival, Westminster Lodge, 1979. The tank contains various species of fish caught in the Ver that morning by Ted Banfield and later safely returned. (JBT)

Advert for Ver House Hotel – note the bathing pool. (JBT)

Cheerleaders at It's a Knockout *Westminster Lodge Meadows 1977. (MoS)*

The river near Holywell Bridge opposite the Duke of Marlborough Pub 1853. JH Buckingham. (MoS)

A medieval wall and fortifying ditch approached St Stephen's Hill at right angles from the Sopwell district. This made a boundary around Eywood Lane and at the junction of the hill, which were diverted towards the river and stopped there.

In 1143, Holywell Hill Bridge over the river is thought to have been the site of a skirmish between King Stephen and his men at arms and the soldiers of St Albans. They arrived at St Albans to arrest William de Mandeville who had been charged with treason and were met by a group of men at the stream called Halywelle Water, where the supporters of Mandeville managed to resist the King's soldiers. In the battle that ensued, the Earl of Harundelle was unhorsed by Walkeline of Oxford in the middle of the stream, where he almost drowned.

The soldiers of St Albans who took part in the battle and protected the church, finally managed to hold back the King and his troops who were made to repay the church which some of the King's men had violated.

The chronicler Matthew Paris reported in the mid thirteenth century that the ford was known as Halliwell Water and *"The Werlam River was once very large and flowed about the city"*. He also wrote of local folklore including the legend of the great dragon of Wormenhert. Doris Joan Baker writes in her book *The Folklore of Hertfordshire*.

Wormenhert was a cave inhabited by a great dragon. Connected to a deep ravine, Wormenhert was surrounded by a mountain which stood above the River Ver and the ruined Roman town of Verulamium, known in Saxon times as Werlamceaster. The Gesta Abbatum tells that around 1007...'Abbot Ealdred, who demolished much of the remaining ruins of Verulamium while collecting stone, brick and other material to rebuild the Abbey, flattened as far as he was able the great ravine and cavern of Wormenhert so dispelling for ever traces of the serpent's lair.

The river then flows under Holywell Hill, an ancient street that is thought to have originated as a footpath to St Albans shrine. Holywell Hill has been known by various names throughout its history which stretches back to long before the thirteenth century, including Halliwellestrate and Halywell Hull. It ran from the former Malt Chepping (chepping is an old name for market) where the market place is today at the top of the hill, to Halliwell Bridge over the river. During the Middle Ages it was known as Halliwell Street and in the fifteenth century the river itself was known here as Halywell. By 1634 it was the Kings Highway leading from St Stephen's to St Albans. The Benjamin Hare map of 1634 names it as Hollowell Street.

There were originally two bridges spanning what was once called Holywell Water here, a narrow footbridge and a wider one for horse and carriages. The wider one crossed the river and was next to a brick wall, at the rear of the cottages near the Marlborough Inn. These bridges were built after 1143 when a bridge over the river at the foot of Holywell Hill was first recorded. Previously only a wide shallow ford existed.

Originally the medieval 'bar' or entrance to the town, before 1800 the site of the Duke of

Marlborough was 'Pondyards Gate', a turnpike house belonging to the Hatfield and Reading Turnpike Trust with two gates, one across the New Road, the present line of Holywell Hill and the other Grove Road, the old route. By 1841 it had become a beer house named after the Duke of Marlborough and kept by Benjamin Taylor. At the turn of the twentieth century it was known as the 'Duke Inn'. In 1994 the name was changed briefly to The Tap and Spile, before returning to its original title.

At the beginning of the twentieth century the depth of the river opposite the Duke of Marlborough was so deep that steam wagons could pump water for their boilers without stirring up the mud or drawing stones.

The structure that was once Holywell Hill Waterworks, currently a children's nursery, stands on

Looking up Holywell Hill from the bridge.
J.H. Buckingham. (MoS)

The Duke of Marlborough and river, late nineteenth century. (DH)

The river, old waterworks and pumping station, Holywell Hill 1980s. (JBT)

the site of the sixteenth century Hallywell House, one of several homes of the wealthy and childless Sir Ralph Rowlett, whose brass is in the Abbey. On his death, the house was passed to his nephew Ralph Jenyns (Jennings), who in turn passed it down to his great grandson, Richard Jenyns and by the mid seventeenth century it had been inherited by his great grandson Richard, father of Sarah Jenyns (1660-1744), later Duchess of Marlborough, who was reputedly born there.

When he died in 1668 his estates went firstly to his two short lived sons and then it was jointly owned by his daughters Sarah and Frances, but in the meantime it had fallen into a state of disrepair until in 1684 Sarah and her husband John Churchill (1650-1722), the 1st Duke of Marlborough, purchased Frances' share, pulled down the old house and hired William Talman (1650–1719) a pupil of Sir Christopher Wren and a renowned English architect and landscape designer whose work included Chatsworth House, to rebuild Holywell House creating a major diversion to the road and diverting the river southwards by the 'New Bar', later the toll house and Duke of Marlborough inn.

Situated near the Ver and its picturesque water meadows, the river was diverted to flow through several ponds all well stocked with fish. Its 20 acre grounds included a tree-lined entrance in Thorpe Road, pleasant flower bordered walks, a kitchen garden stocked with many herbs and plants used for medicinal purposes by Sarah, a practised apothecary, fruit trees and even a bowling green. Maps show The Holy Well to be a focal point of the gardens.

A seventeenth century travel writer, Celia Fiennes, visited St Albans in 1690 saying…*"There are several good houses about the town…one of them, which stands by the bridge, on the river Ver belonging to the Churchills".*

In Oldfield's *Book of St Albans* (c1800) he writes the following:

The River Ver was always an attractive part of town. St Alban's has no artificial promenades or walks to boast of…the walk to Verulam Hills by the Silk Mills is a favourite resort. The river was healthy enough to support a lot of wildlife, especially trout. The Duke of Marlborough enjoyed his "trouts" from the canalized section of the river that flowed through the garden of Holywell House.

The Duchess stayed here for long periods while her husband was fighting on the continent and took an active roll in the politics of St Albans.

Queen Anne and George of Denmark often visited, as did George I. The Dowager Countess Spencer had a green coat charity school until her death in 1814. The 1815 Shaw's guide to the town states, 'The holy-well is still held in some esteem for its purity and salubrious qualities'.

Holywell House eventually fell into ruin and was demolished around 1827 with the original route of Holywell Hill straightened, restored and a new bridge erected prior to building the waterworks. The grounds became overgrown and neglected and less than ten years later only a fishpond and the 'canal', which marked the original course of the river remained.

Today all that can be seen of the formal gardens is a fenced off overgrown hollow in the ground behind De Tany Court which was once part of the canal.

In Iris Butler's 1967 authoritative work on Sarah, Duchess of Marlborough, she writes *"there is now no trace of Holywell House below the Old London Road, only a plaque saying that here dwelt the great Duke of Marlborough"*.

To the east the river has a wooded area on the north bank. Here we come to what was once part of the grounds of Holywell House with the gardens of Prospect Road on the south bank. The new course of the river behind Prospect Road was dug in the eighteenth century when the building of the gardens of Holywell House was carried out.

Bings Orchard seen on old maps was also in this area and is now covered by the old swimming baths and Cottonmill Lane. Its boundary would have been between the river, Old London Road, Cottonmill Lane and part of Thorpe Road.

The Holy Well was deeply respected in medieval times and folklore said that this was the place that Alban's head came to rest after being chopped off and rolling down the hill, but is more commonly reputed to have been where a spring appeared when Alban prayed for water.

It was close to the Ver at Holywell that King Arthur's father Uther Pendragon was miraculously cured of almost fatal battle-inflicted wounds.

John Brompton a fifteenth century English chronicler recorded that he was severely wounded in the battles with the Saxons:

....Uter Pendragon, a British prince, had fought the

Left: *Holywell House from St Stephen's Road 1795. (MoS)*

Below: *Map of St Albans 1810 by J. Roper. Holywell House & its ornamental gardens and lake fed by the Ver can clearly be seen bottom right. (MoS)*

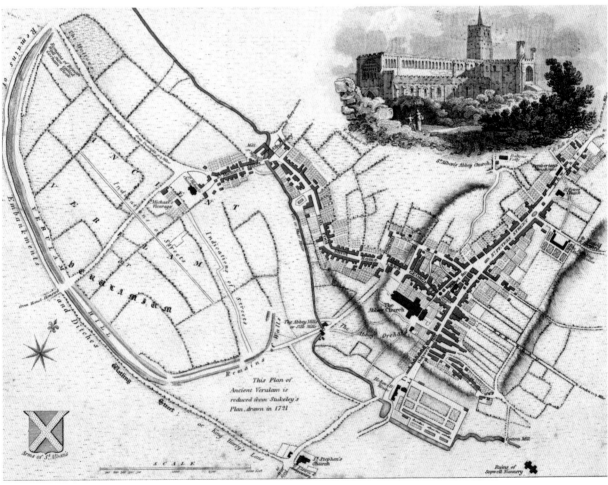

Actor portraying Uther Pendragon at the Holy Well, De Tany Court, Ver Valley Walks Launch 2011. (JBT)

Saxons in a great battle at this place, and received a dangerous wound: and by a long time confined to his bed: until at length he was cured by resorting to a well or spring not far distant from the City, at that time reputed salubrious; and for that reason, and for the cures thereby performed, esteemed holy; and blessed in a peculiar manner with the flavour of Heaven...

In Tudor times it was in the front garden of a dwelling where later Holywell House would stand, on the north bank of the Ver, facing the slope up to Belmont Hill. Although the Holy Well is shown on nineteenth century maps in the garden at the front of Holywell House, Charles Ashdowne's *History of St Albans* published in 1893, reveals that:

It is now remembered only as a muddy depression, sheltered by the remains of a dilapidated wall and a mournful specimen of blackthorn.

In the 1980s a well, thought to be eighteenth century, was excavated but there is no solid evidence of an earlier well except the medieval place name connected with Alban. The supposed site of the Holy Well still exists at De Tany Court, named after Richard de Tany who was granted land called Black Hide in the soke of Tyttenhanger during the thirteenth century, but is covered for safety reasons.

Near the Cotton Mill Bridge 1857. JH Buckingham (MoS)

Flooded allotments next to the river 1979. (MoS)

View of the allotments by the river, looking towards the Abbey 1980s. (JBT)

River Ver near Cotton Mill with St Albans Abbey before restoration, 1879. (AL)

The area running west from near the bottom of Holywell Hill to Cottonmill swimming baths in the east is known as Pocket Park. This area was developed in the early 1990s as an attractive riverside walk.

On the south side of the river was Pond Mead, and in the seventeenth century, as the name suggests, the land had many ponds on it. Today the allotments here still flood and become waterlogged during periods of heavy rain.

Chapter Seven

The Old Cotton Mill to Hedges Farm

*If you're weary, longing for a restful holiday – shun the crowds and spend
your leisure in a quiet way. Find some little river where the shady willows
lean – a river that goes wandering by meadows cool and green…It may not
be as thrilling as the music of the sea – but listen to the gentle water
flowing dreamily. No golden sands, no wheeling gulls, no waves, no rolling
tide – but you'll find rest and peace and beauty by the riverside.*

A Riverside Holiday- Anon

The name Cottonmill derives from the mill that once straddled the river here, with the former Green Lane by which the mill stood and so called for many hundreds of years, renamed Cottonmill Lane after its mill.

The Old Cotton Mills, St Albans. (MoS)

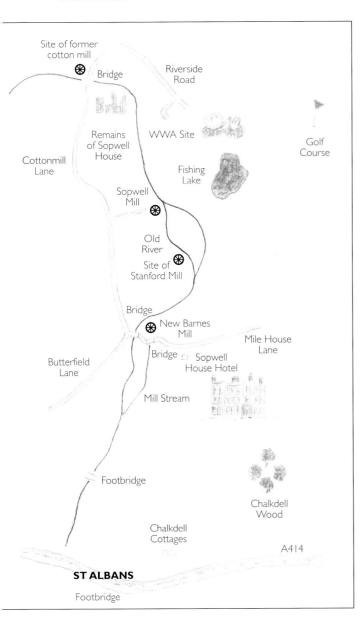

In the middle ages the Abbot of St Albans' granary was at Cell Barnes where the hospital once stood and he had two mills near Sopwell Nunnery; one was Sopwell Mill where Cottonmill Lane crossed the Ver and Stankfield Mill was said to be near where the old St Albans to Hatfield railway line crossed the river. Stank is an old word for a dam or to lay boards, supported by piles or struts at sides of watercourses to strengthen the banks in millstreams and leats for example and also a pond. It is possible Stankfield is a corruption of Stanford which is discussed later in the chapter. Both have now disappeared, the mill we now call Sopwell is of a later date and lies on the south side of the old railway.

From 1680 the former mill on the site of the present day sub aqua club was known as the Cotton Mill and a mill has been recorded on this site for many hundreds of years. From the early eighteenth century it was called 'The Paper Mills' and on the 1766 Andrews and Wren map of St Albans the River Ver was called the Verulam or Muse and a waterworks is shown here; it became a pumping station for the town and was known as the 'water house'. From 1768-79 the mill was used for polishing diamonds and run by Henry Porter.

Another record of bringing water to the town is a 1777 Final Agreement between David Dean and Sir

Alexander Stirling, Baronet, Mary his wife, and John Stirling esq. This mentions two messuages, one mill, one water engine…two acres of land covered in water in St Albans and Sopwell, and the liberty of breaking two acres of land to lay pipes and trunks for conveying water to the Borough of St Albans. Consideration of £100.

In 1794 the Cotton Mill was used as a meeting place for a religious group and a Sunday school for twenty children. By 1810 cotton began to be produced again at the mill that bridged the river. It continued to produce cotton for several decades run by various leaseholders and by 1840 was employing up to sixty people. In 1803 it is referred to by the antiquary H.G. Oldfield as a cotton mill at a small distance from the south side of the old road to London. Until the late nineteenth century cotton wicks for candles along with Berlin wool used for needlework were made at the mill and the 1839 Pigot's *Directory* lists Henry Dupree as a candlewick manufacturer.

A bridge over the river near the mill has been there for many centuries and can be seen in its various forms in the images here. Six years after

being repaired in 1825, a new wooden one was built with a brick structure replacing it just before the mill and river became public swimming baths.

Perambulation of Borough boundaries followed a route that had been in existence since 1635 and was recorded in the town's Corporation Records. When perambulating the boundary of the city in 1804, Thomas Baskerfield the Mayor was required to pass the mace across the river through the Cotton Mill. The Mayor fished the Ver to re assert his mayoral right to do so. In 1863 as well as reporting once again that the Mayor fished the river, costs were mentioned of £4 5s 6d, paid to Charles Owen for *"planking over river and ditches".*

In 1888, the Corporation took over the baths on the site of the former mill. There is evidence that a makeshift swimming pool existed on this site before this date which is believed to have been in the river. The 23 August 1890 edition of the *Herts Advertiser* contained a letter of complaint about this 'new' amenity:

Anyone who visits the present institution in Cotton Mill Lane, dignified with the title of the Albans Swimming Baths will know what a dreadful travesty they are. A beginner who has to touch the bottom to learn is in fear that at any moment his feet may be cut by sharp flint-stone, or else in the next minute he may be up to his knees in mud. The accommodation for diving is wretched, and the wooden planks which line the sides are covered with slime and are most unpleasant.

However fifteen years later a proper swimming baths had been built by George Ford and Mr Bushell at a cost of £1275, it opened on 29 July 1905 and was one of the first outdoor swimming baths at that time with over 6000 people coming to use the pool in the first year, although mixed bathing wasn't allowed until 1924. It was 105ft long by 30ft wide; with a depth of 6ft to 3ft 6ins. Water for the pool was originally taken from the Ver and it was only open for use between May and September in the early 1930s. Many children and adults learnt to swim here and several swimming events took place.

The sub aqua club has used the site since the 1970s. The mill no longer exists and the local swimming baths are at Westminster Lodge.

The Old Cotton Mill footbridge 1853.
JH Buckingham. (MoS)

Nineteenth-century Cotton Mill and bridge.
JH Buckingham. (MoS)

Children playing in the river, Cottonmill Lane 1900.
(Unknown)

The river seems very wide in this image from Ted Banfield's collection marked 'Swimming at Sopwell 1930s' but there is no acknowledgement. Maybe someone out there recognises these young ladies? (JBT)

The Old Cottonmill Swimming Baths. (JBT)

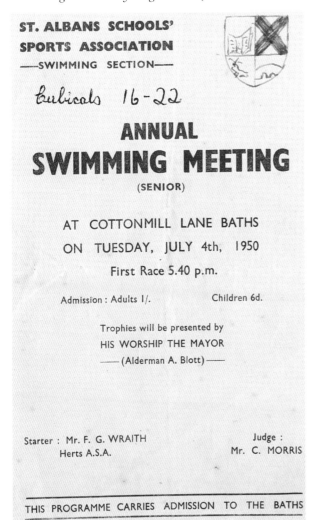

ST. ALBANS SCHOOLS'
SPORTS ASSOCIATION
—SWIMMING SECTION—

Eubicals 16-22

ANNUAL
SWIMMING MEETING
(SENIOR)

AT COTTONMILL LANE BATHS
ON TUESDAY, JULY 4th, 1950
First Race 5.40 p.m.

Admission : Adults 1/.   Children 6d.

Trophies will be presented by
HIS WORSHIP THE MAYOR
—(Alderman A. Blott)—

Starter : Mr. F. G. WRAITH   Judge :
Herts A.S.A.   Mr. C. MORRIS

THIS PROGRAMME CARRIES ADMISSION TO THE BATHS

A 1950 Swimming Event Programme which Ted Banfield took part in. (JBT)

Sopwell Lane is one of the oldest streets in St Albans. First mentioned as early as 1328, it leads to Sopwell Mill and Sopwell House, and was a principal route to London until the end of the eighteenth century.

A deed of 1362 spoke of Sopwell Lane near Sopwell Mill. Considering both the logic and topography, such as the location of the bridge and Sopwell Priory, Cottonmill Lane may once have been a continuation of Sopwell Lane. By 1635, it was the way to Sopwell House and by 1766 the road to Shenley Hill.

Just south of the Ver, in Cottonmill Lane, stand the ruins of the mansion of Sopwell House, built on the site of Sopwell Nunnery.

In the twelfth century, two religious women made a poor house constructed from the boughs of trees covered with bark, near the forest called Eywood, not far from the River Ver.

The ancient Eywood Forest stretched from the edge of St Albans to Park Street and Watling Street to St Julian's and had belonged to the Abbey before the Norman Conquest, being restored back to the Abbey by Abbot Paul (1077-93). It is one of the oldest place names in the area (twelfth century Eywoda) and means a well-watered wooded land.

Here the women began a life of fasting and prayer, and happily continued their religion practising chastity and surviving on a simple diet of bread and water. After many years their laudable behaviour was made known to Geoffrey de Gorham, Abbot of the Abbey of St Albans and he built a cell here commanding that convenient houses be erected for the women, they should be clothed after the manner of nuns and live there under the order of St Benedict and by the assistance of Mary the Blessed Mother of God, to whom it was dedicated. He gave certain possessions and lands to support their honest, though exiled life.

This house was called Sopwell from a neighbouring well where the women are said to have drunk and dipped their bread. Moreover the Abbot, careful of the honour and safety of his nuns, ordered that they should be enclosed in their house under lock and bolt and the seal of the Abbot, and none should be taken into their house but a select and limited number of 13 virgins. He gave to them a churchyard, which he caused to be dedicated, and appointed that none but those of the nunnery should be buried there.

The nuns continued to live their lowly existence locked in the house until Abbot Micheal de Mentmore visited Sopwell and enforced stricter rules. By the fifteenth century Sopwell was very wealthy and fashionable enough for the Duchess of Clarence to be admitted to the priory. It is thought that in 1524 when Anne Boleyn sought peace in the country she joined the nuns for a short time. It has even been said that Henry married Anne here in 1533, but Bletchley Hall, Norfolk and Calais in France, also lay claim to this important historical event. The priory was suppressed in 1537 along with others in the country.

One of the earlier prioresses was Dame Juliana Berners born c1388. Referred to in the original book as Dame Julyans Barnes, she is said to be the author of one of the earliest books to be printed in St. Albans, and the first book to be printed in England about field sports.

The Bokys of Haukyng and Huntyng or the *Boke of St. Albans* as it is also known was first published in 1486 and was a surprising publication for a prioress. The book is of three treatises written to guide *"gentill men and honest persones"* in the arts necessary to an English gentleman; hawking, hunting and heraldry. A second edition published in 1496 added another treatise on fishing and Juliana's surname is now spelt Bernes.

Field sports, about which you would not expect a prioress to write, were popular in the fifteenth century. How a solitary nun knew the sporting terms used by huntsmen and falconers is a mystery although she may have been hawking or at least witnessed the sport first hand before she entered the nunnery as it is written on a flyleaf of a copy of the book originally owned by a Bishop Moore:

This Booke was made by Lady Julian Berners, daughter of Sr. James Berners, of Berners Roding, in Eassex, Knight, and sister to Richard Lord Berners. She was Lady Prioresse of Sopwell, a nunnery neere St Albans, in weh Abby of St Albans this was first printed in 1486.

Therefore she may have come from a wealthy family where these sports would have been practised with some frequency.

Part of the book is about elements to which hawks are prone, including worms, cramps and stones. The cures were often bizarre, including skin of snake, lard of goat, and droppings of sea birds. The chapters on hunting are written in rhyme and are a collection of where, how and when to hunt. These chapters show some evidence of having been written by Dame Juliana Berners, but the parts of the book on angling are thought to be by another author. These are more entertaining and could have been written by an idle monk who much preferred the peaceful pastime of fishing to the weariness of hawking and hunting. The book gives instruction on how to make rods, floats, hooks and line. It is concluded with a request to avoid selfishness and not to fish in a poor man's water, nor

fish for filthy lucre but only for sport. Oh how angling has changed today!

Excavation has shown that Sopwell Priory occupied the same site as the later surviving ruin, which is part of a large sixteenth century house. The earliest feature found was a building with an east apse, presumably Abbot Geoffrey's church, but no associated structures were identified. Perhaps late in the thirteenth century the priory was reconstructed on the usual plan, with a cloister and a larger church built on the site of the apsidal chapel but extending much further east.

Dressed stone with its dating evidence was systematically removed during the Dissolution, when the buildings passed to Sir Richard Lee, the Royal engineer and surveyor, and were converted into a private mansion. This retained the monastic ground plan with a hall, church and courtyard succeeding the cloister. He called his new house 'Lee Hall'. Towards the end of Lee's life (1575) the house was totally reconstructed, this time on a formal and symmetrical plan of the kind then fashionable, but it was never completed. It was passed to his daughter Mary Coningsby upon his death and eventually in 1669 it was sold to Sir Harbottle Grimston.

The north-facing hall block linked two substantial wings, each two rooms wide, and it is the west wing that largely survives today. Ten fine stone medallions from the house depicting Roman Emperors were purchased by the Lord of Salisbury Manor now Salisbury Hall and are still there today.

Circumstantial evidence supporting this was obtained at Salisbury Hall, where excavation by the owner unearthed, together with two more medallions, moulded door jamb stones which are thought to have come from Sopwell. Sir Jeremiah Snow was rebuilding at Salisbury Hall at about the same time as Sopwell was partially demolished by Sir Harbottle Grimston who also transferred some features to Gorhambury.

Parts of the house were inhabited up until the late 1700s and one of its outbuildings was used as a scrap yard and motorbike repair shop until the 1960s.The remains of Lee's house are furthest from the river and today only a single wing, parts of the Great Hall, some of the boundary wall and part of the gatehouse can be seen.

In my early teens an annual adventure for me and a group of girlfriends was to spend the early part of Halloween evening at Sopwell ruins or 'the spuins' as we always called them. Wrapped up against the chilly night, we would take sweets and crisps and sit and try and out scare each other with spooky tales. One particular evening is etched in my mind. It was not only freezing cold but a very thick mist had risen from the river and had cloaked the whole neighbourhood in an eerie, silent miasma. This of course greatly enhanced the creepy tales we took turns in reciting and every time a fox barked or an unrecognised noise cut through the fog we jumped out of our skins! We had been there an hour or so and not only were we by now freezing cold, but had also run out of supplies! I was the last to tell my ghostly tale and was just getting everyone's hairs standing well and truly on end when we heard a strange unearthly noise, piercing the mist from far too near for comfort. We were deathly quiet and listened for what seemed like ages but was probably only 30 seconds or so, but nothing? I carried on and a minute or so later there it was again, seemingly nearer and therefore much scarier – we all shot up and using the one torch we had between us we stood close together and shone the torch through the thickening fog – suddenly a white shapeless form drifted across a gap between the ruins making the noise we had all heard earlier. Being girls of course we screamed our heads off and were just gathering our belongings ready to make a hasty retreat when we heard loud raucous laughter – realising that ghosts weren't renowned for splitting their sides with merriment we took our torch and crept towards the bit of ruin from behind where it seemed to be coming from. There falling around on top of a white sheet with tears streaming from their eyes and holding their stomachs were three boys from the year below us at school, seeing us standing there only made them laugh all the harder! We called them pathetic children and a few names not appropriate for a book such as this and went on our way, leaving them giggling and actually congratulating each other for a job well done! We found out later that they had overheard us planning the evening in our dinner break and thought it would be a wheeze to really give us something to remember Halloween by! Of course we didn't let them get away with it – but that's another story! (The author)

Today, after many hours of work by the local community, the green space surrounding the ruins has been awarded two green flags. These provide a national benchmark for the best green spaces in the country, in association with the government's plans to protect green spaces and launch physical activity initiatives throughout the UK.

It is said that the remains of sewers found between the sites of early religious places and nearby watercourses were looked upon as subterranean passageways by which monks travelled considerable distances underground on errands of wickedness- much believed by local people in the old days.

At the beginning of the twentieth century Rev. H.R. Wilton Hall wrote in his paper on Sopwell Nunnery about his belief in such underground passages in St Albans:

....less than a century ago one was known to exist between St Albans monastery and the River Ver. As the Ver flows between the sites of the monastery and the nunnery, sewers may account for the passages, and well know scandals in both houses, coupled with a love of the marvellous, sufficiently account for the legend that St Albans monastery and Sopwell nunnery, some three-quarters of a mile apart, were connected by an underground passage which must of necessity have passed under the bed of the River Ver!

Indeed the thirteenth century chronicler Matthew Paris writes that tunnels under Verulamium were demolished by the eighth Abbot of St Albans, Ealdred:

Ealdred ransacking the ancient cavities of the old city, which was called Werlamcestre, overturned, and filled

Two women sitting beside Sopwell ruins, 1855. (JBT)

Ruins of Richard Lee's Sopwell House from the river 1875-1900. (DH)

up all the rough broken places, and the streets, with the passages running under ground, and covered over with solid arches, some of which passed under the water of the Werlam river, which was once very large, and flowed about the city, he pulled down, filled up, or stopped; because they were the lurking holes of thieves, night walkers and whores; but the fosses of the city, and certain caverns, to which felons and fugitives repaired as places of shelter, from the thick wood around, he levelled as much as ever he could.

South of Sopwell ruins the high arched bridge built in 1865 for the old St Albans to Hatfield railway crosses the Ver. Although from Hatfield to London Road all the bridges had been built wide enough to allow for eventual doubling of the rail-track, the bridge over the river here was of one-track width only.

Just beyond the bridge towards the Abbey Station there is a pedestrian underpass, and on the London

The old St. Albans to Hatfield railway bridge 1985. (BWHS)

Before construction of Riverside Road Fishing Lakes showing old watercress beds. (VAC)

Road side a small arched bridge that fed water between the two watercress beds each side of the railway. The last passenger train ran across the Ver in 1951, and today it is part of a popular walkway from St Albans to Hatfield.

The earth track between the river and London Road is of small significance today but was once the main road to St Albans from London. London Road was moved to its present route in 1793, but the old road remains a public right of way.

Looking from the railway bridge towards the golf course can be seen the site of a former watercress bed. This was abandoned for many years until in the late 1960s Verulam Angling Club transformed what had become a rubbish dump into a man-made private angling lake. It was designed for the maximum of bank space with the minimum of water and has been extensively landscaped. Many hundreds of hours a year are spent by members on improving the wildlife habitat of this area. Kingfisher, heron, dabchick, reed warbler and many other birds and animals are now present. The lake holds a good head of fish including carp, tench, roach, perch and trout.

The club was formed in October 1934 and one of its first waters was the gravel pits at Moor Mill which was rented for 2/6 per month and cost £15 to be stocked with 300 fish. In 1936, a second lake was rented at Moor Mill at £5 per annum.

The club was involved in the netting of Verulamium lakes from 1939 until the 1960s along with other fishing clubs and volunteers. They were also issued with 36 permits in 1949 to fish the lake at Verulamium on the condition that any pike caught were taken away and no fishing was allowed between the hours of 11am and 6pm.

On the other side of the old railway track in Riverside Road, once called Longmire Road which had once run through park land belonging to Sopwell Priory, lies the site of the old allotments and former location of the watercress beds previously run for several generations by the Pinnock family. This area is now home to a wonderful oasis of peace and calm, in the form of a nature reserve of roughly 4 acres packed full of fauna and flora. The site is run by the Watercress Wildlife Association (WWA), a voluntary

View of the Abbey across the golf-links from VAC Riverside Road Lakes 1980s. (JBT)

Riverside Road from the old railway track 1980s. (JBT)

The Reserve showing the remains of the wooden posts that supported the boards in the cress beds. (WWA)

community group and registered charity, it was formed in 1991 by local residents who were concerned about the future of the site, which since the watercress beds had closed in the 1960s, had become a neglected, overgrown dumping ground for rubbish. During this time, as the water table dropped, the river was often dry and boreholes which had originally fed the cress beds dried up.

A lease was granted to the WWA by St Albans District Council, who owns the land, after they proposed to develop the site as a wildlife conservation area. It was officially opened in September 1992 by the broadcaster, botanist and environmental campaigner David Bellamy.

In the ten years that followed and after much hard work by volunteers, the site was awarded the status of Local Nature Reserve, gaining many awards along the way.

With the help of the Herts and Middlesex Wildlife Trust, a management plan was devised to help look after the site.

The Mere, which was once the main watercress bed fed by boreholes at the northern end was cleared of rubbish and silt and the water now exits by a tunnel and dam system under the Alban Way and back into the Ver. This lake has been known to dry up during periods of drought as in 1997 and 2006, however a variety of aquatic life can be found in and around the water when it re-establishes itself after these dry spells.

The site also includes a butterfly meadow, spinney, orchard, marsh and the pyghtle (a small enclosure of land).

The photo below shows the flag iris, an attractive, long lived and common perennial and a lover of wet soils especially the margins of rivers, lakes and ponds. Established populations spread by means of rhizomes and the seed, which floats in water and colonizes new sites.

Aerial view of opening and David Bellamy giving a helping hand at the opening of the WWA site in 1992. (WWA)

Yellow iris (Iris pseudacorus) *at the WWA site. (JBT)*

The small flood stream between the river and the lake with its stony bed is the habitat of the non native American signal crayfish, which have survived and multiplied throughout most of England over the past few decades as a result of man's carelessness. It is found throughout most of the Ver and is thought to have wiped out the native crayfish with a virus it carries, called crayfish plague (*Aphanomycles Astaci*).

The river between here and Park Street was redirected, narrowed and reinforced with local chalk, flints and wood in the twelfth century to allow a build up of water for the mills at Sopwell and Park Street and to help dry out the marshland in the area.

On the west of the river stands the former Sopwell Mill now Sopwell Mill Farm which also once went under the names of Soppewell or Sapwel. For centuries it was part of the Gorhambury Estate. The existing three storey building and adjoining mill house dates back to the mid seventeenth century and was originally a corn mill although there is evidence of a mill here as far back as the thirteenth century. It

Above and below: *Spring 2010 – the Reserve as a flourishing and verdant wildlife haven. (JBT)*

Behind Sopwell Mill, Abbey in the distance. JH Buckingham. (MoS)

is said that a thousand eels a year came from here and other mills south along the Ver when they belonged to the Abbey.

Sopwell Mill also called 'The Old Fulling Mill', stood below Eywood in 1247. It was built on or near the site of an existing mill which was mentioned in 1381 around the time of the Peasants Revolt with its 'Flotegatestrem and Mullestrem'. Also at this time the fulling mill was 'below the Abbey'.

By 1649 it had become one of Hertfordshire's finest silk mills and it is recorded that a Robert Stanhard was convicted of stealing cloth from the mill. By 1691 it was grinding corn again, thereafter in the late eighteenth century it ground corn alone then was converted to paper making, a method of producing paper in rolls instead of single sheets a process imported from France, before reverting back to corn grinding.

Alfred Climance was the miller in 1861 but after a fire destroyed the mill in 1868 it was occupied by a miller and farmer by the name of Edmund Hinton who died in 1883. Between the fire and when the next occupier George Butterfield, who had previously been a miller in Buckinghamshire moved in around 1884, it had been rebuilt in a different place a short distance upstream. The 1891 Census shows George living at the mill with his wife Eliza and five children ranging in age between five and twenty-one years old. The eldest son, also called George was listed as a miller along with his father and ran two bakeries and a dairy in the town. Then known as Sopwell Mill Farm, there was also a small-holding sited on the adjoining land.

In Brian Waters 1960s' book *Thirteen Rivers to the Thames*, he writes of a 'Miller Butterfield', which is thought to be George Butterfield Senior:

Miller Butterfield enjoyed a river fish on his table no less than his riparian neighbour on the watercress beds below his farm enjoyed an evening beer. The cress gatherer had a small boat and a pitchfork for his occupation, and frequently speared a good trout....and sometimes a pike, for which the miller gave him a shilling which was quickly exchanged for six pints of good Hertfordshire ale. Now there is no mill, no trout, no boat and beer costs more than a shilling a pint!

On a freezing winter's night in 1907 tragedy struck when George was clearing ice from the waterwheel and a falling icicle hit him on the head striking him blind and deaf and never able to work again. He died in 1927. After the accident the mill was taken over by his son George.

By 1931, after being occupied by the Butterfield family for 47 years, the mill was no longer profitable and the lease was surrendered. A sale of 'farming stock, corn mill tools and equipment' took place in September and the family moved to Ramsbury Road. Butterfield Lane, off Cottonmill Lane overlooking the River Ver, was named after the family.

The 1939 *Pigots Directory* shows Samuel Smith as the miller who continued to grind corn until the early 1940s when small scale mills such as Sopwell were gradually ousted by the larger roller-mills such as New Barnes. Between 1943 and 1993 it was leased by

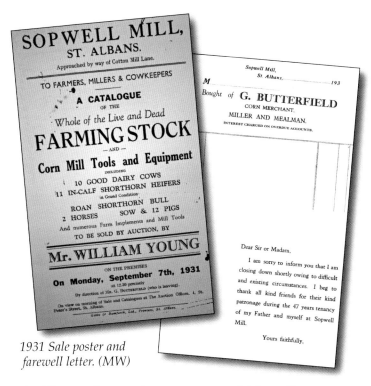

1931 Sale poster and farewell letter. (MW)

the Blower sisters who ran a successful boarding kennels in the grounds of the mill along with a pet shop in London Road.

Now a private house and Grade II listed in 1998, at the time of listing it was said to:

...have a water course and wheel pit to the east end of the site and a gabled sack hoist canopy to centre bay. Against the ground floor wall, a wide, 3 segment low breast water wheel with socketed outer and intermediate cast iron wheel frames with sheet metal buckets bolted to timber bearers carried by the sockets. Rack and pinion gear attached to timber sluice gateway on north side of wheelpit. Stone floor with 3 pairs of stones, but no associated machinery or fittings. Metal gear wheel attached to water wheel shaft engages bevel gearing to drive secondary shaft with further bevel gearing providing power for vertical shafts driving stones above. A near complete example of a mid C19 water-powered corn mill with attached dwelling, retaining its water wheel and primary and secondary drive machinery.

Some of the machinery and the great wheel of 13 ft in diameter and 6ft 6inches wide are still intact.

George Butterfield, last miller at Sopwell Mill. (MW)

The Butterfield family with friends at Sopwell Mill 1920s. Left to right – Bob Clark, Grace Butterfield, Kate Clark, Friend, Fred Fitzjohn, Daisy and Elsie Butterfield. Fred and Grace spent many a romantic hour rowing to and fro between the mill and Park Street during their courting days. (MW)

Two views of Sopwell Mill. (MW)

The river at this point goes round the mill and under a small bridge to the water meadows on the west of the river.

East of the river is Verulam golf course, built on parkland originally leased from Sopwell House estate. The club was formed in 1905 originally with a nine-hole course which was developed into an 18 hole course in 1909 with the lease of a further 136 acres. Designed by James Braid, a renowned golf course designer, the official opening was on 27 April 1912 when Samuel Ryder was Captain. A local wealthy seed merchant and lover of golf, he donated the Ryder Cup in 1926 and to this day, every two years Europe takes on the USA for it. The entrance fee in 1912 was two guineas and visitors could play a mid-week round for 1s 6d or 7½p. The development of the course included raising the riverbank for the fairways and greens. There are still small spinneys of trees, which are said to be remains of the great Eywood Forest.

On the west side of the river below the water meadow is an intermittent spring fed lake, which was once a watercress bed and lined with walkways to tend the watercress. The springs run from the lake but do not immediately enter the river. They run parallel to the river in their own stream as far as New Barnes Mill joining the Ver just before the road bridge.

Around 1085, a Norman Abbot redirected the Ver from Sopwell to Park Street to give a good head of water for the mills at Sopwell, Park Street and Bricket Wood.

There was once another mill between Sopwell Mill and New Barnes Mill, shown on early maps of the area. Stanford Mill appears on several maps from the seventeenth century, one from 1600 'St Stephens Plan of Eywood' showing the ground plans of the mill and a mid-seventeenth century map of 'The Manor of Sopwell in possession of Robert Sadleir Esq' are shown opposite and over page. These maps show formal gardens to the west of Sopwell House with an orchard or garden to the north and the Ver flowing on the west and south. The cultivation and use of the land is depicted in different colours and figures of men and animals showing different aspects of farm work ie ploughing, sowing etc. The mill is sited in 'The Mead' on what is titled the 'old river' and 'below the Paper mill' (Sopwell Mill) which is to the north-west of the house. There is also a mention of a 'New Barnes House'. This map shows an 'Iland' (island), between Stanford Mill and New Barnes Mill between the millstream and river which on the 1890 OS map shows fishponds.

In Chauncey's *The Historical Antiquities of Hertfordshire* he mentions the mill:
In the 33rd year of the reign of Henry VIII (1539) Anthony Denny Esq should have to him and his heirs, all the mannor or Lordship of the King of Parkbury... late in the occupation of John Coningsby... the two water-Mills called Park-mill and the Moor Mill, with all water-courses and profits belonging to them...Appurtenances, in the Parishes of St Stephens, Park...belonging to the Manor of

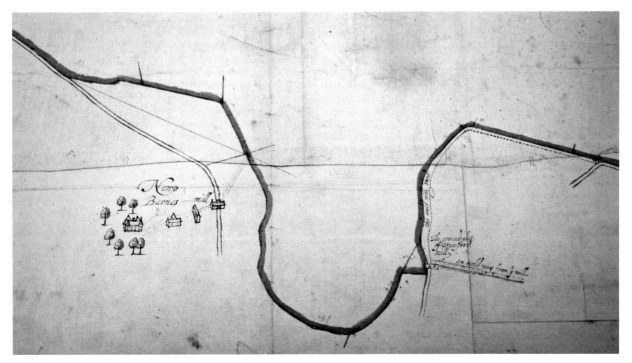

The ground plan of Stanford Mill shown on a 1600 St Stephens Plan of Eywood. (Permission from the Earl of Verulam)

Parkbury…except Cowley Mill, Stanford-Mill, Sopwell Mill…

Although it is also recorded in the Gorhambury Estate records that in 1538 and 1540 respectively the King granted the Manor of Sopwell and Sopwellbury to Richard Lee:

The King grants to Richard Lee the Manor of Sopwell Bury, some time parcel of St Albans Monestary and….Sopwell Myll, Cowley Mill and Staneford Myll….

And in 1540 the King for £477 3s 9d grants to Richard Lee:

The manor of Sopwell Bury….and Sopwell Myll, and Eywood Parke, Parkmeade, Cowley Myll, Stankford Myll….to hold as one twentieth of a knights fee at 53s.1/4d rent with 6s.8d for Sopwell Bury.

By 1581 the two manors were in the name of Humphrey Coningsby and in 1603 the year of his marriage, it had passed to Richard Sadleir, a grandson of Richard Lee.

….re Sopwell Manor and lands, and advowson of St Stephens, and the site of Manor House….Sopwell Mill at New Barnes…a slip of ground environed with water between New Mill and Warren, the massuage lately erected called New Barnes, the old house called New Barnes Farm House and Eywood Field and meadow (Myll Mead or Close east of the river).

By 1627 the manor was settled on Robert Sadleir whose name appears on the map shown below and after whose family a local road is named today.

Sixteenth century Gorhambury records mention Sopwell, Cowley and Stankford Myll. Stankford may be a mis-spelling although there is also mentioned a Stankfield Mill, situated near where New Barnes Mill stands today which was rebuilt 1326-35.

Old documents are a wealth of information and show fascinating and sometimes long lost building and land names as this 1662 Bargain and Sale between Robert and Edward 'Sadlier' in the first and second instance and Joshua Lomax a gentleman of St Albans in the third instance shows:

Robert Sadlier and his son Edward for 5s grant to Edward Sadlier of London, his heirs etc forever, the manors of Sopwell Sopwell Bury and Newlands, with advowson of St Stephens and lands viz. The capital messuage or manor house called Sopwell, the close before the gate, Wall Croft, Bings Orchard and Pond Meade, Little Lawnes, Wood Field, Hill Field, Great Lawnes and Little Warren, St Julians Fields, Eywood and Dry Grounds, Wallnuttree Field and Long Ladders, Betchfield, Bonnace and Newstock Field, Eywoods, Eywoods Hill Grounds, Rush Mead, Nine Acres, Triangle Field and Mill Field, The Paper Mill and two acres near, Paper Mill Meadow, New Barnes Mill, and ten acres near, New Barnes and ninety acres adjoining New Barnes Meade, and all other manors and tenements of said Robert and Edward Sadlier, for purpose of making a recovery, against John Lomax.

Again the Gorhambury records give details of the Sadleir family:

The Sadleirs of Sopwell derived from Sir Ralph Sadleir, Knight Banneret….his second son Edward, married Ann, daughter and coheiress of Sir Richard Lee of Sopwell, and had Richard, upon when his aunt Mary, nee Lee, the other daughter and coheiress of Sir Richard Lee, being childless, settled Sopwell in 1603, Richard Sadleir by his wife Joyce Honywood had Thomas (who settled in Ireland), several other sons and a son and heir Robert, who heavily mortgages Sopwell. After his death his daughter Helen, wife of Thomas Saunders, sold Sopwell to Sir Harbottle Grimston in 1669 for £8550.

The fact that records for Stanford Mill only seem to be present for around 150 years may mean it was a small mill used for work such as cutting wood for the house, especially as there were several other large mills nearby or it could have been destroyed by fire, or the flow of the river just wasn't powerful enough to support three mills in such a small area.

In 1691 a lease by Sir Samuel Grimston to Thomas Dagnall, a millwright from Abbots Langley mentions a decayed mill house and paper mill on which £200 is to be spent rebuilding it as a corn mill and dwelling place. Maybe this was Stanford Mill or if not maybe Sopwell Mill was rebuilt with no need for a further mill so close to it. In 1702 he was mentioned in a lease as Thomas Dagnall of 'New Mills', so it seems he did indeed carry out the building of a corn mill.

In 1736 the St Albans Court Rolls show an indictment of Robert Brantham *"for taking one trout, value 12d at a place called the Paper Mills, in the Parish of St Peters…in the manor of Sopwell, which manor and the right of fishing in all streams therein is the freehold and property of Samuel Grimston esq"*.

Sopwell is in a Conservation Area at a crossing point of the river which runs north south and with a boundary of water meadows, agricultural land and woodland. Near this point on the riverbank stands the Grade II listed three-storey Sopwell House, a country club, spa and hotel surrounded by twelve acres of grounds within the Conservation Area.

Originally known as New Barnes House, a building has stood on this spot since the sixteenth century when it was owned by Sir Ralph Sadleir, but there is the possibility of an earlier building incorporated on the site. It was home to a Duchess called Alice, a member of the distinguished Dudley family. Where Verulam golf course now stands was once part of the extensive grounds. In the eighteenth century Edward Strong, a master mason who had worked on many great buildings including Blenheim Palace and St Paul's Cathedral, crafted several of the houses' stone details.

During the mid 1800s it was the home of the wealthy philanthropic widow Isabella Worley, whose many personal donations to St Albans included Christ Church on Verulam Road and a former

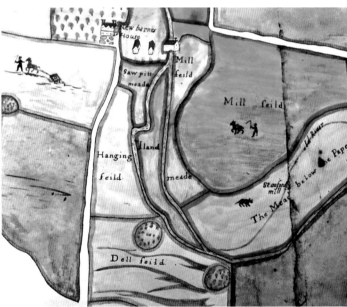

1677 map and close up showing Stanford Mill and the old river – these need to be viewed upside down to make sense. (Permission from the Earl of Verulam)

Near the fishpond, New Barnes (MoS)

religious meeting place, the Wooden Room in Lattimore Road.

The house was extended in Victorian times and in the early twentieth century it was leased to Prince Louis of Battenburg, later to become Marquess of Milford Haven. His daughter Alice married Prince Andrew of Greece and their son Philip married Queen Elizabeth II in 1947 to become Prince Philip, Duke of Edinburgh.

During WWI it became a Remount Depot for Army horses. The War Office, on behalf of the regular artillery, requisitioned horses from their owners – £30

Remount Depot, Sopwell. (JBT)

for a troop horse and £70 for an officer's charger. They played a vital role in the victory of the allied armed forces. A total of 8 millions horses, mules and donkeys died during the war, around 2 million from Britain, many as horrifically as the soldiers whose life often depended on them. The two postcards seen here are from this period.

After WWII the house belonged to the Verulam family, later becoming a home for the elderly then eventually a hotel which has regularly been used by football teams including the English national team before international football events.

I spent many an hour as a girl in the 1970s waiting outside the hotel hoping to glimpse one of the players from Liverpool FC, a team I have supported since I was nine when dad first took me to see them play Arsenal at Highbury. I managed to get many autographs of legends such as Kevin Keegan and 'super sub' David Fairclough and on one very early morning expedition, sitting outside the front of the hotel, manager Bob Paisley must have heard me and my friend – the only ones there at the time – chatting as the next thing we knew two cups of very welcome tea arrived for us! We shouted our thanks and he waved at us and thanked us for coming – a memory that will stay with me always.

There is little left of the former nineteenth century Sopwell Home Farm and its outbuildings. Some have been converted to Sopwell Mews and

accommodation and staff buildings for Sopwell House Hotel. The car park is situated on the former farmyard where as a child I went to feed the pigs that resided there over the little old brick wall by the river that still exists to this day, with pockets crammed full of acorns collected from local trees in the surrounding fields.

There is also an early eighteenth century Grade II listed barn and attached former stable on the east side of the earlier farm. A seventeenth century timber-framed, weather-boarded barn to the south of New Barnes Mill has a large in-filled cart entry on its north-west side and was once used for threshing wheat. It is currently used for private business.

In the drought of 1976, although there were isolated pools on the river above this point, the springs here kept bubbling away and maintained a small movement of water between this point and the Colne.

The river above New Barnes Mill showing 'wild rhubarb' – August 1939. (JBT)

New Barnes Mill when owned by the Co-operative Wholesale Society – the mill from the back showing the boiler house, back of mill, screen room and the old millstream, now covered by the car park, August 1939. (JBT)

Audrey Wadowska daughter of the renowned photographer Arthur Melbourne Cooper by the river at Sopwell bridge, Cottonmill Lane. The view is similar today (MoS)

Sopwell Bridge over the River Ver with its attractive brick parapets seen in the photo above is thought to be late eighteenth century. The parapet wall to the millstream is built of Luton grey brick and dates from the late nineteenth century.

Much seen at Sopwell, Butterbur, also known as bogshorns, bog rhubarb and butter-dock this moisture loving native wildflower, common along the Ver, has pale pink flowers forming a conical shape head from March-May followed by fluffy white seeds. The large kidney shape leaves which can grow up to a metre follow with the plant reaching up to 120cm.

Once called the Plague flower and Pestilence wort it was used in the middle ages as a treatment for the disease as described by Henry Lytea a sixteenth century botanist in his *Niewe Herball*, "a soveraigne medicine against the plague". It has also been used to reduce fevers and as an anti-convulsive with the large leaves used to wrap butter in to keep it cool. The herbalist Culpepper called it "a great preserver of the heart and reviver of the spirits".

A rich source of nectar for bees it is also home to the plant's very own Butterbur moth.

The site of the four-storey New Barnes Mill, previously called Cowley Mill and also confusingly Sopwell Mill is said to date back to at least the twelfth century although an earlier mill is thought to have occupied the site.

In *The History of the County of Hertford Vol. 2* it says:

There were two mills in the parish of St. Peter from the beginning of the twelfth century. They were called Sopwell or Cowley Mill and Stankfield Mill and belonged to the monastery of St. Albans till its dissolution. After this Henry VIII granted these two and Cowley Mill to Sir Richard Lee and they descended with his other property to his daughter Mary. Sopwell Mill, apparently later, took the name of Newbarns, by which it is known now, and Stankfield Mill has become Cotton Mill.

On the 1768 Hares map New Barnes Mills and surrounding land is marked as being owned by Robert New Esq.

The 1850s saw the mill run by Cannon William Smith, Miller & Farmer.

The present group of buildings date from reconstruction in the 1890s when it was converted from the water mill owned by Thomas Hill and a

'The Old New Barnes Mill' 1895. H Winter. (MoS)

New Barnes Mill and loading shed August 1939. (JBT)

Butterbur (Petasites hybridus) Sopwell, March 2011. (JBT)

turbine installed which was in use until the 1960s. The river was diverted under the mill and the mill wheels were completely enclosed.

In the early twentieth century a boiler house was erected as seen in the photo on page 117, to house a steam generator, later to be replaced by electricity from an oil powered generator.

In the 1920s the British Flour Research Committee operated the mill by electricity and it was run 24 hours a day producing up to 1200 sacks a week. In 1931 the mill was acquired by the Co-operative Wholesale Society and flour was milled here until WWII after which it became an engineering works. The small single story building opposite was once the mill workers' canteen.

Although many alterations have taken place to accommodate small industries the main four-storey structure is still in its original state and its corn hoist protrusions at the top of the mill are still in evidence. The wheel no longer exists but the water course remains at the front of the building although

somewhat neglected. The car park at the rear was built where the millstream once was.

In 1795 Royal Assent was given for an Act of Parliament to allow the Rivers Verulam and Colne to be used as a basis for a canal link between the Grand Union Canal at Watford and St Albans. It was reported that *"The Verulam is the only stream with water sufficiently good and pure for the supply of London"*.

The proposed start and a terminal basin for the barges was to be built at Cottonmill near Sopwell Nunnery and to help the boats navigate the narrower parts of the rivers and unsuitable bends, modifications, straightening and by-passes were to be added with locks at Sopwell, New Barnes, Park Street and Moor Mill to help on the hillier parts of the landscape. Opposition to this was strong, especially by the farmers and landowners who would lose valuable farming land with very little in return. Eventually, opposition caused the plans to be dropped.

Set back from Cottonmill Lane near New Barnes

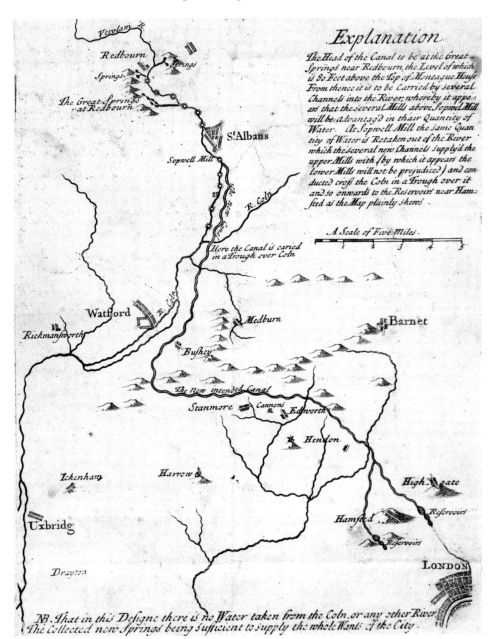

Map of proposed canal in Hertfordshire. (MoS)

Mill and next to the river are two former late Victorian estate cottages, Dhobi Lodge and Laundry Cottage, now residential properties. These were once the laundry and manager's house for the former Sopwell House. Interestingly the Royal Navy website has a section on service slang which mentions dhoby/dhobi as 'to have a wash or wash your clothes'!

The photos below show umbellifers from the Latin 'umbella' a sunshade. This can be a confusing group of plants, often seeming similar they include wild parsnip, hog weed, wild carrot, angelicas and cow parsley with a range of sizes from a few inches to several feet and colours from the purest of white to deep pink. Seen singularly or in frothy drifts they have flowers in umbels – thus their name – in which the flowers arise from the same point in the stem and have stalks of the same length, with a cluster of the youngest flowers at the centre.

After passing round New Barnes Mill, Laundry Cottage and Dhobi Lodge the River Ver winds across the ecologically important Sopwell Meadows towards Park Street. At this point the river has a gravel bottom but where it joins the millstream, often an unattractive and turbid channel, it is very prone to silting and often has little flow. The river carries on with a very high hedge of catkin and hawthorn and many oak trees on the west bank. The opposite bank

New Barnes Mill – from Sopwell Meadows August 1939. (JBT)

Dredging the river at Sopwell 1978 – Butterfield Lane to the left. (PSFS)

An umbellifer bud about to burst open and the lacey white flower which is so attractive to insects, both next to the river at Sopwell. (JBT)

New Barnes Mill and farm buildings where we used to feed the pigs with acorns 1970s. (JBT)

Near New Barnes Mill. (SC/HALS)

Looking towards New Barnes Mill and Dhobi and Laundry Cottages 2011. (JBT)

is open and has been built up to stop the adjoining meadows flooding.

Across the meadow can be seen Chalkdell Woods and the little old flint cottages. Looking back along the river at the north end of the woods, partially hidden behind great trees, can be seen the grand structure of Sopwell House, greatly added to in the past twenty years and between the converted barns of the old Sopwell Farm a view of New Barnes Mill.

Below is an extract from Mrs Terry's memoirs recorded by The Sopwell Residents Association. She lived near New Barnes Mill in the early 1930s:

(Looking at the sketch – not shown here)

....and here were the watercress beds and the lady opposite – I was telling her you were coming and she said her brother-in-law used to work there when he left school at 14 in the watercress beds and when the war came he wanted to join up but they wouldn't let him because he was an agricultural worker. And he used to drive the horses and carts to take the watercress and he said a bomb dropped on the watercress beds but I never heard anything of that. I was in the army during the war so I wouldn't have known what was going on but he reckoned that a bomb had dropped there.

Question: Which watercress beds?

Pinnock's. And here were the willows, sort of a

Top left: *Looking towards New Barnes Mill October 1921. (SC/ HAL)*

Top right: *The same view – the river on left meets with the millstream just down from New Barnes Mill looking towards Butterfield Lane 1980s. (JBT)*

Left: *Modern day view 2011 – these photos show that thankfully, some parts of the river remain virtually untouched across the years. (JBT)*

The author in the Ver near Sopwell – Butterfield Lane on the left. Late 1960s. (JBT)

Boys in the river at Sopwell. (MT)

*Chalkstream Water Crowfoot (*Ranunculus penicillatus subsp. pseudofluitans) *with its white petals, prominent yellow honey-guides and streamers of fern-like parallel deep-green leaves this prolific floating chalk stream plant often dominates the faster flowing parts of the river. Emerging from rhizomes in the river bed, its peak season is early summer but can flower sporadically from April to September.*

round bit in the river and all the boys used to go swimming there and jump off the willow trees. Swimming costumes weren't in, in those days and the girls never went but the boys used to swim there.

And then down here there was Monkey Island we used to call it and there was a big chestnut tree in the middle of it and nothing else but where we spent endless hours. You have to go over stepping stones to get to it and that was Monkey Island.

Question: The river must have been a lot wider in those days?

It was but it was not very deep because my brother fell in it dozens of times of the bridges and things. It was never very deep. I have got a picture here (above) – there are the two boys of the family of Mr Knight who was the head gardener. It was just about here (just up from the storage sheds near the bridge) There was a bridge here you see.

Question: So it was by the fields?

Yes up near the railway bridge.

Seen flying above the river at Sopwell, the little egret measures around 60cm long and weighs 350-450g. This small white heron with its black legs and bill and yellow feet was once common in Britain but over-hunting in medieval times as a bird for the table and the use of its feathers for decorating hats meant it was practically eradicated from Britain until large numbers were observed once again in 1989, breeding in Dorset for the first time in 1996. Mostly silent, it

The Ver, looking towards Sopwell House Hotel 1980s. (JBT)

*Little egret (*Egretta garzetta) *seen flying above the river at Sopwell. (JBT)*

can be heard making a croaking sound and a harsh warning noise if alarmed or threatened. Its food includes fish, reptiles, amphibians and insects and like herons will stalk their prey in shallow waters and can be seen shuffling their feet to disturb small fish. Currently on the Amber List, it is now a British breeding bird with around 150 breeding pairs and also a migrating visitor.

Following the Ver through the meadow you arrive at a small footbridge, from which we played 'Pooh sticks' and caught tiddlers. Here the west bank climbs from the river to the water meadows. There are several very old willow trees along the banks, very battered and bent by many years of storms and winds but very picturesque.

As a personal reflection, it was in the meadows and fields in this area that for many years we would walk along by the river on crisp autumn days (and still do) inhaling with huge pleasure that distinctive smell of nature beginning to prepare for her winter slumber. The 'season of mists and mellow fruitfulness' from my favourite poem by Keats seems to apply so perfectly to our walks by the Ver. Maybe because I was born in autumn I have always been particularly drawn to this time of year. The river gets larger as the bank side foliage begins to decay and die down and the ducks greedily gobble up our titbit offerings knowing that the cooler darker days bring with them a decline in their natural food source. Our family has always gathered some free produce or

Bridge at Hedges Farm near Park Street. A brick bridge, still there today, can be seen further upstream. JH Buckingham 1837-1901. (MoS)

other – acorns to feed the pigs, sweet plump berries for pies and jams and nuts for our garden squirrels and birds to help them through the winter months. The huge mushrooms and puffballs which we would gather on our family strolls in the meadows by the river would on our return home from our long walk be turned into a feast by mum – so large were these fungi treats that our crispy bacon and fresh eggs

The footbridge in Sopwell Meadows. (JBT)

collected from our hens that morning would sit on top of the plate size mushrooms!

Lady's smock may also be observed in Sopwell Meadows. This pretty wild flower is a brassica and related to watercress preferring to live in damp places and beside streams, indeed it was once used in salads. Its cluster of flowers on tall stems with a yellow centre varies in colour from white to pink. The common name of Lady's smock originates from the Tudor period as it resembled smocks worn by women and it was used to make starch for ruffles in Elizabethan times and the tubers were used in love spells. It is also known as Lucy Locket, Pigeon's Eye and Cuckoo flower because it appears at the same time as the cuckoo arrives. In the past it was believed to benefit the heart and with a high vitamin c content was used as an eighteenth century remedy against scurvy. Loved by insects, it is especially attractive to the orange-tip butterfly.

Looking across the meadow to Chalkdell Cottages 1980s. (JBT)

Lady's smock (Cardamine pratensis) *in Sopwell Meadows April 2011. (JBT)*

Looking towards Sopwell from the A414 bridge 1980s. (JBT)

Chapter Eight
Hedges Farm to Moor Mill

I know a spot between the hills
In a valley of flowing streams;
A place where we could happy be
In never ending dreams.
Will you come with me, and bide with me,
Will you live with me for aye;
In the valley that lies betwixt the hills,
Where the silvered waters play?

This spot can never be found by those
Who I love but the brick-lined streets
'Twill be known by you, as 'tis known by me,
In the vale where the waters meet.
Will you come with me, and bide with me,
Will you live with me for aye;
In the valley that lies betwixt the hills
Where the silvered waters play.

The Valley Betwixt the Hills – Rev A.J.Treloar

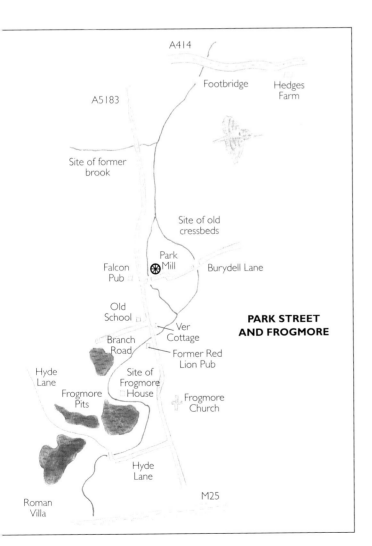

PARK STREET
AND FROGMORE

Just after the river flows under the A414 road bridge erected in the 1930s it reaches an old rambling, red brick foot bridge which once had huge coping stones on the sides, but these have long since disappeared into the river. The riverbank again climbs steeply to the west with water meadows to the east before the fields slope up towards Napsbury and from here can also be seen Hedges Farm buildings.

A farm has been on this site for many centuries. The first known owner was reported to be Thomas Hedge, a Constable of the Manor of Kingsbury in 1572. By 1686 deeds show:

Thomas Aylward holds this farme with gardens, orchards, outhouses etc...for 21 years from Michaelmas 1686.

He also rented Sopwell Farm with a total cost of £200 per annum.

The river carries on south and many of the trees on the banks have been cleared in the last fifty years leaving the river very open and often scarce in wildlife during winter when there is a lack of natural cover.

Park Street and Frogmore village lie in the valley of the River Ver and have been a place of settlement for thousands of years, with evidence of hunter-gatherers in this area around 50,000 years ago. It is thought that the origins of the name Frogmore are derived from the old English 'fog' from 'focga' meaning coarse reeds found in damp areas and 'mor' which is defined as an area of open poorly drained land.

Whilst researching for this book I came across references to a River Tar, which is said to have joined the Ver at Park Street. The first references were in two

125

Above: *A414 road bridge and footbridge 2011. (JBT)*

Left: *View under footbridge by A414 towards Sopwell spring 2011. (BBT)*

Below left and right: *The river downstream from the A414 bridge after dredging in the 1990s. Something that was done regularly up until WWII. Hedges Farm can be seen on the hill in the distance. (JBT)*

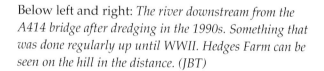

Looking downstream towards Park Street from the A414 bridge, mid 1980s. (JBT)

separate issues of *Hertfordshire Countryside* magazine:

Hertfordshire Countryside Summer 1948 Edition. Article – 'Across Countryside by Iron By-ways' by Douglas Neale.

It is of interest to note that shortly prior to arriving at Park Street we could (and still can) see the rail-less track which was built to carry a line from that point to the main Midland Railway line at Napsbury. That line was smothered before it was christened but the bridge to carry it across the road to Frogmore is still there.

The view across the water meadow of the Ver at Park Street is still the same as in my young days, the stretch below the Tar river junction was one of the few navigable by small craft.

Hertfordshire Countryside Summer 1950, Page 51 *....so to Park Street village, above which the Ver is joined by the jolly little Tar river....*

The second reference is in the St Albans Civic Society booklet 'The River Ver at St Albans', and refers to the 1950 *Hertfordshire Countryside* article above but gives no explanation!

Unable to find any further written information about the mysterious 'Tar' I contacted The Park Street and Frogmore Society who came up with the following information:

If we analyse the first reference we can assume that the journey was from Watford towards St Albans because the rail-less track can be seen prior to arriving at Park Street. Neale says that the bridge to carry the line across the road to Frogmore is still there. The reference is dated summer 1948 and the accompanying picture is dated 19th October 1948, it is clear that the bridge is not there. It does seem that the author is relying on memory with respect to the bridge or that it was removed in the narrow period between spring (assuming the article was written before the summer publication date) and October 1948.

If a 1948 aerial photo is looked at we can see the Ver entering at the top right and crossing the meadow following the line of the buildings until it meets the Mill. To the right between the river and the allotments the faint outline can be seen of the old watercress beds. The beds are fed by springs and water flows through them, under Burydell Lane and on to the watercress beds to the right. Just before the mill the Ver is split into two, one part joins the spring water from the old beds whilst the other section runs through the mill providing the motive power. The water exits the mill race, passes under Burydell Lane, and flows on the left hand side of the triangular meadow to rejoin the other flow whence it curves round to pass under the A5 at the Old Red Lion and into farmland (now the gravel pits).

So it seems that the diversions due to the watercress and milling industries might be the mistaken River Tar and that the water in that area was often used for pleasure by the younger generation.

After kindly putting a piece in their society's *Journal* asking for any memories of the Tar, they were put in touch with Jack Norman, a ninety year old Park Street resident who remembered playing in the River Tar as a boy in the mid 1920s. It was a fast flowing river running from Sopwell and joining the Ver near the area now incorporating the A414 bridge. He also remembers the pike that used to live in the Tar.

He identified the stretch of water he knew as the Tar on a map and it clearly applies to that part of the Ver between Sopwell and the A414. Jack and his friends always accepted the name Tar.

Below is a conversation recorded by the Sopwell Residents Association with Kathy Sinfield and her friend, Joan Forder about the Tar River.

Kathy: *If you are going down Cottonmill Lane, the first bit of the river you came to, we called that the Tar River – before you go over the dog leg.*

Question: *Did your parents call it the Tar River?*

K: *Yes.* (but she has no idea why).

Joan: *I always knew it was the Tar River before I knew Kathy. It was always the Tar River.*

K: *We never called it the Ver River.*

J: *We called the Ver River, the one that runs through the lake, didn't we?*

Q: *Which bit was called the Ver and which bit the Tar, the cutting off point?*

K: *We didn't know that.*

J: *Where you go across the fields and across that little bridge that was the Tar.*

Q: *That's the other side of Cottonmill Lane, Butterfield Lane way?*

J: *Yes.*

Q: *That bit that goes round to Park Street?*

K: *Yes.*

J: *When we went to the bottom of Cottonmill Lane, instead of going round the mill you would go over the stile and just walk across and that was the Tar River.*

Q: *Not the golf course side?*

K: *We did sometimes venture up into the golf course not following the river but that river there either side of Cottonmill they were both Tar Rivers.*

Q: *Your parents called it the Tar River, when were your parents born?*

K: *My mother was born in 1895.*

J: *The second river you go across another bridge don't you. The other river is there that was deeper.*

K: *Ever so deep, you never went there, it was dangerous.*

J: *My mum used to take all the kids in the street down there. There were about 8 or 9 of them. We always used to go down there and we used to swim in that.*

Q: *Which bit are you talking about?*

J: *When you go down the lane and then you go across another bridge where the farm is and the other river joins it further up.*

Q: *The mill stream?*

J: *Yes.*

Q: *Which bit was the deepest then?*

K: *The mill stream. And the little bridge when you got into the field, you could sit on it. My feet didn't reach there but of course the boys' feet reached the river floor.*

J: *It wasn't comfortable as well because it was iron and it had stones and that in it. The second one was because it was a wooden bridge. We used to go across the wooden bridge and over a stile and you were in the farmer's field then and they used to tell you off sometimes.*

It looks like the whole stretch of the river running through Sopwell was the Tar as they cannot pinpoint where it was the Ver apart from in Verulamium.

The 1890 OS map shows a tributary with a dam coming from near the millstream of New Barnes Mill looping across what is now meadowland and through Chalkdell Woods, rejoining the river in the meadow below Hedges Farm and is marked 'Fishpond'. This was presumably the Tar 'River'.

Ted Turner, a Park Street lad remembers as a boy in the 1930s, two deep and wide parts of the river, one

just after the footbridge near the A414 bridge was called the 'Tar wash' and a little further down the river another widened pool called the 'sheep dip'. Here on hot summer days up to 40 children could be found swimming and playing in the river!

However, the reasons for the name Tar are still somewhat of a mystery. The obvious translations are sailor and a thick liquid distilled from wood or coal. In the PSFS piece it also says:

....was this area used for growing straw used in the making of straw hats? St Albans was a major centre for straw hat production in the nineteenth century and at one time we had the contract for producing the straw hats which were part of the Royal Navy's uniform. These hats were coated with tar to protect them from the harsh wet and salty environment. This is how the name Jack Tar was attached to sailors.

Postcard showing Park Street Village Sports Day looking towards Burydell, early twentieth century. The event was held here from the time of Queen Victoria's Diamond Jubilee and included boxing, fencing, and displays by the local fire brigade. Tea was taken in the large marquee shown and prizes presented to the winners, an evening fireworks display ended the day. Note the watercress beds and hut enclosed by the white fence. (JBT)

Postcard showing the river, watercress beds and Bury Dell cottages in the background, taken from the railway embankment. The field beyond the cress beds is now the allotments. (JBT)

I have spoken to other people during the writing of this book who also remember swimming and boating in the Tar.

In Somerset there is an ancient place called 'Tarr Steps' and here the name 'Tarr' is thought to be derived from the Celtic word 'tochar', meaning 'causeway'. The plant wild or tufted vetch is also known by the name tar grass and tar-fitch. Tár is also old English for 'tear' maybe referring in this case to a 'split' in the river?

The river flows towards the old railway bridge and farmyard through Burydell Meadows 1911. (PSFS/CM)

Burydell Forge near the river. (PSFS/CM)

Burydell Forge once stood where the modern Mill Cottages are now next to the Ver Bridge in the lane between the cottages and Park Mill. A forge had been on or near this site since at least the fourteenth century. Members of the local Martin family worked there from the end of the seventeenth century to the mid 1940s when it was closed down. Herbert Martin was the last in the long line of blacksmiths, starting his apprenticeship when he was seventeen and retiring in 1955.

Following the meadow down river we come to the site of the old watercress beds in Burydell Lane, which were created in 1885 from part of the village green and leased by John Sansom. After WWI these beds were bought by the Pinnock family and the River Ver saw many changes, especially once land around it was also converted to watercress growing.

The beds were fed by three artesian wells. These wells allow the water to rise under their own

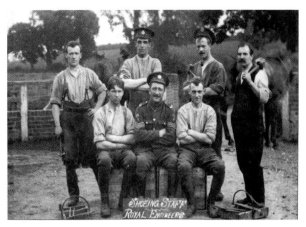

The above postcard shows the Royal Engineers' shoeing staff at Park Street in 1915. They were trained by Herbert Martin far right. Upset by the rough way the horses were treated by the soldiers he chose to join the Navy. These soldiers would have been farriers to the horses of the Remount Depot at Sopwell, just down the river. (PSFS/CM)

pressure once the aquifer is reached. The origins of the name are from Artois in France where they were first developed.

The following is a quote from an interview given to PSFS in 1997 by Claude Pinnock (1916-1997) who owned several watercress beds in parts of Hertfordshire including the one in Park Street.

You want a nice gravel bottom if possible, it's got to have a fall, it must have a fall, see – it's like you in the winter time. If you stand about you get cold, well it's the same with water. When the water comes out of that borehole, that's round about 50 degrees. Well in the summer, when its 80 degrees, it won't go above 51. In the winter time it wouldn't drop below 50. So that's how we can grow the watercress 'ceps when it's very frosty. You've got to have a fall on the bed to keep it moving through them, you've got to have spring water. In the summer time when it was ever so hot, you didn't want nowhere near as much water, therefore you used to have blocks on, we used to have these plugs. They've never gone dry! They must still be going well now.

We started off with seed and when you get the plants, you plant them in hardly any water and they start taking root. Then you let a little drop more water in and they thicken up. Then once you got them up well you can pull them for plants, to plant more up, and once you got a good stock in the summer time you can cut them off – like the tops off – and plant them and they'll take root. You have to plant them thicker. You always plant them heads down the river so the waters running over them and the roots back this way, that's how they come up. It's very interesting.

The Abbey Flyer line used to be known as the "Watercress Line", we used to go to Watford and to...Aston Villa at Liverpool, Barber of Leeds, Irelands of Leicester, Brown of Bedford...Kettering...I used to load me lorry up...go to Park Street Station...back right onto the platform, the train would come in, they'd open the double doors, then we'd work them in there, then

The watercress beds at Park Street c1950. (MoS)

The other side of the bridge from the watercress beds in Burydell Lane 1980s. This area is now inaccessible private land. (JBT)

The mill and Falcon from bridge over the Ver in Burydell Lane, before the car park and houses were built. (© St Albans City and District Council)

Scrap metal yard behind the mill. (© St Albans City and District Council)

that was changed at Watford...I used to go to Midland Station, that was all 'morning gathered', used to catch the 7.30 train to London and the lorries would be waiting there to take them straight to Covent Garden.

Altogether, with the women bunching there, we had over twenty working for us. We were one of the biggest and first people in the country.

In 1984, a whole crop of watercress was washed away in an instant when the local water authority dammed the river which suddenly burst.

Eventually, when watercress production ceased, parts of the beds were filled in and used for building and the river rerouted.

It is mentioned in Cyril Martin's book, *Park Street's Past*, that during WWII, a Handley Page bomber returning to the Watling Street Aerodrome, developed engine trouble and 'pancaked' right over the watercress beds!

Roman Watling Street runs through the village and there were several tributaries to the Ver in Roman times that were wide and deep enough to allow boats to carry produce from the kilns near Mayflower Road to the wharf in the village. Maps between the eighteenth and early twentieth century show a 'brook' running from near Lovett's farmhouse where Oliver Close is now, under the former post office and into the Ver. In Cyril Martin's

book of Park Street and Frogmore he describes this area:

Lovett's farm...was bounded by a fence at the back of the property belonging to the Pilgrim's Rest, along the North side of Park Lane as far as Tippendale. From there it went along a hedge and ditch to a small brook and along the brook back to the village. The brook meandered down from St Julian's Wood, passed under the Watling Street and entered the Ver just north of the house then known as No 1 Park Street.

The whole area between Sopwell and Park Street was once covered by the Eywood Forest as recorded in Saxon times and seen on maps of the area. Much of the forest remained until the mid eighteenth century when it was largely destroyed by fire. The better land was cultivated, but the wet areas were only suitable for pasture. As the waters of the Eywood Estate were unsuitable for mills, the river near Sopwell was divided with a bank of wood, chalk and clay to stop the new stream flowing back over the flat valley. The first mills were probably built of local timber with two floors and a thatched roof.

Mills, owned by the Abbots of St Albans, were erected in Park Street between 1146 and 1167 to assist with the funding of the monastery and, as previously mentioned, locals were charged a fee for grinding their corn.

Park Street Mill, now called Park Mill dates from 1846 and is the successor to Parkmyll, also known previously in the twelfth century as "Le Parkemylle", Parkye Mill or Corville Mill and belonged to the Abbot of St Albans who would grind corn here and be supplied with eels bred and trapped in the river and mill stream. It was rebuilt with its lands extended and the river widened by Abbot John Moote in the fourteenth century at a cost of £22. A blacksmiths was also built on the mill land and would have supplied parts for the mill workings as well as the needs of local people.

The Dissolution of the Monasteries saw an end to mills being owned by the Church and a list of accounts made at this time shows owners and their lands, including mills in and around Park Street:

John Redword, farmer, renders accounts for the farm of two watermills situated in the Soke of Parke Mill and More Mill within the Lordship of Parke. Pastures, waters and all the suite of millterre and other commodities demense to the said John by William Abraham. Total £8.13.4 Parke Mill portion £6.

John Murfynne renders accounts for farm and lands including Soppewell water mill, £13 annually.

In 1539 Henry VIII gave the mill and much of the surrounding land to Sir Richard Lee, who passed it to his son-in-law Humphrey Coningsby and from here onwards the mill was in private hands.

Thomas Babbs owned the mill in 1731 and records show the mill lands consisting of over 7 acres. Taken over by Samuel Dagnall sometime later, it was left to his son, also Samuel, as Park Street water corn-mill and its house with gardens, barns, buildings, Pickbourne meadow and watercourses.

From around 1840, the Beamont family arrived from New Barnes and spent the next five years rebuilding and renovating the mill and its buildings; turning part of it into a bake house and replacing the old flint walls along the river with new brick ones.

The mill used an overshot wheel. When not needed for milling, bypass sluice gates were opened to allow the water to flow into a deep hole below and onwards along a 15 foot wall skirting the garden of the mill joining the millstream near the farmyard. The building that once adjoined the mill was called Corville House and for a while the mill took the same title becoming Corville Mill, named by a previous owner and his wife Captain and Mrs Hopkinson. The bank on the right of the river, which flowed from the mill, was very steep – a mill worker had to be rescued by a farmer in this part of the river one cold winter's day after being chased by an angry bull! This bull apparently lived in a nearby barn and terrified children would creep quietly past hoping they would not be heard and having to run for their lives if they were!

Brimley Villas which still exist across the lane from the mill were built on the site of a timber house that had been used in the past as a place to store and repair the little boats used to keep the river clear. In the early twentieth century a chicken farm was built on the green between the mill by-pass and the river.

Park Mill, also once known as Bury Dell Mill, ceased to function as a flourmill in 1921 and was converted to a very smelly steam-driven glue factory

Park Myll from the Chicken Field. Watercolour painting by J.R.Dunning dated 1895. (MoS)

Workers outside Park Street Mill – early twentieth century. (PSFS/CM)

Below: *C1910. View facing north, before the road was straightened, cottages and Corville Mill House on right of photo on corner of Burydell Lane, before demolition. (JBT)*

by Ronald Christmas.

Cyril Martin describes the river around the mill in the early twentieth century as follows:

When the river wasn't wanted to work the mill, the by-pass sluice gates were opened wide, then the stream burst like a miniature Niagara, into a deep hole below, before rushing a cascade of white foam along the 15 foot wall skirting the mill kitchen garden. It joined the millstream near the farmyard. Between the garden wall and lane-bridge stood the village smithy. The by-pass stream, after leaving the bridge now turns at right-angles to join the mill-stream at the back of the new 3 storey flats. Both sides of the river opposite the smithy went thro' a succession of changes after the ground was acquired by the Pinnock family just after the Great War They had already taken over the first cress-bed from Mr Lewis who had gone bankrupt.

…I spent many warm days paddling in the clear water that flowed each side of the cress. Using our cupped hands we caught green and brown minnows and pink and blue sticklebacks. Kingfishers sat in the willows at the side of the river, awaiting the chance of a quick meal. There were plenty of big fish in the river at that time. When we were tired of fishing we would roll up our shirt sleeves and plunge our naked arms into the soft clay of the bank pulling some out to make clay models.

The river ran deep in some places…we would lay on our belies and drink great draughts of it, suffering no harm.

First came excavation from gravel…Later on the cress beds were filled in, the river deflected and work done to turn the territory into building land.

The flats mentioned above, along with the shops by the bridge, were built where a row of old cottages owned by Browns (Hedges) Farm, used to be by the

Photo taken just after demolition of Corville House, note shop and cottage where the modern shops and flats are now.
(© St Albans City and District Council)

river. One of these belonged to Mr Western who kept dray horses behind his house.

The widening of Watling Street before WWII meant that not only were many cottages pulled down but part of the mill was removed. After the war the mill was used to store aluminium scrap and later the Brookside Metal Company kept salvaged marine scrap on the site. After being lived in privately until 1952 it stood unused for several years and in 1959 during further road widening Corville House was pulled down along with seventeenth to early nineteenth century buildings south of Burydell Lane up to the railway embankment.

During the First and Second World Wars the river was a welcome distraction and source of fun for the children growing up in the area. Again Cyril recalls some lovely memories even though it was a tough and worrying time for many people:

During the long hot summer days we acquired a passion for the river, most of us learning to swim at an early age. Those that couldn't swim made rafts from pieces of wood bound together with some of the buoyant water lily weeds and floated down the river on them…we bathed in the deep mill falls at the back of the mill garden. We found it really exciting diving from the garden wall into the foaming mass of water that plunged from the upper river to the pool below. Passers-by along Burydell Lane would halt on the bridge and watch us. We often tricked them into believing that we'd been drowned by coming up behind the falls out of sight of the watchers on the bridge; then we'd sit there for a few nail biting moments with the raging torrent flowing harmlessly over our heads, before plunging into the back of the falls to suddenly reappear in the middle of the pool, as if we'd been in the water all the time.

In 1984 the mill was sold to Jarvis Development Co. and they converted the mill to offices. During this conversion foundation timbers of previous mill buildings on this site and an old mill key were discovered and in the old blacksmith's garden a WWII bomb was found. The mill wheel and race were preserved and can still be seen today.

In the *Historical Antiquities of Hertfordshire* by Chauncy, another mill is mentioned lower downstream, but any evidence of this would have been destroyed by gravel workings.

On the opposite side of Watling Street to the mill was once a building named the Pilgrims Rest, a place offering accommodation, food and drink to pilgrims on their way to visit the Shrine of St Alban. On this site stands the Falcon Inn, first licensed in 1618 to Walter Ancell. A landlord in 1775, called John Cummings, made over all his goods to a local pawnbroker to pay off his debts together with a letter,

Mill before conversion.
(© St Albans City and District Council)

The Old Mill workings. (TS)

Be so good as to acquaint my wife that I am safe in London.

In 1871 part of a will made out by Nathaniel Hill read:

Also I bequeth unto Thomas Whitehead of Parkstreete in the parish of St Stephen, miller, on surrender of a Message of Tennament with all the outhouses, yards and appurtenances whatsoever, situate in Parkestreete and known by the name of the Fawlkon.

It seemed to have been the most important public house in Park Street and was frequently used for auctions of goods and properties along with local coroner's inquests.

In 1886, local timber merchants George and Harry Boff discovered a hoard of over two hundred fifteenth and sixteenth century gold coins hidden inside an old oak beam they said had been removed from the cottages on the site of the Pilgrims Rest. The find was proclaimed Treasure Trove and the brothers were able to claim the value of the hoard and were given two of the coins as souvenirs, which they wore on watch chains.

Through the meadows to the east of the river, past the mill, you can see the single arched railway bridge with the date '1866' etched on a brick. In 1859 the railway line between Watford and St Albans was laid and the route took it north of Park Street. A station was built at the level crossing at Hyde Lane and a

station cottage was built on the south side of the line, with a view of connecting St Albans to Watford. At Napsbury a line was laid from the station at Hyde Lane across Watling Street and the River Ver. The place where the line was supposed to join the main line was called Park Street Junction and lines were laid for a few hundred yards from Napsbury towards Park Street. Then for no apparent reason the building of the line stopped and the finished part was used as sidings at Napsbury Station until it closed in the 1950s. Therefore this railway bridge over the Ver has never had a train across it!

Past the railway bridge the river runs through the gardens of Ver Cottage, built in 1867 by the Wiggs family as accommodation for teachers who taught at the old Park Street School, which they had founded and stood opposite the Cottage. The rundown school building is still there today. The stone plaque on the front of the house has two dates on it, 1867 and 1878. 1878 was when it was enlarged and it became a private house leased to tenants.

At the beginning of the twentieth century, it was let at £35 per annum and was said to consist of two recreation rooms, four bedrooms, bathroom, kitchen, scullery, WC, woodhouse, greenhouse and garden.

From here the river goes under Watling Street to Park Street Ford.

Ver Cottage mid 1980s. (JBT)

Early postcard of the Ver and River Cottages taken from the bridge. (JBT)

Below is an edited extract from an interview with Mrs Lil Day and her daughter Pauline talking about the river recorded by the Sopwell Residents Association:

Lil: *When I first came to St Albans, I was with my mother-in-law in Park Street until my husband came out of the forces and the River Ver was at the bottom of the garden. Where we lived was right in the main part right opposite the Swan and next door to the Post Office and we had the river down below and somebody had got a boat down there, a really old one, no oars. So there was me, my husband and his two brothers and their wives and we got a picnic with us and we had a wind-up gramophone and we got broomsticks and punted way up to Cottonmill. We went under bridge by the North Orbital and we got out and had our lunch on a grass patch, it was all grass then. And we had music. And then we went back and they put their poles in where it was too muddy and they ended up in the water.*

Pauline: *What about Mum's next door neighbour, she bathed in the river.*

L: *She was the district nurse and had no bath in the house and she had an old fashioned bathing costume and she would get one of these stiff yard brooms, take it down and sweep the bottom of the river.*

P: *The kids used to do it —sweep the floor clean.*

L: *She used to bath herself all over. She kept her swimming costume on. It was an old-fashioned one and it got sleeves and it was over her knees and it was red and white. Nurse Mason her name was and she was the retired district nurse.*

After passing under Watling Street, the river has the former Red Lion inn on the east bank with the two old River Cottages opposite.

Records of the Red Lion first appear in 1786 when Thomas Clutterbuck, a brewer of Stanmore, owned it and it was run by a Mrs Arnold. Between 1786 and 1992 eighteen landlords are recorded including four more ladies, Lydia Rentowl between the 1840s and

The Old Red Lion inn and bridge built in 1884 (AL). The inn and river from the same era. (SMM)

The Red Lion mid 1980s with sign inviting horses to drink from the river. 'Stop brave boy, heed what I say, if the men can't drink, the horses may' (JBT)

1884, Sarah Bruin between 1884 and 1886, Sarah Boffe (after her husband's death) between 1890 and 1900 and Kate Vezy 1902.

Sadly the former pub, where locals and passers-by including our family, refreshed themselves for hundreds of years and children paddled and fished for tiddlers in the ford has gone the way of many of our public houses and was converted for private business in 2009.

The hamlet of Parkye has its origins in the beginnings of a bigger settlement near the ford in around the eighth century. Where the bridge crosses the river the ford is now much smaller and shallower than it once was. Here in the early twentieth century the local chimney sweep Tom Spokes would wash his horse and cart after a day's work.

During 1795 much of Hertfordshire was affected by the thaw of heavy snows causing flooding to many areas and swollen rivers which in some places burst their banks. That same year in the Easter Session Records of the Liberty of St Albans the following appeared concerning damage caused by the floods to Frogmore Bridge:

Order for the erection of a bridge at Frogmore in the Parish of St Stephens, of a plain brick bridge, with one arch of thickness 18 inches, the span of which is to be 18 feet; the bridge is to be 12 feet clear in the carriage way, with brick battlement and oak coping.

It was stated that the late floods had washed away the former bridge. In the Midsummer Sessions there is an order for the rebuilding of the bridge according to an estimate given by a bricklayer from St Albans, Thomas Chambers at a cost of £75 10s although the coping was to be of stone not oak as originally stated. During the Epiphany Sessions in 1796 the accounts for the building of the bridge at Frogmore has been paid in full. However no records exist nor have any traces been found of a Roman bridge at this location. The current bridge is built of brick with stone coping and was rebuilt in 1885.

One year the river overflowed into the field, not far from the Red Lion pub, it froze and made us a great skating rink. My ice skates were just like my roller skating

wheels, they clamped onto the bottom of our shoes or boots.

Colney Street Kids by Sandra Muggleton-Mole.

The inhabitants of houses whose gardens backed onto the Ver, often owned boats and could be seen navigating their way up and down the river especially in warmer weather, occasionally getting stuck in the reeds or, in shallower parts, the mud! Children would earn extra pocket money by wading into the river and helping to push the boats towards the deeper channels of water.

Looking towards Watling Street mid 1980s. The Red Lion pub is to the right of the bridge. (JBT)

The summers of the early twentieth century saw water regattas held on the river, organised by local minstrels who would borrow boats used for keeping the mill water courses clear. The villagers would ride in their own decorated punts with candles and lanterns fixed on the top of tall poles. As the minstrels began to play and sing, the boats would glide up the river in procession, joined by others along the way. Great fun was had by all well into the evening, when the lanterns and candles would be lit, what a wonderful sight this must have been!

The river then winds through what were once the grounds of Frogmore House. Where the gravel pits are today was the private golf links of a wealthy stockbroker, Sydney Brunton and his family who purchased Frogmore House in 1890. Many local people were employed to look after the house, grounds and river of this considerable estate. The golf links came down to the river at one point with paths from the house crossing wooden bridges to the links. Sydney diverted part of the river through an ornamental canal, which had a water chute for his children to play on. There was also a trout hatchery from which the river was restocked and he ensured the river was kept clean with a healthy population of fish.

Sydney also owned horses and they were kept in stables behind the Red Lion inn near the river. During WWI, these stables were used by the Army to accommodate their horses and mules and would have been connected to the blacksmiths and remount depot at Sopwell.

The river was often cleared by the local farmers who would drag it clean with a horse and tanker. The collected material would then be spread on the fields around the village as fertiliser.

At the beginning of the twentieth century, the river was much wider and deeper than today. Many villagers and passers-by quenched their thirst in the clean, clear water. The river would occasionally overflow and flood the surrounding fields, ponds and ditches resulting in a floral oasis of wild flowers including dog daisies, harebells and blue and yellow irises.

View of Frogmore House from golf links across river 1901. (PSFS)

River Ver and parkland around Frogmore House viewed from Hyde Lane (Waterdell). (JBT)

From the early 1950s until 1957, Inn & Co., later to become Redland Aggregates, extracted gravel from where the golf course once stood and Frogmore pits are now. Once work had finished Redlands landscaped the site and leased it with its five lakes to the London Anglers Association for fishing. This continued when the rights were taken over by a local angling club. The lakes have been regularly stocked with fish and baliffed by volunteers who also carry out working parties to help keep the area in a reasonable condition for anglers and visitors alike.

Many species of fish can be caught including specimen bream over 15lb, good size tench, pike and perch along with the infamous 'Toadless', a 40lb+ leather carp, said to be the second biggest in the UK. Fish, some in excess of these weights were netted in the 1960s when they were removed because of

A small rudd (Scardinius erythrophthalmus) *caught in the Ver near Frogmore pits and safely returned 2006. (JBT)*

Reeves muntjac deer (Muntiacus reevesi) *seen near Park Street pits. (JBT)*

Frogmore Pits with line of poplar trees marking the banks of the river in the distance 1980s. (JBT)

pollution. The area is a site of a wide variety of flora and fauna.

Living on top of a seam of gravel (if only it had been gold) had its compensations. When Uncle Charlie made all the concrete paths around the garden and needed sand, he just dug a hole! The other benefits were the lakes it left behind; being so close to the river they filled with water before they could fill them in. So all the fishermen now had more places to fish.

From *Colney Kids* by Sandra Muggleton-Mole

Very similar to the roach with which it is often confused, there are some identifying features that distinguish the beautiful rudd. It has yellow eyes and an upturned mouth, with the bottom lip extending above the upper. The green tinge to its back is accompanied by the beautiful deep golden colour of its body, especially in older fish. Its fins are bright red with the placement of the dorsal fin nearer the rear.

They spawn in May on clean water plants leaving mats of eggs and can hybridise with roach and bream. Feeding on invertebrate and plant material they are susceptible to stunted growth when food is scarce. Although only small specimens have been found in the Ver, in the right conditions they grow quickly and the record for the largest rudd of 4lb 8oz has stood for nearly eighty years and was taken from a Norfolk Mere by Rev. E. C. Alston in 1933.

The Chinese or Reeves muntjac is the oldest known deer on Earth, appearing 15-35 million years ago. Measuring 0.5m high and weighing up to 40lb they originated in South-East Asia and are one of six species of deer in the UK. Introduced into private collections in Britain during the nineteenth century they are thought to have escaped from the Duke of Bedford's herd at Woburn Abbey and a larger number from nearby Whipsnade Zoo. Their habitat includes dense woodland and grass cover. The wild muntjac population in Britain is estimated to be around one hundred thousand and unlike other deer does not have a fixed breeding season. They feed on plants, leaves, nuts, herbs, fruit and will come into gardens and feed on domestic plants if the opportunity arises.

In October 2010 a very large, new wooden footbridge was built over the Ver, which should withstand any modern day floods!

The river in flood, Hyde Lane 1980s. (JBT)

Frozen lake at Frogmore looking towards the river with private apartments and bell tower of Frogmore church in background 2010. (JBT)

The bridge over the Ver at Frogmore c1900, before Frogmore pits. (PSFS /Alpha St Albans Arthur Melbourne-Cooper)

Frogmore ford, Hyde Lane, February 1921. (SC/HALS)

The river leaves the pits and approaches the bridge at Hyde Lane 1982. (JBT)

Himalayan balsam (Impatiens glandulifera) *by the river at Frogmore pits. (JBT)*

...the gravel pits were a short cut home from Park Street School, first we would cut across the meadows that ran along the side of the river. These meadows were so beautiful with cowslips, king cups and milkmaids and lots of other wildflowers, I loved to pick some and take them home to my Aunty Micky. The meadow was very marshy in some spots and you could only walk there in summer. On the banks of the river there stood large weeping willow trees. I'm sad to say these meadows are no longer there, they are covered by a large lake left over from when they removed the gravel, it's sad because it's the only place I knew where king cups grew. It is still a beautiful place, full of wildlife.

From *Colney Kids* by Sandra Muggleton-Mole

The Himalayan balsam is a relative of the Busy Lizzie this attractive but evasive and largely out of control plant with bright pink hooded flowers was introduced into Britain as a garden plant in the 1830s. Common along river banks, it reaches well over 6 feet and spreads with alarming speed. Once ripe, the seed pods explode scattering around 800 seeds up to 25 feet away which are carried even further by rivers!

Although Watling Street crosses the river from east to west, it curves round towards the road near Frogmore church and it is thought that this is the reason why there is a bend in the long straight Roman road, to avoid re-crossing the river.

Hyde Lane was the original Belgic track to their settlement at Prae Wood and from the jetty at Hyde Lane it is believed they were once able to navigate via the river Colne and Thames to the continent.

During the Black Death a pest house was sited near the ford at the bottom of Hyde Lane off Watling Street. It is interesting to note that it was accessible, but down a damp lane well away from everyone else.

It is shown on an 1872 map although by this time these pest houses would have been redundant because of improvements in sanitation and medicine such as smallpox vaccinations, so it's unusual for it to still be shown. It was used for a while as a retaining place for sick animals and by 1898 it is no longer shown on maps.

The river then carries on through a very isolated stretch of wooded area, which is more like the jungle of Brazil than Hertfordshire! This is a fine solitary stretch. Between the pits and the river is an area of quicksand, safely fenced off but avoided at all costs by the more sensible children when I was young, although stories of people getting into trouble and

The river as it flows towards Bricket Wood from Hyde Lane 2010. (JBT)

even getting sucked under were well known and added terror to an already frightening and mysterious place! The river then approaches Moor Mill passing under the M25 motorway.

A Childhood by the Ver
The Memories of Ann Smith (née Jerome)

When I look back at all the happy days I spent either beside, on or in the River Ver around Park Street I realise what a huge part it played in my childhood. Now in my late forties I have trouble enough remembering to pick up milk on the way home from work, but my memories from way back in the sixties and seventies are still vivid, and for that I am grateful. However, I make no guarantee that all place names used are correct although I am quietly confident. It has been a long time!

I have my mother to thank for my love of the river and my memories stem from a very young age. Every Sunday we would go for a walk somewhere close by, and it would invariably involve walking beside some stretch of the river. Some Sundays we would stroll down Bury Dell Lane, past the junk yard and stop to look at the watercress beds. Here on the bridge we would sometimes throw sticks over one side, dashing to the other to see whose stick would emerge first. As I remember it was always mine, or so my mother would kindly have me believe!

In good weather and if time allowed we sometimes ventured a little further. Once we walked along to where the old mill was situated near Moormill Lane. The mill has since been made into a lovely pub.

Another popular route would take us across the

recreation ground, affectionately known as 'the rec', past Park Street School and into the old gravel pits, then and now an area of lakes with the Ver running to one side. We would walk around the first lake, stopping to look for the enormous fish that always seemed to be up near the water's surface in fine weather, and then down to one of my favourite stretches of the Ver.

In years to come I would often meet up with friends from Oliver Close down 'by the pipe'! It was where a large concrete pipe fed into the river. As kids we loved to take our fishing nets as there was also a concrete ledge, big enough for several of us to stand and fish without getting our feet too wet.

From 'the pipe' we would make our way back along the banks of the river in the direction of the Red Lion. Now that was another good place to fish! A couple of hundred yards or so around the bend in the river from 'the pipe' we would arrive at the little wooden bridge. This spanned a little overflow channel from one of the main lakes into the river.

When finally allowed to make such journeys near water without an adult I did so many times, usually with a crowd of kids from the street. We would all be armed with jam jars and nets and it was serious business who caught the most fish, or the largest. And if you should be fortunate enough to catch a frog then you really were considered to be the bee's knees of the day!

However, it was not only fish and frogs we used to catch. One of my most vivid memories is of a day when many of the children from all over the village were fishing in the Ver by the Red Lion pub. One young lass let out such a scream. She had scooped her net into some weed and pulled it up with an adder wrapping itself around the cane. Nearby adults shouted at us children to get out of the water. The fishing cane was promptly dropped and slowly drifted away under the bridge with the current, never to be seen again. The snake too made a hasty retreat, away from the hordes of curious children, all terrified but secretly wanting a closer look.

The Red Lion was a popular spot indeed. Parents supervising children at play could always while away the boredom with a pint once the pub opened.

The site of a ford always meant it was never too deep to paddle. But tiddler bashing was not the only river sport here!

The pub often put on a tug-of-war with teams standing either side of the ford desperately trying to pull each other across and into the water. As I remember there was never anyone left dry anyway, not even the victors.

I think our favourite spot for fishing however was down near the watercress beds in Bury Dell Lane. It was certainly where I spent many a warm summer's day. My mother worked in the village bakery and since this stretch of the Ver was only across the road and down the lane a little it was the obvious choice. We had quite a few adventures too.

One particular summer we started catching large ugly looking black fish with whiskers. We were fascinated yet horrified. My older brother's friend soon identified them as catfish. We had never seen anything like it. And when his father offered to pay 25 new pence each for them to put in his pond we certainly made a killing! I often wonder if the poor things survived being dragged out of flowing water and being rehoused in a large pond. But we didn't give this a thought at the time. It was a precarious task catching those catfish. They only seemed to be in one spot under the bridge. We had to clamber down and shuffle on our backsides along concrete pipes that were set against the bridge and drop down on the far side of the river. From here we would crouch down low and squeeze under the bridge. I can still remember how our voices used to echo under there. There was a narrow concrete ledge and it was here that you would catch them if you were lucky. It was

dark under that bridge and you couldn't see any fish at all, let alone black catfish. You would just whizz the net round a bit and hope for the best.

But my happiest memory of all concerning the Ver was the summer my friend Sharon had a rowing boat. Sharon lived for a while at the post office in the village. The Ver ran along the end of her back garden and was a stretch us kids from Oliver Close could not easily get to because it lay beyond the watercress beds. The river here was sufficiently deep to float a small rowing boat. Sharon and I would row upstream as far as Cottonmill! Deepest, darkest Africa could not have been more of an adventure. From here we would sprawl out in the boat and slowly drift back, enjoying the sunshine as we went and trailing our fingers in the water.

In one part of the river in particular we would notice bits of white pipe lying on the river bed. After noting these several times we decided to stop the boat and investigate. The water was actually a little deeper here and I remember how we had to first go home and change into swimming costumes. The white pipe pieces turned out to be just that. Fragments of old clay pipes that had obviously been thrown into the river many years before. Most were stem pieces but we each found one or two interesting looking bowl fragments. My mother said that she thought she had heard of a time, many years ago, when a clay pipe full of tobacco could be purchased with your pint of ale. If this were the case then the old pipes would have been tossed away as a new one would have quickly replaced it. I think this is a seriously good theory and yet to be disproved. Sadly, I have no idea where this stretch of the Ver is and do not know if it was the site of an old drinking establishment.

I consider myself incredibly lucky to have had both the freedom and the river with which to mould my early years. Nowadays we tend to discourage such adventures because of health and safety issues and the threat from 'strangers'. Very sad, because now instead of making their own entertainment our children seem to go nowhere without some kind of hand held electronic game to take all their attention. I believe they are missing so much.

Chapter Nine
Moor Mill to the River Colne

Little brooklet, can you tell
Whence you come and where you go;
Down the hill through copse and dell,
With a ceaseless flow?

How I love to linger near,
Watching thee on summer day;
Listening to thy murmur clear,
Tracking out thy way.

On through woodland, copse and field,
Round about the labourers cot;
In thy wanderings is revealed
Many a pleasant spot.

Few the feet that track thee out,
Few the eyes that see thy charms;
Flowing here and there about
Woods, and lanes, and farms.

In the valley at thy feet
Thou shall end thy restless flow;
There the river thou shalt meet,
And together go.

Little brooklet on the hill,
This the story that you tell;
Happy they who seek thee still,
They who know thee well.

The Brooklet – A.J.Treloar

The final village on the Ver's journey before it joins the River Colne is Bricket Wood, said to originate from Bricket meaning 'Bright Islet'. However the Rev. H Hall in 1858 says it originates from 'Brachinges', either the meadow with the brook (from the A.S. 'broc') or the badgers meadow (from the A.S. 'broc', a badger).

Situated south west of St Albans on a 'till', a protruding sediment-covered spur, with a history that goes back to at least the Bronze Age, the Domesday Book records 165 inhabitants at Heanhamstede (place of the high heath). Up until the Dissolution of the Monasteries the area was under the rule of St Albans Abbey when as with much of the land throughout England it was split into different manors including Burston and Hansteads. The area has long been associated with farming and milling.

Its various spellings can be traced as far back as 1228 and include:

Bruteyt (bright coloured small island or piece of marshland) – thirteenth century
Brutethte – fourteenth century
Briteyghtwood/Bosco de Brygteyght (bright islet) sixteenth century
Brickett/Bricket Wood – seventeenth-twentieth century

In the early twentieth century many outsiders would visit the famous fairgrounds, usually by train which stopped at the local station opened in 1861.

The 1930s saw the start of the construction of many houses and bungalows and of course the infamous nudist camps – Spielplatz being Britain's oldest naturist reserve and one of two remaining sites. Surrounded by major roads including the M1 (opened in 1959) and M25 (opened in 1986), the village is also home to a wonderful 70 hectare wooded common which is a Site of Special Scientific Interest.

When the M25 was taken over the Ver, the river was deepened but over time it become silted with little flora and fauna. It was under this bridge in 2007 that a man became buried waist deep in mud whilst attempting to rescue his dog that had also become trapped. The dog managed to escape but the man had to be dug out by firemen resulting in many calls to clear this part of the river. A band of thick mud is still seen during low water levels today.

The river then approaches Moor Mill. 'Moor' originates from an old word 'more' which is a corruption of 'mere', meaning lake. Also once known as Frogmore Mill, this Grade II building was listed in 1953. It is thought to be over five hundred years old;

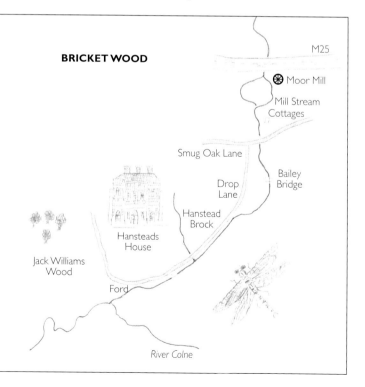

BRICKET WOOD

M25

Moor Mill

Mill Stream Cottages

Smug Oak Lane

Bailey Bridge

Drop Lane

Hanstead Brock

Hansteads House

Jack Williams Wood

Ford

River Colne

The river approaches Moor Mill in the nineteenth century. JH Buckingham (MoS)

Ted Banfield by the M25 Bridge mid 1980s. (JBT)

Above left and right: *Rear views of Moor Mill and weir 1980s. (JBT)*

although it is believed a mill has stood on this site for over a thousand years and is mentioned in the Domesday Book as Moremylle. The first mill was thought to be an early wooden Saxon structure.

At the beginning of the twelfth century it was known as "le Moremyll" and belonged, like most mills in and around St Albans, to the Abbey.

In 1350, at a cost of £11, Abbot John Moote totally rebuilt the mill. The millers were given permission to fish the river and the eels caught proved to be so popular at the Abbot's table that they were used to pay the millers' tolls. However local records list many poachers caught stealing fish from the Abbot's waters here and along the river, sometimes being caught on several occasions. In the fifteenth century, Richard de Wallingford, Abbot of St Albans cleared and relined the mill pool and dam.

Eels.

It is said the eels disappeared from the river in the early twentieth century when the roads were tarred.

As mentioned in many old local documents the eel (*Anguilla Anguilla*) was once prolific everywhere in Britain including the Ver but has long since disappeared from our river largely due to unpredictable water levels, pollution and lack of food. Able to move over land for short distances, the colour of an eel indicates its age and it can grow to over 1.5m. Preferring to live on the bottom of lakes and rivers in well aerated water, it feeds on small fish, crustaceans, amphibians, larvae and blood worms. The eel has two small fins either side of its body behind its head with its dorsal fin extending to the tip of its tale.

The larvae eel drift for around 300 days from the Sargasso Sea towards Europe before becoming "glass eels", swimming up estuaries and upstream. They then become elvers and as they age their colour changes to a browny yellow giving them the name "yellow eel". They mature between five and twenty years (although can live way beyond this age in captivity) turning a more silvery colour and it is at this stage they begin their long journey back to the Sargasso Sea to breed before dying.

An endangered species, it is thought that in the past forty years there has been a 90% decrease in eels reaching Europe. Reasons for this decline aren't fully understood and studies are currently taking place to try and find the causes, but reasons are thought to include overfishing, parasites, pollution and barriers to migration.

Once an important and plentiful food going back many centuries, it was also used to pay rents to landlords especially by millers who would set traps in the rivers and millstreams. Even now jellied eels are part of East London's traditional fare and glass eels are a delicacy in many parts of Europe.

In 1559, after the Dissolution of the Monasteries, ownership of the mill passed to the Manor of Park (Park Street) and by 1630 it had been incorporated into the estate of the Earl of Essex.

A 1735 will of William Fuller named him as the miller of Moor Mill. In the late eighteenth century it is documented that the Woodward family were masters of the mill and there was still a Thomas Woodward there in 1845. Before 1886 the mill was run by Alfred and Ebenezer Cook. Thomas Gee took over and ran a sizable poultry farm and was well known at the time for his prizewinning chickens.

The current structure was built in 1762 and has an eighteenth century two-storey mill house attached. There is mention of two mills on or near this site belonging to the Manor of Hanstead in the Domesday Book, thought to be Moor Mill and Park Street Mill.

A List of Moor Mill Tenants and Owners from AD 800 to 2010

800-1066	Lord of the Manor of Hanstead
1399	John Moote, Abbot of St Albans
1401	John Wyndsor
1529-1542	John Redwood
1670	John and Elizabeth Beldon
1686	Abraham Pruden
1722	Briant Marlborough
1735	William Fuller
1769-1845	John, James and Thomas Woodward
1845-1875	Alfred and Ebenezer Cook
1875-1923	Tom Gee
1923-1980	Leonard Taylor and Geoff Taylor his son (from 1944)
1980-1984	Department of Transport
1984-1989	Joe Carter
1989	Regents Inns
1992	Whitbread plc

The last miller and farmer at Moor Mill was Geoff Taylor whose family had been there for three generations. It was a flourmill with two paddle undershot wheels, one of ten foot six inch in diameter and six foot wide, the other of ten foot six inch diameter and seven foot six inches in width, driving three sets of stones which are still on show. It ceased producing flour in the early twentieth century and was used to grind corn for cattle feed until WWI when it became part of a farm for dairy herds, poultry and finally arable.

On the farm Mr Taylor had a very old punt...and he used this to keep his part of the river clean, free from weeds and reeds. The river in most parts was very shallow, and we would be allowed to paddle this punt up and down the river, it was great fun.

One day fed up with the river and feeling

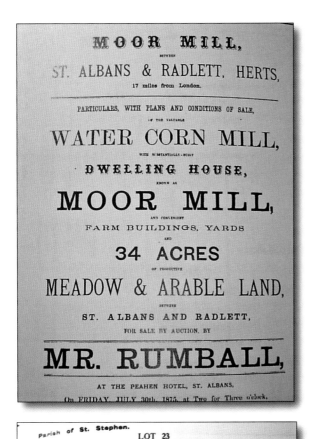

Sandra Muggleton-Mole outside Moor Mill late 1940s. (SMM)

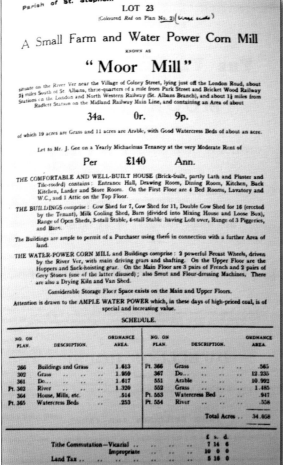

An 1875 for sale poster for Moor Mill. (JBT)

A male orange tip butterfly (Anthocharis cardamines) by the river at Moor Mill 2011. (JBT) Seen on warm spring days and fond of river banks and damp meadows, the white females lay only a single egg on a flower stalk as the larvae are cannibalistic and for this reason it is thought the female is able to detect eggs that have already been laid. Only males have orange tips to their wings.

Moor Mill late nineteenth century. (JBT)

Moor Mill, Mr Garment on right hand side next to fence. (BWHS)

adventurous, we dragged the punt over the field at the back, paddling the punt over the channel that was used to make the old mill work, over some more ground and launched it into the lake at the back. This lake was man-made. When they had removed the gravel and being so close to the river, the gravel pit had filled up with water. We paddled the punt over to the other side of the lake and back again, and then dragged it back to the river. Shortly after, while paddling back to the mill it sunk in one foot of water. If it had sunk while we were on the lake who would know? None of us could swim!*

From *Colney Kids* by S. Muggleton-Mole

Once the farm and its assets were sold it passed through several hands before being opened in 1992 as a restaurant and public house by the then mayor, Peggy Hughes. Still named Moor Mill it has some of the original machinery intact and the overshot water wheels are a moving feature within the restaurant.

The river is diverted down a very wide sluice before the mill, skirts the pub garden and is joined by the millstream and flows under the road bridge on Smug Oak Lane, which was a ford up until the middle of the twentieth century.

One memory of Vinegar Hill was not a good one. There were a lot of us kids playing together on our bikes. I would have been very young, maybe three or four years old as I was still riding my three-wheeler bike. They were all racing bikes down the hill, so I thought I would do the same. Now the problem was my three-wheeler bike didn't have brakes…once off I soon realised I was in trouble, never having gone at such a speed before. On reaching the bottom of the hill I half fell and half jumped just before hitting the water, it was a close call as the bike ended up in the river and I ended up in tears with skinned knees and hands. It was also a great place for a sledge; we would play until we got so cold we got hot aches. Later on Vinegar Hill had the steepness taken out of it, as the lorries from the gravel pits had a job to climb it!

From *Colney Street Kids* by Sandra Muggleton-Mole

Moor Mill and the M25 Bridge from across the river mid 1980s. (JBT)

Cows in River Ver by Moor Mill 1950s (unknown)

Moor Mill and the river in the snow c1950s. (RH/BWHS)

Vinegar Hill (Smug Oak Lane) and the ford 1922. Named because it was so steep (sharp like vinegar). Once the white iron bridge was built the wooden bridge seen here was removed. (SMM)

Family on road bridge near Moor Mill c1900. (BWHS)

This 1939 photo (above) of one of the Fitzsimons girls was taken looking down the Lane away from the mill – towards the white bridge, on the far side…was our swimming pool. It looks as if the river had recently been cleaned out…the council had teams of men that would go along in boats and remove reeds, weeds and any rubbish from the river.

The boys would often try and build dams across the river, much to everyone's relief they never worked! It was a double dare to go under the bridge – the boys told us there were great big leaches under there.

I loved it when the summer days were long and hot, we would lie on the edge of the river in the shallows wallowing, giggling and chatting just letting the water flow over us to keep cool.

My uncle Bill Grey lived down in the village…and every spring he would go down to the river and prepare the ford next to the old white iron bridge (now replaced). Once raked out and free from weeds it became our swimming pool for the summer. The river bed was made up of brown and white stones, overhung in some parts by willow trees it made its way through banks lined with weeds and wildflowers. The river weed was and still is a vivid shade of green – almost fluorescent. We would try and skip stones over the water and see how many times we could get them to jump. We probably put back all the stones Uncle Bill raked out. Many hours were spent exploring the river fishing for minnows and stickle backs with our fishing nets. It wasn't always the ideal weather for being in the water, but we would brave it until someone's mother told us to get out as our lips had turned blue and we could no longer speak because our teeth were chattering so much.

From *Colney Kids* by Sandra Muggleton Mole

It was along this stretch to the confluence that Ted Banfield last saw a water vole on the Ver in the early 1980s. Apparently they were pointed out to me on our walks along the river when I was little by him, but I only have scant memories of them. However I have seen these adorable little creatures throughout my life mainly on my fishing expeditions on other rivers around the country. To date there are no water voles along the Ver, where the last reported sightings were in the 1980s, but I, like many others live in hope of their return.

The water vole (*Arvicola amphibious*), is Britain's fastest declining mammal with populations in some areas falling by over 90% in the past 100 years. Throughout Hertfordshire small populations are

The adorable water vole. (RC)

known to exist on the rivers Chess, Mimram, Purwell and Rhee, although there could be other undiscovered colonies.

Their habitat includes the tall flora of rivers, streams, lakes and ditches where they feed on over 200 kinds of vegetation leaving tell tale signs of their 'feeding stations' with little heaps of nibbled leaves and stems that have a distinctive 45 degree angle at the cut ends. They also marks their territory with small piles of droppings usually on clear areas near where they enter the water. The burrows along their territory are not just in the water but above it and away from the water's edge but they dive into the river with a distinctive 'plop' alerting other voles of possible danger, often stirring up river bed sediment to cause a cloudy patch to hide in as they race to their burrows.

'Ratty' in Kenneth Grahame's beautiful book and my childhood favourite, *The Wind in the Willows* was actually a water vole! They are the largest of the three vole species found in Britain, being around the same size as a brown rat for which it is often mistaken as rats are also good swimmers.

The main differences to look for are:

Water voles	Rats
Small hidden ears	Large ears
Blunt nose	Pointed nose
Mid brown coloured silky fur	Brown/grey fur
Tail that is shorter and furry	A long pink hairless tail, often scaly
Oval 8-12mm long, fibrous, almost odourless droppings	Scattered, larger, darker, offensive smelling

Their demise has been caused by many factors including the drying up of rivers, destruction of habitat and pollution but the main culprit is the American mink (*Neovison vison*) an escapee from fur farms throughout the country. Mink control schemes exist through much of Hertfordshire including the Ver in the hope that eradication of this mammal will help to encourage the return of the water vole by introducing captive-bred animals. Parts of the river Ver are certainly healthy enough at the time of writing to support the water vole.

The Ver then winds on to the Water Authority's flow weir, and under a Bailey-type bridge, which was used by lorries for gravel extraction to Riverside Way. The diversion of the River Ver and destruction of its surrounding water meadows for extraction in the 1970s was fought against by many local people but the land had been sold by the estate of Miss Yule to the St Albans Sand and Gravel Company years before so little could be done to stop it. The new, straightened channel of the Ver was dug only 10 feet away and parallel to Drop Lane previously known as Hansteads Lane and the water meadows destroyed. For many years the river suffered from this rerouting and the dust created from the gravel extraction. In

1980 Hertfordshire County Council purchased three quarters of a mile stretch of disused riverbank alongside the Ver adjacent to the old gravel pits between Moor Mill and Drop Lane. The Green Belt Management Experiment developed the site into a recreation area assisted by volunteers. Today after many improvements 'Riverside Way' has been greatly enhanced, with the continued planting of trees and hedges and the river in better condition with the return of flora and fauna. Managed by the Countryside Management Service, the area is monitored and maintained creating a popular riverside walk. Nearby is a pumping station built in 1950 which supplies water to parts of Watford and London.

Flow weir looking towards Smug Oak Lane 1980s. (JBT)

The gravel pits works were owned by Inns and Company. The small "train" was a little diesel shunting engine that pulled around 10 small tipping wagons between the excavators in the top fields, down to the washer. Each wagon would hold about 2 tons of dug material…Once down and alongside the washer grid, which was situated underneath the washer, the raw material, a mixture of sand, stones and clay would be transported up to the top of the washer via a long conveyor belt. From here it would tumble through various sieves at the same time being drenched with water. The sieves were different 'grades'. The biggest stones came off first and the finest…would be sand which came in two grades:

Sharp sand – used for concrete.
Building sand – used for brick laying.
The slurry…was run via pipes into holes in the ground…these were dangerous areas that we tried to avoid as it stained clothes, shoes…and knickers!

When the boys were bigger they would make short runs from sections of discarded track..and they would get a wagon chassis on to the rails, and ride the length of it, jumping clear before it crashed into the stop.

Sandra Muggleton-Mole

During a talk on the history of Bricket Wood by Meryl Parker in 1977 she mentioned that near the ford in Drop Lane:

There is a very, very deep part of the river, which all the local boys used to know because they used to swim in it, and it's called Quickies Hole because a gentleman

These two delightful pictures of the Ver are taken from glass slides owned by the author dated 1906. The top one entitled 'General View Bricketts Wood' and the bottom one 'Bricketts Wood Ladies Toilet'. (JBT)

called Mr Quick, a brewer from Watford came down and committed suicide in it one winter.

It is near here, just above the confluence that Hanstead Brook, the Ver's small and intermittent second tributary, joins the river. Thought once to have contributed a more significant amount of water to the Ver, its two branches emanate from near How Wood and the grounds of Hanstead House meeting and flowing into the Ver by Lower Stud at Drop Lane.

Looking up the hill to the right, a lovely view of Hansteads House can be seen. Hansteads is recorded in the Domesday Book of 1085 when the estate was under the jurisdiction of St Albans Abbey. It then consisted of twenty hides, approximately 2400 acres and in Lordship another six hides (720 acres), 34 households, woodland for a thousand pigs and two

mills one probably on the site of Moor Mill. An area of 3120 acres around the present site of Hansteads House would have covered a great length of the Colne and Ver in this area. There is evidence that the area was inhabited during Roman times.

In the sixteenth century it was home to the wealthy Day family and called Great Hansteads Farmhouse built to the east of the medieval village of Heanhamstede and covered land from Station Road down to the ford.

The estate was split into two during the eighteenth century, the original house – Great Hansteads – and another building called Little Hansteads. From 1877 until 1899 the occupants were the Peareth family who then sold it to Frank Woodhouse Forester before being bought by David Yule.

Old course of the river showing gravel extraction machinery in background, 1975. (BWHS)

Flowing towards the ford 2008. (JBT)

Daphne Clements and Betty Sawers fishing in the river near the stepping stones in Drop Lane c1934. (DB)

Near the ford at Drop Lane 1965. (BWHS)

A view obscured by trees today, horse and riders, where the stepping stones are now, Drop Lane mid 1980s. (JBT)

Hansteads House 1980s. (JBT)

Stepping Stones, Drop Lane, summer 2011. (JBT)

As well as owning the house he also purchased angling rights to the River Ver. By 1912 with business interests at home and in India the Yule Company, with David at its head, became the largest British-owned enterprise in the Empire and he was rewarded with a knighthood by King George V. The old house was demolished and a new mansion was completed in 1928, the same year as Sir David died and was buried in the grounds. His wife Lady Henrietta Yule was left an estate worth around £10,000,000, which she added to throughout her life buying up large areas of local land, two film studios – financing over 70 films – and a luxury yacht once used by Edward VIII and Mrs Simpson. She also owned a private zoo and aviaries at Hansteads and bred Arabian horses. Her daughter, Gladys, born in 1903, took over the estate on Lady Yule's death in 1950 making her the heiress who had inherited the most money ever to that date. Sadly she was the last of the Yule family and her fortune was left to a female companion. Evidence of the Yule's interest in breeding racehorses can be seen in the old converted stable buildings in the area, whilst Waterside Cottage or Bottom House as it was once called, on the opposite side of Drop Lane (called Hansteads Lane until the 1880s) by the river, was the laundry for the stables

The house and estate were bought by a religious group, The World Wide Church of God, who renamed the house Memorial Hall. In 1979 it was bought by the CEGB as a staff training college and the sports complex built by the religious group was until 2010 leased to St Albans City and District Council as the Bricket Wood Sports Centre. It is at the time of writing the HSBC training college, although there are plans to sell it.

At the end of Riverside Way there is a footbridge followed by a road bridge. This is the last crossing on the River Ver.

In the UK there are about 20 species of damoiselles and the largest is the banded with a wingspan up to 70mm. This metallic blue/green winged beauty can be found flitting and fluttering along the river from May to late August.

They lay up to 450 eggs on emergent and floating

Male banded damoiselle (Calopteryx Splendens) *near confluence 2011. (JBT)*

plants which hatch after 14 days, overwintering buried in mud. Climbing up reeds and water plants they moult into an adult, living for around two years, mostly spent in the aquatic larval stage feeding on small insects caught on the wing. Preferring the slower moving areas of water, they are a good indicator of water quality as they are very sensitive to pollution.

Two views from Drop Lane across to Jack Williams Wood, the second after the rain at the end of October 2000. (BWHS)

After a small water meadow on the bend of the river there is the last of the fords. The Ver as it approaches its confluence with the Colne is normally the major river, but there is a noticeable difference in the depth of the Colne once the rivers converge. It has often been said by many throughout history that as the Colne joins the Ver and not vice versa the river as it flows onwards from this point, should be called the Ver, not Colne!

Chauncey comments:
The Colne, which springs forth near Tittenhanger, thence passes the road at Colney-Street and running above two miles in length, meets the Verlume near Park - Street, but 'tho the Verlume is much the greater stream, yet the Colne usurps the glory of her own name and floweth thence to Watford.

In *South Country Trout Streams* by George Dewar he explains the retaining of the name Colne thus:
The River Ver's water is crystal clear and lusty in its flow; the River Colne is torpid and murky. Following the rivers confluence the river water remains in the state of the latter, hence it retains the name 'Colne' as it flows onwards to the Thames at Staines.

A 1962 aerial view showing the confluence of the Ver with the River Colne.
(Copyright restricted www.blueskymapshop.com)

Rivers meet 1980s. (JBT)

It is thought the name 'Colne' originates from the Celtic 'Cul-an' meaning the 'narrow or confined river'.

From here the Ver unites with the River Colne, flowing onto the Thames and eventually the sea to begin the cycle of our most precious commodity – water.

Rivers are one of the most beautiful features of our island an essential part of the character of our towns and villages; they provide inspiration to writers and painters, challenges to conservationists, landowners, engineers, anglers and boatmen. The River Ver, a rare and fragile chalk stream is more than that often-used title for waterways 'liquid history': it is by its very rare nature 'liquid gold'. Yet the greatest challenge facing everyone who uses and loves the river today is increased concern for the natural and historic conservation of this very special and rare environment. It is threatened by a catalogue of problems, not least the lack of water – chalk streams are wonderful places but we all need to save water to help ensure their future survival. Each person uses an average of 150 litres of precious water per day and with just a little effort this can be reduced to help make a real difference to the future of our waterways! I, as I know Dad was, am keen to make people aware of how valuable and important our chalk streams are and raise their profile and that of their rich diversity of wildlife.

Geographically our story ends, but the life and history of our river continues to tell its tale of a beautiful, vulnerable and precious chalk stream that must be protected and enjoyed to ensure its continued existence.

We are all part of our river's long and varied history but it relies on us to help ensure its survival. If this book inspires people to take an interest and help care for the River Ver and the flora and fauna that could not survive without it, it is a job well done!

To pass on is as great a joy as to inherit.

Some Modern Day Societies and People Associated with the River Ver

Bricket Wood History Society was formed in 1977 and explores all aspects of the local area its history, environment and natural history. Contact Anne Carter, Secretary: 01923 279870 or Mr Laurie Hart, Chairman. email: hartlj@supanet.com

The Chilterns Conservation Board looks after this unique area of Southern England. Check out the Chalk Stream pages. www.chilternsaonb.org

Flamstead Village Website – A good source of local information and contacts.

The Herts & Middlesex Wildlife Trust works to protect wildlife, managing an area spanning 1900 acres, with 43 nature reserves from beautiful wetlands and woodlands to rare patches of heath and orchard. www.hertswildlifetrust.org.uk/

Markyate Local History Society. Formed in May 1990, the society holds meetings with local speakers and visits local houses and museums. Exhibitions are usually held biennially and the society produces newsletters and a yearly journal.
http://misc-histories.info/markyate-hist/

Park Street and Frogmore Society was formed to promote interest in local history and nature conservation and covers the three villages of Park Street, Frogmore and Colney Street. It holds six open meetings each year, with speakers, organises guided walks and publishes four Newsletters and two Journals per year.
Contact:Tony Stevens, 33 Ringway Road, Park Street, St Albans, Herts AL2 2RE. email: tsteve33@btinternet.com

Redbourn Village website is packed with information on the village including history, photos and interesting facts. www.redbourn.org.uk

Redbournbury Fishery was founded by John Dunckley in 1987. The fishery covers approximately seven acres and consists of a stretch of the River Ver, a well stocked trout lake and a coarse lake and provides day ticket river and lake fishing. http://redbournburyfishery.co.uk/default.aspx

Redbournbury Mill lies 2 miles north of St Albans. It is established as a museum and the only working mill on the Ver producing a range of stone ground organic flours and hand-crafted breads. www.redbournmill.co.uk

Red Kites. Helen Olive is part of the South of England kite monitoring group, and was responsible for the welfare of almost 40 red kite chicks before they were successfully translocated to Aberdeenshire in 2008/9. Along with the website she raises public awareness, and is the main point of contact for the public if they discover dead kites in the Chilterns. Her hand-made red kite greeting cards are sold in local shops and selected National Trust outlets. www.redkites.net

St Albans & Hertfordshire Architectural & Archaeological Society (Arc & Arc) was formed in 1845 to promote an interest in local history, and to encourage research and its publication. www.stalbanshistory.org

The Chiltern Society. The Chilterns cover a 650 square mile area across Oxfordshire, Bucks, Herts and Beds. Half of this area forms the unspoilt Chilterns Area of Outstanding Natural Beauty (AONB). Much of the remainder is protected by Green Belt status. The society's vision is to maintain the uniqueness of the Chilterns in the face of growing pressures on this part of the country. www.chilternsociety.org.uk

The Countryside Management Service works throughout Hertfordshire to enable local communities to enjoy care for and enhance their local environment. www.hertslink.org/cms/

The Ver Valley Society exists to protect and promote all aspects of the River Ver and its valley. Originally founded in 1976 to promote the Ver/Colne Walk, shortly after the river, and its valuable water meadows, began to decline due to over abstraction of ground water and climate change. In 1993 they were instrumental in having one of the many pumping stations put onto standby status. The 24km river is divided into 12 stretches which are regularly patrolled by volunteer bailiffs. As well as measuring the flow, they send in reports on wildlife, plants, invasive species, pollution, blockages, the state of the paths etc, with relevant bodies contacted when necessary. A quarterly newsletter is produced and there are four Open Meetings a year. www.riverver.co.uk

Veolia Water Central serves over 3.5 million people with around 940 million litres of water every day and is committed to producing a reliable, safe supply of high quality drinking water to customers. https://central.veoliawater.co.uk/index.aspx

Verulam Angling Club was formed in 1934 by local businessmen and has been providing quality fisheries and sport for its members ever since. Members can enjoy a vast array of fish and fisheries. www.verulam-angling.co.uk

The Watercress Wildlife Association is a beautiful and peaceful local nature reserve in St Albans occupying the site of old watercress beds and allotments and partially bounded by the River Ver. It contains a number of important habitats. www.watercresslnr.org.uk

---

Image Credits

A big thank you to all those who allowed the use of their images in this book. Some from Dad's collection were unusually for him, devoid of any ownership details. Every attempt has been made to identify owners and copyright holders where applicable. Images may have passed through many hands before being given to Dad or me and the original donors or copyright holders of some images were at the time of writing, untraceable.

AB Allen Beechy

AL Andy Lawrence

Alpha St Albans (Arthur Melbourne-Cooper)

AS Ann Smith

BBT Bruce Banfield-Taylor

BWHS Bricket Wood History Society

CM/PSFS Cyril Martin/Park Street and Frogmore Society

DB Daphne Bunker

DH Dilys Hudson

EE Eric Edwards

GW Geoff Webb

HALS Hertfordshire Archive and Local Studies

HL Helen Olive

ITV/GI ITV/Granada International

JB/AM John Buckingham/Alan Malin

JBT Jacqui Banfield-Taylor

JC J Cunningham

JT Joanne Turner

MoS Museums of St Albans

MR Mike Richardson

MT Mrs Terry

MH Margaret Harrington

MW Margaret Wickens

NG Noel Godman

PSFS Park Street and Frogmore Society/Tony Stevens

RC Roger Cave

RH Richard Hale

DH Richard Hogg

RM Redbournbury Mill

SA Stuart Antrobus

SC/HALS Stingemore Collection/Hertfordshire Archive and Local Studies

SKC/HALS Stanley Kent Collection/ Hertfordshire Archive and Local Studies

SMCES St Michaels CE School

SMM Sandra Muggleton-Mole

St Albans City and District Council

TS Tony Stevens

VAC Verulam Angling Club

VVS Ver Valley Society

VWC Veolia Water Central/Ellie Powers/Rob Sage

WT Wendy Timberlake

WWA Watercress Wildlife Association/ Steve Simpson

Bibliography

Information has been observed in many books and documents over the years by Dad and myself. Those that I have used and am aware Dad read are listed below. I apologise if I have missed out a source of information through my own error or simply by not being able to find the source or being unaware of where Dad gleaned his information.

A Civil Parish of St Stephens.
A History of Hertfordshire. Tony Rook.
A History of St Albans. James Corbett.
A New History of Flamstead. Eric Edwards.
A Redbourn Commoner. Geoff Webb.
A Source Guide to the River Ver & its Valley. VVS.
A Souvenir of Bricket Wood.
Albans Buried Towns: An Assessment of St Albans' Archaeology up to AD 1600. Rosalind Niblett and Isobel Thompson.
An Edwardian Village. Cyril Martin.
Around St Albans. Geoff Dunk.
Bricket Wood Village Guide.
Cathedral & City, St Albans Ancient & Modern Excavations at Park Street 1954-57. AD Saunders.
Fishpool Street, St Albans. Gerald Sanctuary.
Friars Wash Point-to-Point Races. Eric Edwards.
Ghostly Hertfordshire: True Ghost Stories. Damien O'Dell.
Gibbs Illustrated Handbook to St Albans 1866. Fred B Mason.
Gorhambury. St Albans Architectural & Archaeological Society.
Haunted Hertfordshire – A Ghostly Gazeteer. Ruth Stratton and Nicholas Connell.
Hertfordshire A Guide to the Countryside. Shirley David.
Hertfordshire County Geographies. FHH Guillemard.
Hertfordshire Geology and Landscape. John Catt et al.
Hertfordshire in History. Ed by Dr Doris Jones Baker.
Hertfordshire. W Branch Johnson.
Herts Advertiser.
Historic Herts. W Percival Westell.
History of Verulam & St Albans. (1815).
Kelly's Trade finder of St Albans 1975.
Know St Albans – Three Watermills in St Albans. M Leamy and E Parker.
Mysterious Ruins. Donald Pelletier.
Oldfields Book on St Albans c1800.
Park Street's Past. Cyril Martin.
Pebbles and Puddingstones. St Albans Museum.
Redbourn Memories. Geoff Webb.
Redbourn through Time. Geoff Webb.
Redbournbury Mill. Justin James.
Redbourn's History. Alan Featherstone.

Remember Markyate, Flamstead & Trowley. Reg A Nelsey and Rosslyn French.
St Albans & Harpenden Review.
St Albans A History. Mark Freeman.
St Albans Almanac & Guide 1931.
St Albans as it was. Elsie Toms.
St Albans Directory: A-Z of St Albans Place Names Over 2000 Years. Tony Billings.
St Albans Historical and Picturesque. Charles H Ashdown.
St Albans the City & its People. Edited by JH Brett.
St Michaels Manor 1886-1986. Betty Ream.
The Battles of St Albans. Peter Burley, Michael Elliot and Harvey Watson.
The Book of Markyate. MLHS 2002.
The Book of Park Street and Frogmore. Cyril Martin.
The Character of Redbourn. Geoff Webb.
The Civil Parish of St Stephen – A History of People & Places Vol. 1.
The DIA Cautionary Guide to St Albans. Clough Williams Ellis.
The Hertfordshire Village Book. Herts Federation of Women's Institutes.
The Hills and Streams of Hertfordshire and Other Poems. Rev. Albert J. Treloar, B.D.
The Historical & Topographical Description of the Municipium of Ancient Verulam. Frederick Lane Williams.
The Historical Antiquities of Hertfordshire.
The History of Redbourn. May Walker.
The Little Ver Book. Judy Green.
The Mills of Redbourn. Alan Featherstone.
The New Book of St Albans. Dr Elsie Toms.
The Story of Redbourn. Redbourn Local History Society.
The Story of the English Towns – St Albans. W Page.
The Story of the River Ver. Elizabeth Delaney.
The Victoria History of the Counties of England. Edited by William Page.
The Witches of Hertfordshire. Simon Walker.
Verulamium since the Wheelers. Rosalind Niblett.
Verulamium. Rosalind Niblett.
Westminster Lodge Leisure Centre, St Albans, Hertfordshire Archaeological Evaluation Report February 2010. Wessex Archaeology.

Index